READINGS IN
MEDIEVAL POLITICAL THEORY

D1565752

READINGS IN
MEDIEVAL POLITICAL THEORY
1100-1400

Edited by
Cary J. Nederman
and
Kate Langdon Forhan

Hackett Publishing Company, Inc.
Indianapolis/Cambridge

Copyright © 1993 by Cary J. Nederman and Kate Langdon Forhan
First published 1993 by Routledge
Reprinted 2000 by Hackett Publishing Company, Inc.

06   05   04   03   02   01   00   1   2   3   4   5   6   7

For further information, please address:

> Hackett Publishing Company, Inc.
> P.O. Box 44937
> Indianapolis, IN 46244-0937

> www.hackettpublishing.com

Cover design by Brian Rak

Library of Congress Cataloging-in-Publication Data

Readings in medieval political theory : 1100-1400 / edited by Cary J.
Nederman and Kate Langdon Forhan.
         p.   cm.
    Includes bibliographical references and index.
    ISBN 0-87220-489-8 (cloth)—ISBN 0-87220-488-X (paper)
        1. Political Science—Early works to 1800. I. Nederman, Cary J. II.
Forhan, Kate Langdon, 1949- III. Title.

JC111 .R4 2000
320'.09'02—dc21   00-047291

For Arlen, Mitchell and Daniel
and
for Joseph, Langdon and Nicholas

CONTENTS

Preface   ix
Acknowledgements   xiii
Introduction: the formation of medieval political culture   1
Further Reading   16

Part I The twelfth century   19

1 Bernard of Clairvaux, Letter to Pope Eugenius III   21
   Translated by Kate Forhan

2 Marie de France, *The Fable of a Man, His Belly, and His Limbs*   24
   Translated by Kate Forhan

3 John of Salisbury, *Metalogicon* and *Policraticus*   26
   Translated by Cary Nederman

4 *Treatise on the Laws and Customs of the Kingdom of England
   Commonly Called Glanville*   61
   Translated by Cary Nederman

5 Philip of Harvengt, Letter to Henry, Count of Champagne   64
   Translated by Robert Ziomkowski

   Further Reading   67

Part II The thirteenth century   69

6 Brunetto Latini, *The Book of Treasure*   71
   Translated by Kate Forhan

7 Thomas Aquinas, *On Kingship, Summary of Theology* and
   Commentary on Aristotle's Politics   97
   Translated by Susan Ziller, Cary Nederman and Kate Forhan

CONTENTS

8 Giles of Rome, 'On Civil Government'   149
   Translated by Kate Forhan

   Further Reading   153

Part III The fourteenth century   155

9 John of Paris, *On Royal and Papal Power*   157
   Translated by Cary Nederman

10 Dante Alighieri, *The Banquet*   168
   Translated by Kate Forhan

11 Marsiglio of Padua, *The Defender of the Peace*   173
   Translated by Cary Nederman

12 William of Pagula, *The Mirror of King Edward III*   200
   Translated by Cary Nederman

13 William of Ockham, *Whether a Ruler Can Accept the Property of
   Churches for His Own Needs, namely, in Case of War, even
   against the Wishes of the Pope*   207
   Translated by Cary Nederman

14 John Wyclif, *On the Duty of the King*   221
   Translated by Cary Nederman

15 Christine de Pizan, *The Book of the Body Politic*   230
   Translated by Kate Forhan

   Further Reading   248

   Name index   250

   Subject index   254

PREFACE

In the popular imagination, Western Europe during the Middle Ages is often equated with the 'Dark Ages', a period wherein culture and reason gave way to social disintegration and the excesses of mystical faith. This character-ization of the Middle Ages might seem especially appropriate to the study of political theory. After all, unlike the ancients, medieval authors seldom produced great systematic analyses of politics or philosophically sophis-ticated defences of political ideals. And unlike political theory in the modern age, the Middle Ages yielded none of the intellectual constructs from which arise contemporary ideological and intellectual disputes. Or so we assume.

In part, this unfavourable estimation comes from a failure to realize that historical periodization involves judgements of value which are themselves political or ideological. The very term 'Middle Ages' stamps an entire civil-ization as a kind of interregnum between what was 'really' important, namely, the classical period, usually meaning Plato and Aristotle, and the moderns. Yet reality is much more muddled than such tidy categories would imply. In fact, our civilization, like any other, is inextricably linked with the past, however despised or revered. The great twelfth-century scholar and churchman John of Salisbury reminds us that we, like the students of any age, can see farther only because we are standing on the shoulders of the giants who came before us.

Individuals born during the period we term 'medieval' continued to think and write about political questions and problems: their texts abound in archives and libraries. Moreover, the theoretical observations generated during the Middle Ages form an important contribution to the Western tradition of political thought. Medieval theorists repeatedly addressed many of the issues which scholars regard as 'perennial' elements of the West's political identity. The intellectual in the Middle Ages, no less than in other eras, wanted to discover the qualities of the good society and the proper roles and functions of the individual within that society. He or she was concerned with specific problems found within those societies – problems of violence, of corruption, and of the abuse of authority, for example. Medieval scholars sought to expound and defend ᴄoctrines and ideas unknown to previous generations and to make sense of them in the light of the past. The hegemony of a revealed Christian religion, the persistence of pagan classical texts and ideas, and the development of a feudal social and political structure – all of these factors shaped the distinctive theoretical outlook on politics typical of writers during the Middle Ages. In turn, it ought also to be emphasized that numerous attributes of medieval political practice and thought exercised a decisive influence upon the more recent history of the West. Principles of law, government, liberty and rights so cherished by modern citizens may be traced to medieval sources.

The primary goal of the present volume is to disseminate to a non-specialist audience a representative sampling of the political ideas and arguments which theorists of the Middle Ages bequeathed to the West. The editors' preference has been to include lengthy selections from texts in order that students and scholars may have collected together in a basic sourcebook the 'masterpieces' and 'classics' of medieval political thought. But we have also included shorter excerpts from less well-known authors, including women, that have never before appeared in translation. It is also our belief that a thorough comprehension of the theories of politics arising from the Middle Ages requires an appreciation of the political culture in which medieval authors were immersed. Thus, we begin with a brief introductory survey of the intellectual, ideological and historical context which animated the political reflections of Western Europe during the Middle Ages.

FURTHER READING

A bibliography designed for further student reading, containing a survey of recent primary and secondary literature for the period from 1100 to 1400 available in the English language, will be found following each major section. In particular, we have tried to focus on works appearing since *c.* 1980. A more complete bibliography, citing Latin and vernacular editions of original sources, older English-language literature, and non-English secondary scholarship, may be found in J.H. Burns, ed., *The Cambridge History of Medieval Political Thought*, Cambridge, Cambridge University Press, 1988.

TEXTUAL SOURCES FOR TRANSLATIONS

Bernard of Clairvaux, Epistola 256, in *Sanct Bernardi, abbatis Primi Clarae-vallensis, Opera Omnia*, ed. F.J. Mabillon, Venice, 1750, vol. 1, 258–9.

Marie de France, *Fabilaux*, ed. Harriet Spiegel, Toronto, University of Toronto Press, 1987.

John of Salisbury, *Metalogicon*, ed. G.B. Hall and K.S.B. Keats-Rohan, Turnholt, Belgium, Corpus Christianorum, 1990.

John of Salisbury, *Policraticus*, ed. C.C.J. Webb, Oxford, Oxford University Press, 1909.

De legibus et consuetudinibus Angliae qui vocatur Glanvill, ed. G.P.G. Hall, London, Thomas Nelson, 1965.

Philip of Harvengt, Epistola 17, in J.P. Migne, *P.L.* Paris, vol. 203, 1844–64, 152b–153b.

Brunetto Latini, *Li Livre dou Tresor*, Berkeley, University of California Press, 1948.

Thomas Aquinas, *Summa Theologiae*, ed. Cambridge Blackfriars, New York, McGraw-Hill, 1964–80.

Thomas Aquinas, *De Regno*, ed. J. Mathis, Turin, Marietti, 1924.

Thomas Aquinas, *In octos libros politicorum expositio*, ed. R.M. Spiazzi, Turin, Marietti, 1951.

Giles of Rome, *De regimine principum*, lib. iii, ed. Hieronymum Samaritanium, originally Rome, 1607, photographic reprint Frankfurt, Minerva GmbH/ Unveranderter Nachdruck, 1968.

John of Paris, *De potestate regia et papali,* ed. F. Bleienstein, Stuttgart, Klatt, 1969.

Dante Alighieri, *Il Convivio*, ed. E. Moore, in *Tutte Le Opere di Dante Alighieri*, Oxford, Oxford University Press, 1904.

Marsiglio of Padua, *Defensor pacis*, ed. C.W. Previté-Orton, Cambridge, Cambridge University Press, 1928.

William of Pagula, *Speculum regis Edwardi III*, ed. J. Moisant, Paris, Picard, 1891.

William of Ockham, *An princeps*, ed. H.S. Offler, in *Opera politica*, vol. 1, 2nd edn, Manchester, Manchester University Press, 1974.

John Wyclif, *Tractatus de officio regis*, ed. A.W. Pollard and C. Sayle, London, The Wyclif Society, 1887.

Christine de Pizan, *Le Livre du Corps de Policie*, ed. Robert H. Lucas, Geneva, Droz, 1967.

ACKNOWLEDGEMENTS

This book arose out of numerous discussions with many colleagues in both hemispheres about the problems connected with teaching the political thought of the Middle Ages to undergraduate students. One of the recurrent issues raised by college and university teachers reluctant to teach medieval theory was the absence of a collection containing a wide range of lengthy selections from texts of the period. Having heard this objection posed so often, the editors resolved to rectify the lacuna. Our thanks are due to these colleagues – far too numerous to be named – for stimulating and encouraging us to move forward with this project.

The editors must also thank Siena College, its Arts Division, and its Department of Political Science, for material and personal support for the volume. In particular, we wish to credit the aid of Dean Thomas Bulger, Dr Leonard Cutler, Head of the Department of Political Science, Ms Theresa Pardo and Ms Jamie Bult from Academic Computing, and Ms Ellen Johnson from the Faculty Support Office. All the translations in this volume are the work of the editors, except for the letter by Philip of Harvengt, which was translated by Robert Ziomkowski; and Thomas Aquinas' *On Kingship* and the *Commentary on Aristotle's Politics*, which were translated by Susan Ziller. Both are former students of Siena College.

By far our greatest debt rests with our families, and it is to them that this volume is dedicated. Without the support, patience, and love of Joseph Cousins, Langdon White and Nicholas Forhan-White, Arlen Feldwick, and Mitchell and Daniel Hooper, none of our accomplishments as scholars would mean very much.

Round Lake, New York

INTRODUCTION: THE FORMATION OF MEDIEVAL POLITICAL CULTURE

BETWEEN HEAVEN AND HELLAS: THE CLASSICAL TRADITION

The story of medieval political thought properly begins with a discussion of the fate of the tradition of philosophy which had been founded in ancient Greece. After the conquest of Greece by Rome, the Greek language continued to be read by the intelligentsia of the West and the texts of Plato and Aristotle were thereby available without necessity of Latin translation. Moreover, the Romans themselves contributed to the development of political thinking: Cicero (106 BC–43 BC) wrote Romanized variants of Plato's *Republic* and *Laws*; Seneca (4 BC–AD 65) composed essays and letters which surveyed the moral dilemmas confronting the intellectual in politics; and Plutarch (*c.* AD 46–*c.* AD 120) fashioned a series of parallel biographies of famous Greek and Roman political figures. In short, Roman culture preserved, revered and expanded the theoretical teachings of the classical Greek philosophers.

This tendency was gradually reversed, however, during the final phase of the Roman Empire. Two reasons may be cited to explain the change. First, beginning with the Emperor Constantine (*c.* 280–337), the empire adopted Christianity as its official religion, which led to an increasingly hostile attitude towards pagan ideas. Christian intellectuals like St Jerome (354–420) discouraged the unbridled use of non-Christian texts and concepts on the grounds that these were tainted with the stain of worldliness. Some authors, like the classically educated St Augustine of Hippo (354–430), continued to draw heavily upon the pagan materials available to them. But the more typical perspective seems to be that of Tertullian (*c.* 160–*c.* 220), who asks his readers: 'What is there in common between the philosopher and the Christian, the pupil of Hellas and the pupil of Heaven?'

The second important factor in the erosion of the influence of ancient thought upon the Western intellect pertains to the fissure between the two

1

imperial capitals at Rome and Constantinople. The creation of twin Emperors in the East and West, dating to the late third century, had ultimately produced a vast cultural and political gulf between the Greek and Latin worlds. One consequence of this separation was the death of Greek literacy in the Western world, even among the best educated scholars. St Augustine, for instance, seems to have possessed little, if any, facility in Greek despite his excellent education. Indeed, it is often said that when Boethius died in 524 – his intention to translate into Latin all the works of Plato and Aristotle unfulfilled – the West's knowledge of the Greek language died with him. Thereafter, for nearly one thousand years, whatever the Western mind grasped of the philosophical heritage of Greece was acquired through Latin translations and intermediaries.

The limited transmission of classical texts to the Middle Ages held especially staggering implications for the field of political thought. For instance, while Plato's name and ideas were not completely unknown to medieval authors, none of his political works – including the *Crito, Republic, Statesman* and *Laws* – survived in the West. The fact that medieval texts sometimes cite or even quote from the *Republic* reflects the access which Roman sources such as Cicero enjoyed. The only work of the Platonic corpus to be translated into Latin was the *Timaeus*, a late dialogue on cosmology. But because the *Timaeus* was purportedly a continuation of the *Republic*, its early pages include a summary of Plato's views on the tri-partite structure of the soul and the city, as well as on the specialized virtues particular to each sort of citizen. These introductory remarks to the *Timaeus*, coupled with an available commentary on the dialogue by Calcidius (fl. early 300s), seem to have exercised a considerable influence upon the political concepts elucidated by the early Middle Ages, such as the doctrine of the 'three orders' (namely, those who fight, those who pray, and those who work). Only much later, however, did the main body of Platonic political writings return to circulation.

While the impact of Plato's philosophy can still be measured after the fall of Roman domination, the fate of Aristotle's social and political thought followed a different trajectory. Prior to his execution, Boethius had managed to translate two Aristotelian treatises – the *Categories* and *On Interpretation* – into Latin, and these provided the primary source for knowledge of Aristotle well into the twelfth century. While the *Categories*, in particular, contains some of the main tenets of Aristotle's moral theory, his political doctrines were inaccessible (at least directly) to early medieval thinkers. Then, because of renewed contact between Christianity and Islam in Southern Europe during the 1100s, the bulk of Aristotle's work, which Islamic and Jewish scholars had studied for generations, rapidly became available to Western readers. Parts of the *Nicomachean Ethics* were translated into Latin before 1200 (a full text appearing around 1250), while the *Politics* was disseminated about 1260. While it overstates matters to regard the flood of Aristotelian texts as the cause of an intellectual 'revolution' in

Western Europe, medieval political theorists quickly adopted much of the linguistic and conceptual apparatus of the *Politics*. Indeed, we may properly characterize Aristotle as the predominant classical figure in the political philosophy of the Middle Ages from the mid-thirteenth century onwards.

The influence of the political ideas of pagan Roman culture upon medieval thought, while not so dramatic as in the case of Aristotle, was ultimately just as pervasive. Many Latin texts of political significance were familiar to the Middle Ages, even prior to the cultural Renaissance experienced by Europe in the twelfth century. For instance, Cicero's thought was widely known and admired throughout the West, at least in part because of his eminent reputation as a political theorist. During late antiquity, Christian authors quoted at length from his *De res publica, De legibus, De officiis* and other political, moral and rhetorical treatises. Indeed, St Augustine and Lactantius (*c.* 250–325) are still the two most reliable authorities for the contents of those portions of *De res publica* which remain missing; they transmitted a wealth of Ciceronian materials to medieval Christians as well. Especially popular among political authors throughout the Middle Ages were Cicero's *De officiis* and *De inventione*, both of which taught a doctrine of political naturalism (adapted from Stoicism) long before the recovery of Aristotle's *Politics*. Even after the writings of Aristotle returned to general circulation, Cicero continued to find an audience and to be cited for his political ideas.

Elements of classical political thought were also conveyed by means of less overtly theoretical sources. The renewal of interest in Roman civil law during the 1100s reacquainted the West with ancient conceptions of justice, sovereignty, legislation and, perhaps most important, the ideal of imperial majesty. When later monarchs and their supporters cited the dictum 'The king is emperor in his own realm', they did so in full awareness of the powers which an emperor could claim for himself. The revival of interest in Roman law also stimulated theoretical investigations into and practical applications of the notion of a corporate community; the introduction of a legal basis for collective identity encouraged the proliferation of such new social forms as the urban commune, the guild and the university. While the impact of Roman law was felt most in the areas of public administration and justice, medieval political texts composed by lawyers and non-lawyers alike were imbued with its doctrines and terminology.

In general, the Middle Ages viewed and used the ancients far differently than would the European Renaissance of the fifteenth and sixteenth centuries. Where Renaissance Humanism sought to study antiquity as the distant historical past – emphasizing textual and contextual accuracy – medieval thinkers perceived themselves as the direct heirs of classical Greece and Rome. As such, political theorists in the Middle Ages were usually most concerned to adapt the lessons of ancient writing to more immediate circumstances and problems. Fidelity to the original author's intentions meant considerably less during the Middle Ages than did the quest for truths which

3

were ultimately rooted in Holy Scripture. St Augustine had remarked in *On Christian Doctrine* that Christian intellectuals should treat those pagan ideas which are true and compatible with the faith as objects held by 'unjust possessors' that ought properly to be removed from them and converted to the use of believers. In this, Augustine set the tone for the interpretation of the classics by political theorists for a thousand years to come.

THE PHILOSOPHICAL ROOTS OF MEDIEVAL POLITICAL CULTURE

In any account of the formation of medieval political culture, Augustine of Hippo is a towering figure. Born of a pagan father and Christian mother during the last days of the Roman Empire, Augustine's own life reflected the disintegration of the old classical world and the birth of a new one. The confusion and turmoil of his intellectual and spiritual journey from paganism to philosophy and from Manicheism to Christianity parallel the tumult of his age. His prodigious intellectual curiosity and scrupulous honesty are reflected in his written works, which have inspired thinkers from many cultures and many times. The *Confessions* represent a new kind of writing – an introspective look at the development of an individual. *The City of God* is a discussion of Christian society and thus attempts to show the place of that individual in the world.

Augustine also influenced medieval political culture via his analyses of the ideas of his age, such as Manicheism, Platonism, Stoicism, and Scepticism, as well as by his works on ethics, all of which provided a link with pagan culture. Through his works the medieval thinker could learn about classical ideas during a time when many books written by ancient authors were unavailable.

Three aspects of Augustine's thought will be outlined here: a view of the human person, the idea of order, and, later in this introduction, some of Augustine's practical advice on life in society.

First, for Augustine, the human individual is a kind of bridge between two different kinds of being: a rational animal, ranking between the angels who are entirely spirit and the beasts which are entirely flesh. Humanity is the pivot in creation – the joining together of spirit and flesh. At its creation, both elements of its being were able to work together harmoniously, the body under the control of the spirit. A human being was able to enjoy the pleasures of the senses without being enslaved by them. This harmony within human nature was the consequence of a willingness to live according to God's vision of what a human being was supposed to be. The result of that conscious intention to live 'according to God' was that humans lived in an earthly paradise that provided the good things of the body as well as of the mind (*City of God* 14:11 329).

But after the Fall this condition changed. In Augustine's view, humans chose to violate their own being in order to embrace something they thought

4

better. Sin, which to Augustine was the decision to disorder one's proper and natural relationship with God, could only have been followed by a dislocation of one's relationship with oneself. Thus the consequence of the first sin was the divided self and a body that was out of control, with ungovernable appetites and insatiable desires. Reason lost the ability to govern the body because it had lost the authority to do so. 'For the evil act could not have been arrived at if an evil will had not gone before' (*City of God* 14:11 337). The cause of an evil will was the desire to exist completely on one's own terms, without reference to other human beings. The evil will was the will to choose one's own nature, to behave like a god and not like a created being. This, to Augustine, was a form of vanity, called pride.

The decision to turn away from the good has consequences for the individual, not only in his relationship with God, but in his own integrity and authenticity, since

> by turning to himself he ended by having less true being than he had when he was rooted in him who has the highest being. Therefore to leave God and to have being in oneself... is not to be nothing already but to come nearer to being nothing.
>
> (*City of God* 14:13 338–9)

The solution to this problem, and thus the recovery of self, is to be found in the proper ordering of one's loves. It is not the act of loving that has moral stature but the object of love. Love is an activity of the will which, like the rest of our nature, was created good and correctly directed at our creation. A right will is therefore love of a good object and a wrong will is love of a bad object (*City of God* 14:3 271). The solution to the recovery of self is to direct the will towards those things that are objectively good and away from those things that lack goodness. Foremost among these goods towards which the will should be directed is God, since God is by definition the Good. The rest of our loves should be loved in their proper order. Virtue and happiness follow from the recovery of self which is consequent upon a right ordering of loves.

Among Augustine's many contributions to the history of medieval philosophy, this refusal to accept the philosophical dichotomization of the human person is surely one of the most important. While the Augustinian view acknowledges inner conflict – the duality of flesh and spirit – it denies that the only resolution to the dilemma is dichotomization. Augustine's view is that an individual must not choose to be either body or spirit, but must be both, with his will as a mediator between them. The Augustinian solution to the problem of dualism was able none the less to provide a philosophic basis upon which medieval thinkers were to build, and which persisted until Descartes (1596–1650) divided body from mind once again.

Boethius (480–524) was another transitional figure who did much to transmit pagan philosophical ideas and values, thus aiding in the foundations of a new political culture. Not only were his commentaries and translations of Aristotle's logical works and of Porphyry's introduction to Aristotle the primary source of Aristotelian philosophy before the twelfth century, but his *Consolation of Philosophy* was of inestimable influence even much later. The *Consolation* was often translated; the English King Alfred the Great produced one of the more famous medieval renderings, but versions were also made by Chaucer and Queen Elizabeth I, among many others.

A problem that puzzled medieval thinkers concerned human freedom. If God is good, one must be able to make free choices. Yet if God is omniscient, He knows the choices one will make in advance – before even one knows them oneself. Are people then really free? If not, how can God punish or reward them for their choices? By his unique understanding of time, Boethius sought to solve the problem of reconciling God's goodness with his foreknowledge. In the sixth chapter of Book V of *The Consolation of Philosophy*, Boethius turns the discussion to the nature of eternity, and thus, via the problem of foreknowledge, to the consideration of necessity. In the form of a beautiful woman, the character Philosophy appears to Boethius, who is awaiting death in a prison cell. Eternity, begins Philosophy,

> is the complete, simultaneous and perfect possession of everlasting life, this will be clear from a comparison with creatures that exist in time. Whatever lives in time exists in the present and progresses from the past to the future....
>
> (*Cons.* 163–4)

It is the fact of living in time that gives human beings their fear of God's foreknowledge. If, by seeing into the future, God can know what our choices will be before we ourselves have decided, how can we be said to choose freely?

Eternity is not, however, an infinite progression from past through present and into future, but rather the simultaneous comprehension of the whole of life. God, who lives outside of time in eternity, lives in the eternal present. God's knowledge of an action is very like ours when we watch a play – we are outside the time of the characters on stage. God's knowledge then is not properly speaking 'fore' knowledge at all, but knowledge of the eternal present. This view of God's knowledge in the eternal present obviates the problem of necessity. Since God views us as we are making choices as well as seeing the consequences of those choices, our actions cannot be said to be determined. As Philosophy argues in the *Consolation*,

> Men see things but this certainly doesn't make them necessary. And your seeing them doesn't impose any necessity on the things you see present.... And if human and divine present may be compared, just as you see things in this your present time, so God sees all things in his eternal present.
>
> (*Cons.* 167)

The idea of the eternal moment restores free will to human beings.

> God sees those future events which happen of free will as present events;... All things therefore whose future occurrence is known to God do without doubt happen, but some of them are the result of free will.
>
> (*Cons.* 167)

A God of justice and of goodness could therefore be reconciled with the omniscient God who could see the future.

THE SEARCH FOR THE GOOD

Augustine and Boethius had ensured the transmission of certain Greek philosophical questions, as well as their answers to them, which, we must remember, are questions that have been asked by many political theorists. What is the good? What kind of society will best provide the good? The simplicity of these questions is deceptive. The primary issue was a very old one. Augustine advocated the Platonic notion that the highest good is found in God. To be happy is to be virtuous, know God and be like him. To be a philosopher means to love God. But how is a philosopher to live? And what is his relationship to society to be? Understandably, the medieval thinker understood the question within the framework of his own culture. Quite commonly, the monastic movement and its primarily clerical, celibate, and male spokesmen portrayed the search for the good as dependent on the choice of the right lifestyle – considered to be the contemplative monastic life. Other individuals, including women as well as men living in the world, saw education and learning as more important than monastic life in the desire for the good.

Augustine's *City of God* was very influential in this debate. The distinction between earthly and heavenly lives and the discussion of the nature of the good led to an exploration of the various kinds or states of life that an individual might lead. Faced with a decaying and degenerate empire, on the one hand, and the fears of both Christians and pagans that the virtuous life can only be lived in a life of asceticism and self-denial, on the other, Augustine believed that the individual had to choose an actively Christian life within the confines of a very human world. To express this he used the metaphor of the heavenly and earthly cities. For Augustine, the choice was between a life of leisure 'spent in considering or enquiring into truth' as the Greek philosophers had advocated, and a life of activity 'engaged in administration of human affairs', which provided an arena for the expression of charity to others, or alternatively, some mixture of the two (*City of God* 19:2). Moreover, Augustine thought that the risks of temptation to despair and commit suicide were sufficient in a life of inactivity as led, for example, by the Stoics, to warrant the statement that they that believe that the life of the wise man must be social, we approve much more fully. For how could the City of God... reach its appointed goal, if the life of the saints were not social?

(City of God 19:5)

However, Augustine had not been alone in discussing the active and contemplative lives, nor was he even the first to discuss the issue in Christian terms. Other early figures, such as Origen (185?–254?) and Gregory of Nyssa (331–91), tended to emphasize withdrawal from active life towards a renunciatory asceticism. This subordinate view of activity was important in giving Eastern Christian spirituality its monastic and ascetic flavour, quite pronounced in comparison with Augustinian or 'Western' spirituality with its more generally positive view of life in the world.

By the late sixth century, due to the enormous influence of Pope Gregory the Great (540–604), the Augustinian distinction between inactive and active, or as Augustine sometimes called it, contemplative and administrative, remained, but the ideal of a mixed life began to disappear, which had a profound effect on political ideas. Gregory's own life and career were dominated by the aspirations of Eastern asceticism and his own incompletely fulfilled desire to embrace monastic life. When in 573, Gregory, the son of a Roman senator, sold his extensive properties in order to found seven separate monasteries, he anticipated a life spent within them, a desire that was not to be satisfied. Before his own reluctant elevation to the papacy in 590, he was called to administrative responsibility by both Pope Benedict I and Pope Pelagius II, and consequently was later filled with nostalgia for his relatively brief life as a monk.

Critically important to the development of Gregory's thought, and indeed to the entire monastic movement, was the *Rule of Saint Benedict* (480?–543?). While the *Rule* itself was written about 525 and was known in Gaul in the sixth and seventh centuries, it did not become predominant in the Empire until imperial and papal decrees made it obligatory. It was not until the extraordinary rise of the Benedictine order in the tenth and eleventh centuries that monasticism took an institutionalized form.

Throughout the intervening centuries, the various so-called 'states of life' (that is, modes of religious life outside of the secular community) formed an ill-defined and sometimes curious, but not yet institutionalized, mixture of experiences. Experimentation with varied lifestyles was common; some groups of lay people lived communally, often near a monastery, and monks themselves lived by informal and *ad hoc* collections of rules. This period of experimentation belies the neat categories of lay, clerical, and monastic living that were later to be so important to medieval thinking. Those categories only began to have concrete meaning with the tenth-century development of the Benedictine rule and the period of organization and institutionalization that followed it, culminating in the Gregorian reform movement at the end of the eleventh century. Thus, Benedict's influence was substantial, both because of the *Rule*, which provided a conduit for a modified Eastern asceticism into the West, and also because of his more direct influence on the ideas of Gregory the Great. The rise of monasticism, which formalized and institutionalized the ascetic traditions of the Eastern fathers as transmitted by Benedict and Gregory I, encouraged the development of renunciatory and separatist sentiments within the Church. Thus, by the twelfth century the monastic tradition held that the achievement or acquisition of the highest good was attainable only within the confines of monastic life.

This is of course extremely significant for political life. It presents a radical departure from the classical views of Aristotle and Cicero that political life is an important component in the search for the highest good. If by 'political' we understand some ideas about the importance of the whole community – prescribing the roles of men, women and children, citizens and foreigners, and merchants, farmers and soldiers – then ideas about the perfect society or the attainment of the good life that exclude certain groups become very troublesome. This is especially true if the good is equated with God, as it was during the Middle Ages.

Because of this dilemma, we find throughout the medieval period evidence of a competing understanding of the good life and of knowledge that fostered the development of formal education as well as a great deal of speculation about how the good society should be organized. The definition of philosophy as love of wisdom, and therefore as love of God, inspired the creation of schools. Beyond monastic schools, one encounters numerous attempts during the Middle Ages to create institutions of learning which were more broadly accessible to secular priests and lay people. Thus, for instance, royal and papal decrees called for the establishment of schools, whether as part of religious reform movements, or under enlightened monarchs such as the Frankish Emperor Charlemagne (742–814), or simply out of need for various kinds of professional training. Some of the most famous universities, those of Oxford, Cambridge, Paris, and Bologna, for example, were founded and nurtured during the Middle Ages. However, many smaller local schools, attached to noble households or to cathedral chapters, also flourished during this period, only to disappear with the Reformation.

One of the effects of educational reform, particularly in the eighth and twelfth centuries, was the devotion of attention to ideas about how the good life should be lived and the good society organized. The so-called Carolingian Renaissance of the eighth century, when the court of Charlemagne actively promoted learning and assembled scholars from throughout Europe, saw the production of a number of short works, called *speculae* or 'mirrors', that were intended as handbooks for princes on the art of ruling. This 'mirror-of-princes' genre was to continue to be a popular way to advise kings and their subjects about the nature of good government throughout the Middle Ages and Renaissance. While the actual counsel offered in the *speculae* was often highly conventionalized and afforded little room for independent reflection, later medieval authors such as John of Salisbury and Giles of Rome were able to extend the genre in order to construct original political observations and arguments.

OPERATIVE POLITICAL THOUGHT: FEUDAL SOCIETY

Another factor crucial to the formation of medieval political culture stems from the language and concepts associated with the dominant social and political system of the period, feudalism. Such ideas as contract, reciprocity, liberty, consent, representation and so forth, all of which were derived from feudal society, constituted the common currency of political life in the Middle Ages. These doctrines were employed by the great rulers and prelates of Europe during their political struggles, by propagandists and publicists in the pursuit of one or another cause, by literary creators of prose and poetry who idealized and romanticized medieval politics, and most especially by the political philosophers of the age. It is thus highly artificial to separate 'operative' political thought (that is, the precepts and language of practical political affairs) from the more intellectually sophisticated expressions of medieval political culture. When the Middle Ages attempted to frame responses to such 'perennial' questions as 'What is the good life?' or 'What is the good society?' the answers invariably depended on the conditions and assumptions imposed by the operative ideas of feudal society.

Our identification of operative political doctrines is aided by the fact that the medieval world yields a treasure trove of written records. With customary obligations and services to be rendered, manors and estates maintained careful financial accounts, many of which have been preserved to this day. Local churches registered baptisms and other significant social information, while the chroniclers of the great religious houses committed to writing the deeds of kings, princes and similar prominent men. Secretaries dutifully collected and collated the decrees and correspondence of their ecclesiastical and lay masters. Charters and concessions specifying the rights and tenures of feudal lords were solemnized by formal documents. In turn, such record keeping permits us an unprecedented opportunity to glimpse the operative political ideas arising from feudalism.

In the strictest sense, feudalism was a formalized but personal relationship of trust and loyalty obtaining between two free persons of unequal rank established for the purpose of mutual protection and benefit. More broadly, feudalism was a means of distributing and controlling land tenure and the political rights attached to it. Ideally, feudalism required that every estate, village or tract of property have a ruler who not only profited economically from his holding but also exercised primary jurisdiction over it. By no means was this lordship to be absolute or independent, however. On the contrary, direct mastery of the land and those working it was itself acquired and legitimized by the master's submission to a superior in a public act known as homage. In the ceremony of homage, the inferior (or vassal) pledged to follow and obey his superior lord, while the lord promised to cede property and jurisdictional liberty (a fief) to his vassal. Thus, the swearing of an oath of homage entailed a conditional exchange: land and power on the condition of loyalty and obedience, the latter normally expressed through the performance of military service. Moreover, the superior lord of one vassal was himself likely to be the vassal of a yet greater lord and subject to the same feudal relationship. As a hierarchical network of interconnections between greater and lesser lords, the idealized system of feudalism resembled a massive pyramid with a single and final ruler residing at its pinnacle. Generally, the peak of the pyramid was occupied by the king or emperor, whose duty was to warrant the fiefs endowed to his feudal inferiors.

Seldom did this image of the feudal pyramid match actual practice, however. In the conquered kingdoms of England and Sicily, as well as in the Crusader states of the East, the imposed structure of feudalism approximated the ideal, primarily because it was introduced 'from above'. But in the rest of Western Europe, where feudalism had evolved less artificially, feudal institutions were hardly so regularized or coherent. Instead, many lords who were technically obliged to give obedience and loyalty to superiors in fact behaved as though they were autonomous: dukes and princelings, not to mention mere castellans, acted impudently and ignored their sworn duties to the lords from whom their fiefs were held.

This reflects the disordered fashion in which feudalism had emerged out of previous Germanic, Roman and Christian practices. Both the early Germans and the Romans had employed systems of private patronage analogous to the personal association of the lord with his vassal. Roman society traditionally relied on clientage relationships in order to further the interests of patrons and retainers alike. The Germanic invaders of late antiquity and the early Middle Ages had attached to the clientage structure a military connotation: young warriors submitted to an elder by pledging to obey and serve him in return for training and maintenance.

The Church apparently contributed that other essential component of feudalism, the conditional concession of a fief. Although a great landholder by the close of the first millennium, the Church was forbidden by canon law to protect itself by violent means. Hence, in order to defend its properties during dangerous times, the Church granted benefices to laymen, which allowed them the use of certain holdings without concession of title in return for military aid. By the year 1000, these developments seem to have been sufficiently generalized that it is possible to speak of Europe as predominantly feudal, in the sense that most property was held on condition of the performance of military service to some superior. But because of the utterly disorganized manner in which feudal institutions spread and were implemented, disconformities abounded: jurisdictions overlapped,

11

boundaries were disputed, and obligations were ignored or challenged. The early practice of feudalism in much of Europe was thus characterized by fragmentation, absence of political control and a general attitude of independence from superior authority.

This context contributed to the formulation of the medieval concept of liberty. To the feudal epoch, a liberty designated a sphere of jurisdiction within which an individual was free to act without external interference or constraint. Normally, particular feudal lords were said to enjoy liberties, although the grant of a liberty might be made to a guild or urban community in the form of a special privilege. But this medieval sense of liberty was in all cases different from earlier classical and Christian notions: to Greeks like Plato and Aristotle, liberty conveyed the negative connotation of the licence to do exactly as one pleased without regard for moral or political rectitude; in the Christian tradition, liberty denoted the submission of one's private will to the will of God expressed by His law. In contrast, feudal liberty was understood as freedom from a servitude, that is, the right of an individual or group to exercise its own judgement separate from and in the absence of any determination by a superior. Thus, when the English document Magna Carta (1215) declared that the liberties of all subjects are to be respected by the king, it meant that the ruler cannot unilaterally or arbitrarily infringe upon or withdraw those prerogatives specifically conceded to lords and communities. This is not to say that the possessors of liberties could exercise power indiscriminately. The grant of a franchise never entailed the delegation of unlimited authority and abuses could always justify suppression of a prerogative. But broadly speaking, liberty functioned in feudal society like the doctrine of subjective natural rights would in early modern European politics: it guaranteed to private persons a proper realm of action apart from and outside the direct influence of a suzerain or sovereign.

The medieval idea of liberty also illustrates one of the essential features of feudalism, its tendency towards political disintegration. Liberty was often invoked by the rebellious subjects of kings and princes in order to assert their autonomy from superior powers. Indeed, the feudal system itself made provision for action against the superior lord who insisted upon denying the liberty of those beholden to him. In a famous letter dating to 1020, Bishop Fulbert of Chartres (d. 1028) proclaimed that in the various duties and obligations required of the vassal, 'the lord must also in all things do similarly to his vassal'. Thus, reciprocity was the hallmark of the feudal bond, and the specification of mutual obligation gave a measure of security to the vassal. If the vassal was alleged to have violated his oath by failure to perform his service, or by disloyalty, the lord could not punish him without first securing the judgement of the vassal's peers in a formal court proceeding. If the lord broke the contract by depriving the vassal of his rights or liberties, the vassal could properly renounce allegiance once he had publicly withdrawn his homage and fealty. The operative political thought of the Middle Ages was constructed around an agreement between the ruler and the ruled such that the subject retained the option to resist any of his ruler's commands which were pronounced arbitrarily.

In view of these doctrines, one might expect feudal society to be constantly on the verge of dissolution and collapse. In fact, feudalism proved to be a remarkably stable and resilient political system, due in large measure to its corresponding conceptions of law and justice. The legal process in feudal society rested on a high degree of involvement by those over whom law was enforced. In the first place, the law administered in a feudal court was essentially customary. Precepts were deemed valid depending upon whether they had persisted 'from the time when the memory of man runs not to the contrary', to cite a popular medieval phrase. This reflected the presumption that any custom of long standing would already be well known and as a consequence would be more easily enforceable. The notion of law as the product of a positive legislative enactment was thus largely neglected during the Middle Ages, even once the rationalistic principles engendered by canon and Roman legal systems had become widely disseminated. The content of law was to be found or discovered, not created anew. Law was thus what people generally accepted through usage to be proper and fit, instead of what rulers or their expert advisors considered to be just. And judgement in accordance with law depended upon the reports of individuals as to the relevant established custom and procedure. Admittedly, unusual circumstances might force the clarification or modification of customary precepts. Yet even this was undertaken collectively, in consultation with those over whom the law was enforced. Because law within feudal society was conceived to be the result of generations of common agreement, no individual could claim to be above the law by virtue of having propounded it. Regardless of Romanist teachings about the absolute supremacy of the royal will, the king or prince was expected to subject himself to the same laws which governed the deeds of his subjects.

The primary mechanism which assured that the medieval monarch behaved in accordance with law was his feudal obligation to seek the consent of his vassals prior to undertaking any novel or important action. Fulbert of Chartres had admonished the vassal of his duty to 'counsel and aid his lord', and the obligation pertained no less to the lord to accept 'counsel and aid' from vassals. When royal governments extended their authority during the course of the twelfth and thirteenth centuries, the traditional requirement of 'counsel and aid' was pressed by members of the feudal aristocracy as a remedy to the growing independence of kings. In response, rulers began to consult publicly and collectively with greater subjects on matters of common concern by convening royal councils. The forum of the council allowed grievances to be heard, judicial cases and principles of law to be settled, plans for peace and war to be discussed, extraordinary taxes to be imposed and, in general, the policies of the Crown to be fixed. Initially, attendance at such royal assemblies was strictly limited to the king's closest advisors and officials, in conjunction with dukes, barons, abbots, bishops and analogous lay and ecclesiastical magnates. But eventually the composition of the council in most European nations expanded to encompass delegations from lesser landholders, the lower priesthood and even larger urban centres. By the close of the thirteenth century, the feudal requirement of 'counsel and aid' was transformed into the basis for full-fledged parliamentary institutions. Such medieval assemblies retained all of the functions of earlier royal councils, while incorporating into the process of governmental decision-making an unprecedented range of voices and interests. Although it is too soon to speak of these parliamentary convocations as truly 'popular' in nature, feudalism nevertheless generated the principle that the prior consent of the governed is necessary for the king to act on a wide variety of fiscal, legal, judicial and military initiatives.

THE BIRTH OF TEMPORAL POLITICS

One of the most striking features of public life during the early Middle Ages was the extent to which the functions of secular politics intermingled with ecclesiastical affairs. This interpenetration of spiritual and temporal realms arose to a great extent out of the Christian tradition itself, which stressed the sacral basis of kingship and the character of the prince as minister of the Church. Scriptural texts declared the king to be the 'servant of God' (see Romans 13:4), a view that was reinforced by clerical participation in the process of royal consecration. Consequently, early medieval rulers styled themselves protectors of the Church and defenders of the faith, and they often encouraged the clergy to reform itself by adopting a more spiritual tone. Thus, kings felt well qualified to intervene in ecclesiastical matters, since their involvement was so widely sanctioned by Christian doctrine and practice.

This pattern of spiritual–temporal relations shifted drastically in the second half of the eleventh century, however, in the wake of a series of events usually grouped together under the label of the Investiture Controversy. The issue at stake was the unity of secular and religious functions with which ecclesiastical magnates (ranking officials like bishops and abbots) were endowed. Throughout the Middle Ages such officials were not only leaders of the Church but also amongst the most powerful and wealthy of feudal lords, administering vast tracts of land and prerogatives on behalf of their parishioners and orders. Not surprisingly, secular rulers took a strong interest in the appointments made to these posts. While in theory bishoprics and abbeys could only be filled through an election by the canons or brothers, in practice temporal princes usually authorized the appointments in order to secure loyal incumbents. Thus, bishops or abbots often seemed more concerned to serve the interests of their temporal rulers than to seek the welfare of their churches or the care of souls. Moreover, kings were easily tempted into the sale of ecclesiastical offices (the sin of simony).

The secular character of many Church offices became controversial over the course of the eleventh century, when the Church experienced several waves of reforms. The culmination of this reforming urge came with the elevation of Pope Gregory VII (1073–85), who prohibited the appointment of clerical officials by temporal rulers (so-called lay investiture) in a 1075 decree. Gregory's prohibition was unequivocal:

> No one of the clergy shall receive investiture with a bishopric or abbey or church from the hand of an emperor or king or any lay person, male or female. But if he shall presume to do so he shall clearly know that such investiture is bereft of apostolic authority, and that he himself shall lie under excommunication until fitting satisfaction shall have been rendered.

This proclamation sparked off a conflict with the Roman Emperor Henry IV (1056–1106), who viewed the Gregorian position as a direct affront to his customary rights as a temporal ruler and to his ability to maintain political order within German society. In the course of the ensuing controversy, Gregory and Henry each asserted the ultimate authority of his respective office over the other, to the extent that they both issued proclamations of deposition against one another. Gregory's case was founded on the doctrine of the independence of the Church from the control of secular powers, and of the spiritual right of the pope to 'bind and loose souls', that is, to judge the faithful. Henry based his defence upon the claims that secular rulers were the immediate agents of God, that their supremacy was confirmed by their anointment, and that they were therefore subject solely to God's judgment.

The emergence of this conflict was significant for the development of medieval political thought in several ways. First, the Investiture Controversy stimulated a vast polemical literature dedicated to the examination of the bases of temporal power – the earliest instance of such an investigation in the medieval West. These pamphlets, which incorporated arguments on behalf of both papal and imperial causes, were composed by some of the finest minds of the late eleventh century and articulated a number of themes which were to continue to be important in Western political thought. Some authors, like Hugh of Fleury, extended the thesis of the secular ruler's divine mission, while others (like Honorius Augustodunesis) propounded the view that since God conferred royal power by means of the priesthood, secular princes were beholden to the clergy for their offices. Other participants in the war of propaganda appealed to rudimentary versions of social contract theory to support their positions. On the one side, Manegold of Lautenbach argued that Christian subjects had a duty to withdraw their allegiance from any ruler who refused to submit to the Church and its doctrines, since 'he who disdains Christian obedience should be judged unworthy of ruling Christians'. On the other side, the anonymous tract *On the Conservation of the Unity of the Church* (*c.* 1090) asserted that only the common consent of the great men of the realm was adequate to create or depose kings. In sum, the Investiture Controversy provided an early opportunity for thinkers to begin to speculate about the nature and origins of government and rulership, and thus created an intellectual climate within which secular political thought might emerge.

The eventual resolution of the conflict was no less important for the evolution of medieval political ideas. The contest between papal and temporal authorities persisted into the early twelfth century, spreading to other Western European countries. Although it may be too simplistic to say that the views of the Gregorian reformers were victorious, the Church did succeed in establishing its independence from secular control in a manner analogous to that originally proposed by Gregory VII. In 1107 King Henry I of England renounced his rights of investiture, although on condition that ecclesiastical magnates continue to perform feudal homage to the Crown. Similar terms were accepted by the German Emperor Henry V (1106–1125) in 1122, after another prolonged period of strife between the imperial and papal powers. The effect of this resolution was more profound than it might appear. For thousands of years, the pre-modern societies of Rome, Egypt, China, Mexico, Peru and Japan, for example, were essentially theocratic, that is ruled by a God-King or by a priestly caste. The distinctively different character of Western and modern politics developed in part through the separation of secular from religious power. For in freeing the offices of the Church from the direct control of princes, the secular rulers had also succeeded in liberating themselves from immediate responsibility for religious and ecclesiastical affairs. Likewise, religious leaders liberated themselves from the burden of secular responsibilities. Henceforth, the world of medieval politics was understood to be composed of two mutually independent coordinate powers: the *regnum* (secular kingdom) and the *sacerdotium* (spiritual realm). Each of these spheres enjoyed its own distinct concerns and interests which, while somewhat overlapping, were fundamentally separate. This lent to temporal politics a measure of autonomy which it had not enjoyed previously during the Middle Ages. It also created a political climate within which theoretical speculation about uniquely human, earthly public affairs could commence. Thus, the resolution of the Investiture Controversy in the early twelfth century simultaneously heralded the dawning of a more strictly secular tradition within medieval political theory.

FURTHER READING

Primary sources (cited here)

Augustine, *The City of God*, trans. Henry Bettenson, London, Penguin, 1984.
Boethius, *The Consolation of Philosophy*, trans. V.E. Watts, London, Penguin, 1969.

General works

Black, A., *Guilds and Society in European Political Thought from the Twelfth Century to the Present*, Ithaca, Cornell University Press, 1984.

Black, A., *Medieval Political Thought, 1250–1450*, Cambridge, Cambridge University Press, 1992.

Brown, Peter, *The Body and Society*, New York, Columbia University Press, 1988.

Burns, J.H., ed., *The Cambridge History of Medieval Political Thought*, Cambridge, Cambridge University Press, 1988.

Kantorowicz, H., *The King's Two Bodies: A Study in Medieval Political Theology*, Princeton, Princeton University Press, 1957.

Kretzmann, N., A. Kenny and J. Pinborg, eds, *The Cambridge History of Later Medieval Philosophy*, Cambridge, Cambridge University Press, 1982.

Lewis, C.S., *The Discarded Image*, Cambridge, Cambridge University Press, 1964.

Lewis, E., *Medieval Political Ideas*, 2 vols, London, Routledge and Kegan Paul, 1954.

Morrall, J.B., *Political Thought in Medieval Times*, New York, Harper and Row, 1962.

Myers, H.A., *Medieval Kingship*, Chicago, Nelson Hall, 1982.

Nederman, C.J., 'Aristotle as Authority: Alternative Aristotelian Sources of Late Medieval Political Theory', *History of European Ideas*, 8, 1987, 31–44.

Nederman, C.J., 'Nature, Sin and the Origins of Society: The Ciceronian Tradition in Medieval Political Thought', *Journal of the History of Ideas*, 49, 1988, 3–26.

Skinner, Q., *The Foundations of Modern Political Thought*, 2 vols, Cambridge, Cambridge University Press, 1978.

Smalley, B., ed., *Trends in Medieval Political Thought*, Oxford, Basil Blackwell, 1965.

Stock, Brian, *The Implications of Literacy*, Princeton, Princeton University Press, 1982.

Tierney, B., *The Crisis of Church and State 1050–1300*, Engelwood Cliffs, Prentice-Hall, 1964.

Tierney, B., *Religion, Law, and the Growth of Constitutional Thought, 1150–1650*, Cambridge, Cambridge University Press, 1983.

Tierney, B. and P. Linehan, eds, *Power and Authority*, Cambridge, Cambridge University Press, 1980.

Tuck, R., *Natural Rights Theories: Their Origin and Development*, Cambridge, Cambridge University Press, 1979.

Part I

THE TWELFTH CENTURY

1

LETTER TO POPE EUGENIUS III
Bernard of Clairvaux

INTRODUCTION

Bernard of Clairvaux (1090–1153) was a fiery preacher, an inspiring correspondent, and a prayerful 'father of souls' who had tremendous influence on
medieval life and ideas. He was born into an aristocratic family in France and
received the education appropriate to his age and class, and, presumably, his
family expected him to have an influential career as well. But in 1111,
Bernard entered a poor and strict monastery at Citeaux, accompanied by a
number of young noble friends. Three years later, he was sent by his abbot
to found a 'daughter house' at Clairvaux, the monastery associated with his
name. From there he began a career that would influence popes, kings,
scholars, lay people and monks. He had a burning desire to extend the
reforms of the monastic movement to the whole Church – emperors and
popes included. His zeal for reform, his charisma, intelligence, and, one
suspects, a touch of self-righteousness, led him to accuse the philosopher
Peter Abelard of heresy, to rebuke Emperor Lothair for his support of the rival
Pope Antecletus, to preach (at the request of Pope Eugenius III) in favour of
the Second Crusade. Throughout his long and influential career, he wrote
hundreds of letters of instruction, rebuke, encouragement, consolation, and
common sense to a varied audience of the poor and humble as well as the
rich and powerful. He was canonized in 1170.

   The letter included here had far more influence on medieval political ideas
than would appear. It was long considered to be written about 1146 and to
be describing the Second Crusade. Today some scholars believe it was
written later, about 1150, and that it was to encourage the Pope to launch a
new expedition to recapture the 'Holy Lands' and the city of Jerusalem. In
any case, the letter articulates the doctrine of the 'two swords' which was
used to justify the Pope's temporal as well as spiritual authority. Told in
slightly different versions in each of the four Gospels, the story of Jesus' arrest
in the garden of Gethsemane was understood by Bernard to signify the

origins of Christian political power (Matthew 26:51–6, Mark 14:47, Luke 22:49–52, John 18:10–12). At the end of the meal which Jesus was eating with his followers, he warns them of the dangers to come and tells them that they should sell what they can to buy swords. The disciples show him that they already have two swords and Jesus says 'It is enough' (Luke 22:36–8). During the scuffle in the garden later that same evening, Peter drew his sword to defend Jesus, at which time Jesus commanded Peter to sheathe his weapon. Consequently, although Peter had the right to the 'sword' of temporal power, and therefore political authority, he and his successors were not permitted to shed blood.

LETTER TO POPE EUGENIUS III

The news is not good, but is sad and grave. And sad for whom? Rather, for whom is it not sad! Only for the sons of wrath, who do not feel anger, nor are they saddened by the sad events, but rejoice and exult in them. For everyone else, it is sad because it is a cause that affects the community. You have done well to praise the just zeal of the Church in France, and to corroborate its authority with your letters. I tell you, such a general and serious crisis is not an occasion to act tepidly nor timidly. I have read [in the book of] a certain wise man: 'He is not brave whose spirit does not rise in difficulty.' And I would add that a faithful person is even more faithful in disaster. The waters have risen to the soul of Christ, and touch the very pupil of his eye. Now, in this new suffering of our Lord Christ, we must draw the swords of the first Passion. And by whom else, if not you? Peter has them both to draw when necessary; one by his command, the other by his hand. One of them was not to be used by Peter, since he was told 'Put your sword in the scabbard.' Therefore, they were both his, but one was not to be drawn by his hand.

I believe that it is time for both to be drawn in defence of the Eastern Church. You hold the position, you ought also to have the zeal. What is it to hold the chief position and decline the responsibility? A voice is heard, 'I go to Jerusalem to be crucified again.' Some may be indifferent to it, others deaf, but the successor of Peter may not ignore it. He will say therefore, 'All may be offended by you, but I am not.' He will not be dismayed by the prior defeat of the army, but rather will do his best to restore it. Is there any reason for a man not to do his duty, just because God does as He wishes?

Truly, as I am a Christian and a believer, despite all the evils, I will hope for better, and I believe it to be a great joy, that we will find the way through various tribulations. Truly, we have eaten the bread of sorrow and drunk the wine of compunction. Why are you distrustful, friend of the Bridegroom, as though the kind and wise Bridegroom had not, as usual, delayed serving the good wine? Who knows, if God changes His mind, perhaps He will forgive, and leave behind a blessing? And certainly, as you know, the highest Divinity is accustomed to judge in this way. When has great good not been preceded

22

by great evil? To mention nothing else, was not the unique and singular benefit of our salvation preceded by the death of our Saviour?

You therefore, friend of the Bridegroom, prove yourself a friend in need. If you love Christ with that triple love about which your predecessor was questioned [cf. John 21: 15–17] – with all your heart, with all your soul, with all your strength – then it is necessary to have no reservations, no inattention, while the bride is in danger; but watch over her with all the strength, with all the zeal, with all the care, with all the authority, with all the power that you have. An extraordinary danger demands an extraordinary effort. The foundation is shaken, and imminent ruin follows unless resisted. I have written boldly, but also truthfully for your sake.

You have heard by now that the assembly at Chartres chose me (in an amazing decision) leader and head of the military expedition, which, you may be sure, was not then nor is it now my wish. I am not capable (as I measure my strengths) of accomplishing such a thing. Who am I to set up camp efficiently or lead forth armed men? There is nothing more remote from my vows, even if I had the strength and the skill. But you know all this, it is not for me to lead you to wisdom. I ask humbly, by the love you particularly owe me, not to abandon me to human caprice; but ask eagerly for divine counsel, as particularly incumbent on you, and work diligently, so that as His will is done in heaven, it will also be on earth.

2

THE FABLE OF A MAN, HIS BELLY, AND HIS LIMBS

Marie de France

INTRODUCTION

Stereotypes about the Middle Ages abound, and the writings of Marie de France (fl. *c.* 1160) disprove several of them: she was a woman who was literate yet probably not a nun, she knew Latin as well as French, she was proud of her work and willing to take steps to defend it from others' claims. Although details of her life are few, tantalizing bits of information can be found in her work. Scholars speculate that she was educated in Latin as well as French, and that she knew some English. It is believed that she had some connection with the literate, sophisticated Anglo-Norman court of Henry II of England and his queen Eleanor of Aquitaine.

We know today of three works composed by her: a collection of narrative poems, 'Lais'; a translation from Latin of a twelfth century tale about a trip to the underworld, *St Patrick's Purgatory*; and her collection of fables. But 'facts' about her life – who she was, where in France she was from, or how she lived, are very few.

The selection we have chosen from Marie's works is a fable, the theme of which enjoyed great popularity in the Middle Ages. It was considered to have a political 'moral' stemming from the metaphor of the body politic, a metaphor that was often used to express ideas about politics. The story that the fable tells has two major classical sources: Livy's *History of the Romans* which was the more 'scholarly' and philosophical source; and the Greek fabulist Aesop, whose work was translated into Latin in the fourth century by Romulus. Marie's French version of the story made it accessible to non-scholars as well. It is even possible that Marie's contemporary, John of Salisbury, heard her tell the story at Henry II's court.

THE FABLE OF A MAN, HIS BELLY, AND HIS LIMBS

Of a man, I wish to tell,
As an example to remember,
Of his hands and of his feet,
and of his head – they were angry
Towards the belly that he carried,
About their earnings that it ate.
Then, they would not work anymore,
And they deprived it of its food.

But when the belly fasted,
They were quickly weakened.
Hands and feet had no strength
To work now as they were accustomed.
Food and drink they offered the belly
But they had starved it too long.
It did not have the strength to eat.
The belly dwindled to nothing
And the hands and feet went too.

From this example, one can see
What every free person ought to know:
No one can have honour
Who brings shame to his lord.
Nor can his lord have it either
If he wishes to shame his people.
If either one fails the other
Evil befalls them both.

3

METALOGICON AND *POLICRATICUS*

John of Salisbury

INTRODUCTION

The twelfth century is commonly considered to be a period of intellectual renaissance in such fields as philosophy, literature and law. One of the beneficiaries of this revival was political theory. By the mid-1100s, sustained and systematic reflection about the nature and purpose of political society, and about the normative standards by which political institutions ought to be judged, was a feature of the medieval intellectual landscape. No one contributed more to this renaissance of political theory than John of Salisbury (c. 1120–80). A native of Old Sarum (the original site of Salisbury), John received the best education available during the 1130s and 1140s: studying at Paris (and possibly Chartres), he encountered the lessons of Peter Abelard, Thierry of Chartres, William of Conches, and many other outstanding minds of his time. In 1148, after a dozen years in France, John entered the service of Theobald, Archbishop of Canterbury, as his secretary and confidant. Theobald's household attracted a large pool of talent, including Thomas Becket, the future Archbishop and martyr, whom John may first have met in Paris. When Becket left Theobald's service at the end of 1154 to become Chancellor to King Henry II, John composed a satirical poem, the 'Entheticus on the Teachings of the Philosophers', which warns of the dangers and pitfalls of court life. John himself was soon to discover how precarious public service could be: falling into disfavour with the King for some unspecified reason, he withstood a period of internal exile in 1156/1157, during which time he seems to have conceived and begun to write his two major works, the *Metalogicon* and the *Policraticus* (both completed in 1159). Restored to royal favour, John found himself taking on increasing responsibility in Theobald's household as the Archbishop's health declined. In the wake of Theobald's death in 1161 and Becket's appointment as his successor, John remained in the service of the new Archbishop, and eventually (if less than wholeheartedly) followed his master into exile during the course of his conflict with Henry II over the rights of the Church. The tale that John was present at and wounded in the assassination of Becket at the altar of Canterbury Cathedral in 1170 is merely fanciful. After the Archbishop's demise, John remained active in ecclesiastical affairs, and was appointed Bishop of Chartres in 1176.

John stood at the pinnacle of learning in the mid-twelfth century, and was an influential figure in the cause of humanistic instruction. His *Metalogicon*, a survey of the state of academic education and a critique of current pedagogical attitudes, stressed the capacity of human beings to enhance the gifts of nature and divine grace by way of concerted study and practice. Attacking the so-called 'Cornificians', a pseudonym for his opponents who maintained the rigidity of intellectual endowments, John pointed out that the fruits of social and political association only became possible as a result of the progressive refinement of the rational and linguistic skills of humankind. In this regard, John reveals himself to be a devoted adherent to Cicero's political and rhetorical thought.

The *Policraticus*, John's 'mirror' of the moral and political standards by which governments are to be evaluated, places a similar emphasis on edification, in this case on the education of rulers and their servants. Subtitled 'Of the Frivolities of Courtiers and the Footprints of Philosophers', the *Policraticus* is often described as the first complete work of medieval political theory. John begins with a long satirical critique of the temptations associated with public life, surveying the many forms of courtly entertainment which distract officials from the performance of their duties. He stresses the importance of the moral instruction of the ruler and the necessity for the king to surround himself with literate and wise counsellors; an evil prince with equally vicious advisors will necessarily be a tyrant who enslaves and oppresses his people. John asserts that a well-organized political community will resemble a healthy human body, guided by the soul (priesthood), ruled by a wise head (the king), and populated by all the limbs and organs (from the counselling heart to peasant feet) necessary for the efficient, just and mutually beneficial functioning of the entire organism. When this is achieved, the *Policraticus* states, the order implicit in nature is realized, the divine will is obeyed, and the earthly as well as eternal happiness of all members is assured. A badly arranged body politic, in which some or all of the parts seek their own good in separation from the common welfare, is impious, unnatural and ultimately miserable. John insists that when the lesser members of the body politic stray from the public good, the king is ultimately responsible for their correction or punishment. Should the ruler himself behave in a tyrannical manner, however, his subjects (if they are just) are equally bound by their duty to guide him back to the proper path or, failing that, to replace him. On these grounds, John takes the important step of defending the political and religious legitimacy of killing the incorrigible tyrant.

METALOGICON

BOOK 1

Chapter 1

...To all who are truly wise, there is no doubt that nature, the most merciful parent and the best disposed moderator of all affairs, has raised up human beings, among the other animated creatures it has brought forth, by the privilege of reason and has distinguished them by the faculty of eloquent speech, arranging by obliging diligence and well-disposed law that man, who is burdened and drawn down by the weight of base nature and the sluggishness of the bodily mass, may rise to the heights, borne aloft as though by beating wings, and that by this fortunate advantage he may surpass all others in obtaining the pinnacle of true happiness. Therefore, while grace makes nature fertile, [natural] reason watches over the investigation and examination of various matters, searches the inner depths of nature, and measures the fruits and accomplishments of individual persons, and by the love of goodness innate in everyone, urged along by one's natural appetite, reason strives entirely or above all else for that which seems to be well-suited to taking hold of true happiness. Since no one who is unaware of communal life or who stands outside society can even conceive of true happiness, whoever attacks that which brings about the unification and fostering of the right of human society (which is in a certain way the unique and singular fraternity among the children of nature) would seem to obstruct everyone's path to the attainment of happiness, and the route to peace is so blocked that the depths of nature combine to incite the destruction of the world. The effect of this is to propagate discord among brothers, to hand out weapons to the peaceful, and lastly to encourage a new and great chaos between God and human beings. For the creative Trinity, the one and true God, has so ordered the parts of the universe for the sake of a more firmly joined connection and protective charity that each one requires the assistance of the others and a defect in one is repaired by the others, insofar as each individual part is like a member of the other individual parts. All things are, therefore, incomplete if they are disconnected from one another, but otherwise they are perfected if they are associated, because everything stands in a firm relation of reciprocal aid. What is more trustworthy and useful for the sake of acquiring happiness than virtue? What is more profitable? For virtue is almost the singular and unique path which grace has provided for the sake of happiness. For those who are blessed without the merits of the virtues do not so much attain to it by themselves as are carried off to it. Consequently, I do not marvel enough (because I cannot) at what is intended by someone who denies that eloquent speech is to be studied, and who asserts it to arise from nature as a gift to those who are not mute, just as sight is a gift to those who are not blind or hearing to those not deaf, but who insists that even if the gift of nature is reinforced by training, still no benefit is offered by such art, or the art is of less worth than the effort expended. For just as eloquent speech is not only defiled but also dense when not illuminated by reason, so also wisdom which is not proficient in the use of words is not only disarmed but is in a certain manner crippled. For although speechless wisdom can sometimes reveal itself to a considerable extent within the confines of the solace of self-awareness, still seldom and to a small extent does it contribute to the utility of human society. For reason – the parent, wet-nurse and custodian of knowledge and virtue – which frequently conceives by means of words and which gives birth more prolifically and more fruitfully through words, either remains entirely sterile or at least unproductive if its fruitful conceptions were not brought forth into the light by the practice of eloquence and the prudent activity of which the human mind is cognizant were not made known everywhere. It is this sweet and fruitful marriage of reason and words that has engendered so many distinguished cities, has reconciled and allied so many kingdoms, and has united and tied together in love so many peoples, so that whomever endeavours to separate that which God has wedded for the sake of the common utility is universally condemned to the punishment accorded the public enemy. He who excludes the lessons of eloquence from the study of philosophy begrudges Philology to Mercury [the god of eloquence] and tears Mercury from the embrace of Philology. And although he may seem only to persecute eloquent speech, he disrupts all liberal studies, he assails all the works of every one of the philosophers, he breaks apart the covenant of human society, and he leaves behind no opportunity for charity or reciprocity of duties. Human beings become beasts if they are deprived of the gift of speech granted to them, and their cities would seem rather like enclosures for livestock than assemblies of human beings joined together by a certain covenant, so that by its law they may live according to shared duties and reciprocal friendship with one another. For what contracted would be properly honoured, what instruction in faith and morals would be esteemed, what voluntary obedience or sharing would occur, were verbal intercourse to be removed? Therefore, our Cornificius, that ignorant and evil opponent of the study of eloquence, attacks not one person, not a few people, but all cities at once and the whole of political life.

POLICRATICUS: OF THE FRIVOLITIES OF COURTIERS AND THE FOOTPRINTS OF PHILOSOPHERS

BOOK 4

Chapter 1: On the difference between the ruler and the tyrant, and what the ruler is

There is wholly or mainly this difference between the tyrant and the ruler: that the latter is obedient to law, and rules his people by a will that places itself at their service, and administers rewards and burdens within the republic under the guidance of law in a way favourable to the vindication of his eminent post, so that he proceeds before others to the extent that, while individuals merely look after individual objects, rulers are concerned with the burdens of the entire community. Hence, there is deservedly conferred on him power over all his subjects, in order that he is sufficient in himself to seek out and bring about the utility of each and all, and that he may arrange the optimal condition of the human republic, so that everyone is a member of the others. In this, nature, that best guide to living, is to be followed, since it is nature which has lodged all of the senses in the head as a microcosm, that is, a little world, of man, and has subjected to it the totality of the members in order that all of them may move correctly provided that the will of a sound head is followed. The ruler is raised to the apex and becomes illustrious, therefore, as a result of his many and great privileges which are as numerous and extensive as are thought to be necessary for him. Certainly this is proper because nothing is useful to the people except that which fulfils the needs of the ruler, since his will should never be found opposed to justice.

Therefore, according to the general definition, the ruler is the public power and a certain image on earth of the divine majesty. Beyond doubt the greatest part of the divine virtue is revealed to belong to the ruler, insofar as at his nod men bow their heads and generally offer their necks to the axe in sacrifice, and by divine impulse everyone fears him who is fear itself. I do not believe that this could have happened unless it happened at the divine command. For all power is from the Lord God, and is with him always, and is His forever. Whatever the ruler can do, therefore, is from God, so that power does not depart from God, but it is used as a substitute for His hand, making all things learn His justice and mercy. 'Whoever therefore resists power, resists what is ordained by God' [Romans 13:2], in whose power is the conferral of authority and at whose will it may be removed from them or limited. For it is not even the ruler's own power when his will is harsh to his subjects, but a divine dispensation at His good will to punish or train subjects. From this we see that during the persecution by the Huns, Attila was questioned by the holy bishop of a certain city about who he was, to which he responded: 'I am Attila, scourge of God'; the bishop venerated him (it is written) as a divine majesty. He said, 'The minister of God is well honoured'; and also, 'Blessed is he who comes in the name of God.' The gates of the church were mournfully unbarred to admit the persecutor through whose hand martyrdom was attained. For he had not the audacity to exclude the scourge of God because he knew that His cherished son had been scourged and that there was no power to scourge him except from the Lord.

If, consequently, power is regarded as venerable by those who are good, even to the degree that it is a plague upon the elect, who ought not venerate what is instituted by God for the punishment of wrongdoers, for the approval of the truly good, and for the enforcement of devoted service to the laws? 'It is indeed an adage worthy', as the Emperor has it, 'of the majesty of kings that the ruler professes an obligation to his own laws. Because the authority of the ruler is determined by the authority of right, and truly submission to the laws of rulers is greater than the imperial title' [Justinian, *Codex* 1.14.4], so it is the case that the ruler ought to imagine himself permitted to do nothing which is inconsistent with the equity of justice.

Chapter 2. What law is; and that the ruler, although he is an absolutely binding law unto himself, still is the servant of law and equity, the bearer of the public persona, and sheds blood blamelessly

Rulers should not suppose that they are disparaged by the belief that the justice of God, whose justice is eternal justice and whose law is equity, is preferable to the justice of their own statutes. Furthermore, equity (as the experts in law assert) is a matter of what is appropriate, according to which reason equalizes the whole and seeks just equality in matters of inequality; what is equitable to all is what grants to each person that which is his own. Its interpreter is law, in as much as law makes known the will of equity and justice. And thus Chrysippus asserted that law has power over all divine and human affairs, for which reason it presides over all good and all evil and is ruler and guide of things as well as of men. Papinian, a man of the greatest experience in matters of jurisprudence, and Demosthenes, the influential orator, would seem to support this and to subject all men to its obedience because all law is a sort of discovery and gift from God, the teaching of the wise, the corrective to excesses of wilfulness, the harmony of the city, and the banishment of all crime. It is proper for all who dwell in the community of political affairs to live according to it. All are, for this reason, obligated to be restrained by the necessity of observing the laws, unless perhaps someone imagines that he is granted the licence of iniquity.

Still the ruler is said to be an absolutely binding law unto himself, not because he is licensed to be iniquitous, but only because he should be someone who does not fear the penalties of law but someone who loves justice, cherishes equity, procures the utility of the republic, and in all matters prefers the advantage of others to his private will. But who in public affairs may even speak of the will of the ruler, since in such matters he is not permitted his own will unless it is prompted by law or equity, or brings about judgements for the common utility? For in fact his will in these matters should have the force of judgement; and that which most rightfully pleases him in all matters has the force of law because his determination may not be inconsistent with the design of equity. 'From your visage,' it is said, 'my judgement proceeds, your eyes must look at equity' [Psalms 17:2]; for indeed the uncorrupted judge is one whose determination is on the basis of the assiduous contemplation of the image of equity. The ruler is therefore the minister of the public utility and the servant of equity, and in him the public persona is borne since he punishes all injuries and wrongs, and also all crimes, with moderate equity. In addition, his rod and staff, exercised with the moderation of wisdom, return all deviations and errors to the way of equity, so that the Holy Spirit may meritoriously congratulate the ruler, saying: 'Your rod and your staff, they are comforts to me' [Psalms 23:4]. While his shield is also strong, still it is a shield for the feeble and one which deflects the darts of malignance from the innocent. Those who are advanced most by his duties of office are those who can do least for themselves, and those who most desire to do harm are those who draw the greatest hostility.

That sword with which blood is shed innocently is therefore not borne without cause, so that one may frequently kill and still not be a man of blood nor incur the accusation of murder or crime. For if one may believe the great Augustine, David is called a man of blood not as the result of war, but as a result of Uriah. And Samuel is nowhere indicted as a man of blood or a murderer, although he killed Agag, the obese king of Amalek. This is indeed the sword of the dove, which quarrels without bitterness, which slaughters without wrathfulness and which, when fighting, entertains no resentment whatsoever. For since law will prosecute the blameworthy without personal animosity, the ruler most properly punishes transgressors not according to some wrathful motive, but by the peaceful will of law. For although it may be seen that the ruler has his own public executioners, we ought to think of him as the sole or primary executioner to whom it is permitted to allow a substitute hand. And we may agree with the Stoics, who have diligently investigated the reasons for names, when they say that 'public executioner' (*lictor*) is derived from 'stick of the law' (*legis ictor*) because it is the aim of his duties to strike down whoever the law adjudges must be struck down. And, for this reason, those officials of antiquity by whose hand the judge punished the guilty would be told, 'Comply with the will of the law' or 'Satisfy the law', when they hung the sword over the criminal, so that the grief of the situation might be mitigated by the mercifulness of these words.

Chapter 3: That the ruler is a minister of priests and their inferior; and what it is for rulers to perform their ministry faithfully

This sword is therefore accepted by the ruler from the hand of the Church, although it still does not itself possess the bloody sword entirely. For while it has this sword, yet it is used by the hand of the ruler, upon whom is conferred the power of bodily coercion, reserving spiritual authority for the papacy. The ruler is therefore a sort of minister of the priests and one who exercises those features of the sacred duties that seem an indignity in the hands of priests. For all duties of sacred law are in fact the affairs of the religious and the pious, yet that duty is inferior which executes the punishment of crime and which seems to be represented by images of executioners. And for this reason, Constantine, the most faithful emperor of the Romans, when he had convened the Nicean Council of priests, neither ventured to take the foremost position nor allowed himself to mingle with the presbyters, but occupied the hindmost seat. The decisions which were heard to be approved by them were venerated by him, just as if he supposed them to emanate from the court of the divine majesty. And when written accusations involving the crimes of priests were presented in their turn to the emperor, he accepted them and placed them unopened in the fold of his toga. After he called them back to charity and concord, he himself said that in as much as he was a human who was subject to the verdict of the priests, it was not allowed for him to examine divine cases which none except God alone could adjudicate. Those rolls which he had accepted he consigned to the flames uninspected, fearful to publicize the crimes or abuses of the Fathers and to incur the same curse as Cham, the reprobate son, who did not share in the reverence of his forefathers. And thus, in the writings of Nicholas, the Roman pontiff, it is narrated that the same Constantine had said:

> Truly if my own eyes had seen a priest of God or any of those who wrap themselves in the robes of the monastery sinning, my cloak would have been stretched out and would have covered him up, so that no other would see him.

The great Emperor Theodosius was suspended by the priest of Milan from the use of regalia and imperial insignias because he deserved punishment (although not on account of a serious error), and the emperor patiently and solemnly did the penitence for homicide imposed upon him. Indeed, according to the useful testimony of the Gentile Teacher, he who blesses is greater than he who is blessed, and he who is in the possession of the authority of conferring a dignity takes precedence over he who is himself conferred with a dignity. Furthermore, by the law of reason, whoever wills is he who nullifies, and he who can confer rights is he who can withdraw them. Did Samuel not impose a sentence of deposition upon Saul by reason of disobedience, and substitute him with the humble son of Jesse atop the kingdom? If the properly constituted ruler administers faithfully the office undertaken, such honour and such reverence are exhibited for him as to match that superiority which the head has over the other members of the body. In addition, he administers his office faithfully when, mindful of his special situation, he remembers to cherish the unique character of the community subject to him, and when he is cognizant that he does not owe his life to himself but to others, and when he allots things to them according to the order of charity. Therefore, he owes the whole of himself to God, most to his country, much to his parents and relatives, and less (although still a little) to foreigners. He is thus duty-bound 'to the wise and to the foolish, to the insignificant and to the great' [Romans 1:14].

Inspection of such persons is common to all prelates, both those who administer care in spiritual matters and those who exercise temporal jurisdiction. Consequently, we have Melchizedek, the first whom Scripture introduces as king and priest (making no mention at present of the mystery by which he prefigures Christ, who was born in heaven without a mother and on earth without a father). It may be read of him, I say, that he had neither father nor mother, not that he was deprived of either one, but because according to reason kingship and priesthood are not generated of flesh and blood, since in founding either one, respect for lineage should not prevail apart from respect for the merits of the virtues, but the desire for the benefit of the faithful subjects should be prevalent. And when someone ascends to the summit atop either mountain, he must be oblivious to carnal desires and must do only what is demanded for the welfare of those subject to him. Accordingly, he is father and mother to his subjects or, if he knows of a more gentle form of affection, he should use that; he desires love more than fear, and reveals himself to his subjects as someone whose life they would out of devotion prefer to their own, so that they count his safety as equivalent to the life of the people; and then all affairs will proceed properly for him, and a small body of obedient guards will prevail (if necessary) over innumerable adversaries. For love is stronger that death; and the military formation that is tied together by the bonds of love will not break easily.

Before the Dorians fought the Athenians, they consulted an oracle regarding the outcome of the battle. It was responded that they were to be victorious, unless they killed the king of the Athenians. When they reached the point of making war, their soldiers were commanded before all else to safeguard the king. The king of the Athenians at that time was Codrus. It was he who, deliberating upon the response of the deity and the command to the enemy, changed his royal dress, entering the encampment of the enemy carrying kindling around his neck. The throng there blocked his way and he was slain by a soldier whom he had struck with his pruning hook. Once the body of the king was recognized, the Dorians departed without a battle. And thus, in this way, the virtue of the Athenian leader, by which he offered his own death in exchange for the safety of his country, delivered Athens from war. Similarly, Lycurgus during his reign laid down decrees affirming the obedience of the people to their rulers and of the rulers to rulership in accordance with justice; he abolished the use of gold, silver and all other wicked materials; he consigned the safeguarding of the laws to the Senate and the power of choosing the Senate to the people; he resolved that virgins should marry without a dowry, so that wives would not be chosen for pecuniary reasons; he willed that the elderly have the greatest honours according to the degree of their age; certainly in no other place on earth did the elderly have such great honour. Then, in order that his laws would be bestowed eternally, he placed the city under the obligation of a solemn oath that they would not change one of his laws until after he had returned. He departed afterwards for Crete, went there into a perpetual exile, and commanded that upon his death his bones be thrown away in the sea so that the Lacedaemonians would not suppose that the bonds of their sacred oath were dissolved by the return of his remains. I use these examples so freely because I find that the Apostle Paul used them while he preached to the Athenians. That remarkable preacher strove to impress Jesus Christ and His crucifixion upon their minds, so that by a multitude of gentile examples, they would learn that deliverance is obtained solely through the ignominy of the cross....

Chapter 4: That the authority of divine law consists in the ruler being subject to the justice of law

But why do I stoop to examples of human improvement, in spite of the fact that they are numerous, when everyone can be more appropriately propelled towards action through laws than through examples? One ought not, however, hold the opinion that the ruler himself is constantly released from law. Attend to the law which is imposed upon rulers by the Greatest King who is an object of fear over all the earth and who takes away the breath of rulers:

> When you have come to the land which the Lord your God will give you, and have possessed it and dwelled therein, you will say, 'I will select a king over me, like all the nations that are around me'; you will select him king over you, whom the Lord your God will choose from among one of your brethren. You cannot make a foreigner king over you, someone who is not your brother. And when he has been selected, he should not multiply horses for himself, nor return the people to Egypt in order that he may multiply the number of horses; for the Lord has said to you that you shall not henceforth return that way any more. He should not have many wives who will improperly influence his mind, nor should he have a large weight of silver and gold. And afterwards he will sit upon the throne of the kingdom and he will write for himself a copy of this law of Deuteronomy in a book, drawing from the exemplar of the priests of the tribe of Levi, and it will be with

him and he shall read therein all the days of his life, that he may learn to fear the Lord his God, and to keep all His words and ceremonies which are prescribed by the law. His heart should not be lifted up haughtily above his brethren, nor should he incline in his direction to the right or to the left, in order that he and his children may reign a long time over Israel.

[Deuteronomy 17:14–21]

Need one ask whether anyone whom this law constrains is limited by law? Certainly this is divine and cannot be dismissed with impunity. Each word of this text is thunder in the ears of the ruler if he is wise. I keep silent about selection and its forms, which is required for the creation of the ruler; my attention is turned for a brief period to that formula of living which is prescribed for him.

It is said that when someone is empowered who declares himself a brother of the whole people in matters of religious worship and in the feeling of charity, he should not multiply his horses, since the greatness of their number is a burden to subjects. To multiply horses is really to collect more than necessity requires, whether by reason of vain glory or because of another error. For 'too much' and 'too little', if one follows the Prince of the Peripatetics [Aristotle], signify the excess or diminution of legitimate quantities within particular genera of things. Is it to be permitted, therefore, to multiply dogs or birds of prey or savage beasts or any monstrosities of nature you please, when horses, which are necessary for military purposes and useful in all aspects of life, are limited in number to a legitimate quantity? Certainly there is no mention made in the law of actors and mimes, clowns and prostitutes, pimps and similar prodigal men whom the ruler ought rather to exterminate than to encourage; not only are all these abominations to be excluded from the court of the ruler, but they are to be eliminated from the people of God.

The name 'horses' may be understood to include everything useful for the household and all of its necessary supplies; a legitimate quantity of such things is that which is rationally demanded by necessity or utility, provided that the useful and the honourable are made equivalent, and that a civilized person always chooses what is honourable. For philosophers were long ago satisfied that no opinion is more pernicious than the opinion of those who separate the useful from the honourable; and the truest and more useful judgement is that the honourable and the useful may at all times be converted into one another. Secular histories report that, when it was observed that Dionysius, the tyrant of Sicily, surrounded his person with guards, Plato inquired: 'Have you committed so much evil that you need to have so many guards?' This is in no way fitting for the ruler, who in doing his duty so wins the affection of all that every one of his subjects would expose his own head to imminent peril for him – just as nature urges the limbs to expose themselves for the relief of the head – and would sacrifice his own skin for the sake of the royal skin; and all that a man has he will give up for the life of the ruler.

It is stated next that 'he should not return the people to Egypt in order that he multiply the number of horses'. Indeed, all who are established in roles of authority are to take precautions with the greatest diligence in order that inferiors are not corrupted by their example, nor by their abuse of things, nor by following the path of pride or luxury which returns the people to the darkness of confusion. For frequently it happens that subjects imitate the vices of superiors because the people strive to be in conformity with their magistrates, and everyone aspires to that which is perceived to be illustrious in others. The thoughts and words which the great Theodosius expresses are celebrated by that eminent versifier:

> If that which one has decreed is commanded in common, one ought
>   first to order one's own subjection; then greater observance of equity
> by the people will occur, nor will they refuse, when they see for
>   themselves
> the author subjected to his own dictates. The world is arranged
> after the example of the king, nor is an effect upon the judgements
> of men a matter of powerfulness of edicts instead of the life of the ruler.
> The changeable masses are always altered by the ruler.
>
> [Claudian, *Panegyricus*, ll. 296–303]

The actual wealth of individuals is by no means comparable to the wealth of all. Any given person spends out of his own private coffers, but the ruler draws upon the public treasury or riches; if perhaps there should be a deficit, he has recourse to the wealth of individuals. It is necessary, however, that private persons be content with their own goods. Should these be diminished, he who can now merely aspire to splendour blushes at his own sordid poverty and the darkness of his confusion. For from the decree of the Lacedaemonians, the parsimony of rulers in the use of public goods is ordered, while the common law does nevertheless permit the use of their inheritance and those things that fall upon them by adornment of fortune.

BOOK 5

Chapter 1: Plutarch's letter instructing Trajan

There exists Plutarch's letter instructing Trajan, which describes the idea of a certain sort of political constitution. It is said to be thus:

> Plutarch sends greetings to Trajan. I know that in your moderation you do not desire rulership, which yet is always merited by devotion to good morals. You are of course judged so much the worthier insofar as you are seen to be more removed from the accusation of ambition. I

accordingly congratulate your virtue and my fortune, if you yet administer carefully that which you properly merit. I do not doubt that you are in other respects subject to danger, and that I am subject to the angry tongues of detractors, since not only does Rome not suffer the weaknesses of emperors, but also common gossip is accustomed to refer the transgressions of disciples back to their teachers. Hence, Seneca was slandered by the tongues of his detractors for the offences of Nero, the recklessness of Quintilian's young charges was referred back to him, and Socrates was accused of being too indulgent towards his pupils. Yet you administer everything most correctly, if you do not desist from knowing yourself. If you first of all compose yourself, if you dispose all your affairs towards virtue, everything proceeds properly for you. I have written out for you the strengths of the political constitution of our forebears through which you will have Plutarch as an advisor in living if you comply with it. Otherwise, I invoke the present letter as witness that you do not advance the advice of Plutarch in the destruction of the empire.

Chapter 2: According to Plutarch, what a republic is and what place is held in it by the soul or the members

The parts of this political constitution follow thereafter in a pamphlet entitled *The Instruction of Trajan*, which I have sought to incorporate partially into the present treatise, yet in such a way as to reproduce the outlines of its meaning rather than its actual words. It is first of all required that the ruler evaluate himself entirely and direct himself diligently to the whole body of the republic, whose condition he enjoys. For a republic is, just as Plutarch declares, a sort of body which is animated by the grant of divine reward and which is driven by the command of the highest equity and is ruled by a sort of rational management. By all means, that which institutes and moulds the practice of religion in us and which transmits the worship of God (not the 'gods' of which Plutarch speaks) acquires the position of the soul in the body of the republic. Indeed, those who direct the practice of religion ought to be esteemed and venerated like the soul in the body. For who disputes that the sanctified ministers of God are His vicars? Besides, just as the soul has rulership of the whole body, so those who are called prefects of religion direct the whole body. Augustus Caesar himself was constantly subject to the sacred pontiffs until the time when he created himself a Vestal pontiff and shortly thereafter was transformed into a living god, in order that he would be subject to no one.

The position of the head in the republic is occupied, however, by a ruler subject only to God and to those who act in His place on earth, in as much as in the human body the head is stimulated and ruled by the soul. The place of the heart is occupied by the senate, from which proceeds the beginning of good and bad works. The duties of the ears, eyes and mouth are claimed by the judges and governors of provinces. The hands coincide with officials and soldiers. Those who always assist the ruler are comparable to the flanks. Treasurers and record keepers (I speak not of those who supervise prisoners, but of the counts of the Exchequer) resemble the shape of the stomach and intestines; these, if they accumulate with great avidity and tenaciously preserve their accumulation, engender innumerable and incurable diseases so that their infection threatens the ruin of the whole body. Furthermore, the feet coincide with peasants perpetually bound to the soil, for whom it is all the more necessary that the head take precautions, in that they more often meet with accidents while they walk on the earth in bodily subservience; and those who erect, sustain and move forward the mass of the whole body are justly owed shelter and support. Remove from the fittest body the aid of the feet; it does not proceed under its own power, but either crawls shamefully, uselessly and offensively on its hands or else is moved with the assistance of brute animals.

In his manner, Plutarch asserts much more about the qualities of the body, which he develops diligently throughout the tract towards the end of teaching the republic and instructing magistrates. One who follows everything in the text syllable-by-syllable is a servile interpreter who aims to express the appearance rather than the essence of an author. And because much in him regarding the worship and praise of gods, which he had thought to press upon the religious ruler, is examined according to superstition, let us disregard that which pertains to the practice of idolatry. Instead, we may touch briefly upon the ideas of the man when he instructed the ruler and officials of the republic in the practice of justice.

Chapter 7. What bad and good happens to subjects on account of the morals of rulers; and that the examples of some stratagems strengthen this

'He who gives honours to the unwise', it is said, 'is like he who casts a stone upon Mercury's pile' [Proverbs 26:8]. This is explained in different ways by different people. Requesting the indulgence of wiser men, I believe that Mercury's pile consists in the calculation of accounts, since Mercury is the deity of those who are occupied with business affairs and who keep diligent watch over their ledgers. Therefore, to cast a stone upon the pile, which aids in the calculation of accounts, is to upset totally the computation of the accounts, and to confer honour on the unwise is to subvert the life of the republic. And it is impossible that one governs others usefully when he is subverted by his own errors. For it is said: 'Where there is no governor, the people are brought to ruin' [Proverbs 11:14]. And elsewhere:

An unwise king is the ruin of his people, and cities will be inhabited according to the judgement of the prudent.... All the powerful are short-lived, a languishing illness lays down the physician. The physician cuts off the illness rapidly; so whoever is a king today will be a corpse tomorrow. For when a man dies, he will inherit serpents and wild beasts and worms.

[Ecclesiasticus 10:3, 11–13]

To what purpose, I ask, are the poor oppressed with injuries, enfeebled by exactions, despoiled by extensive pillaging, commanded to meet peoples in battle and to terrify the world, except in order that the powerful will be succeeded by their heirs? For in fact their heirs succeed to everything according to their right; they do not even require a solemnized will and testament, for they put themselves forward on the basis of intestacy; wish it or not, you will have these heirs.

In the field of secular literature, Plato has said:

When the magistrate oppresses subjects, it is just as if the head of the body had swollen up so that it is impossible for the members of the body to endure it either at all or without difficulty. It is impossible, however, to tolerate or cure this affliction without the most extreme pain among the members. Yet if the affliction would be incurable, it is more miserable to live than to die. For nothing is more useful to those in misery than to end their misery, no matter how.

It is read that the same writer also has said:

When an official brutalizes subjects, it is the same as if a legal guardian had persecuted his ward, or if you had slaughtered with his own dagger someone for the sake of whose defence you had been handed and had accepted his sword. For indeed, it is a very celebrated fact that the public enjoys the rights of a ward, and public affairs do not proceed well until the time when it is acknowledged that a head is useless to them unless he faithfully coheres with the members.

These are Plato's views, which are elegantly and truly expressed. But, as it appears to me, there can be no faithful and firm coherence where there is not a tenacious unity of wills and a virtual joining together of souls themselves. If this is missing, men harmonize their works in vain, since deceit advances into catastrophe without an attitude of helpfulness. 'Deceivers and cunning men', says Job, 'provoke the wrath of God, and they ought not complain when they are vanquished; their souls perish in calamity and they live among the weak' [Job 36:13–14]. For works are sometimes manifested by reason of shame, or occasionally fear. But the most solid union is the one which proceeds by the openness of faith and love, and subsists solely upon the foundation of virtue. Yet works, because they are a sign of character, generate favour, since there is nothing is more useful and more efficacious for the status and the improvement of magistrates....

Chapter 11: Of the eyes, ears and tongue of the powerful, and of the duties of governing, and that judges ought to have a knowledge of right and equity, a good will and the power of execution, and that they should be bound by oath to the laws and should be distanced from the taint of presents

Next follows the contributions of the eyes, ears and tongue, which were said above to consist of the governors of provinces. Accordingly, a governor is one who governs the province by conferring legal right. Thus, he should have knowledge of equity and iniquity, and his skills and mind set are to be directed to the execution of justice. For while the physician should not be blamed for the eventual outcome of death, still, if something mournful happens as the result of one's rulership, one is deservedly blamed. If a person knows something and does not act upon it, he is accused not by reason of ignorance but by reason of malice. Indeed, the end of either one is damnation, although the punishment of ignorance is more mild, except perhaps for that ignorance which has arisen from negligence. For if ignorance is unalterable, it does not carry the penalty of death but is excused by innate dimness. Still if a governor knows and wishes to serve equity but cannot, the fault is the ruler's rather than his. But most assuredly, the judge is to incline towards the direction of his sacred calling, since he ought to have his own knowledge of right, a good will and the powers of execution; and he should be obligated by sacred oath to the laws so that he will recognize that it is illicit for him to diverge in any matter from their integrity. For Wisdom teaches us about his wisdom. 'The wise judge', it says, 'will judge his people, and the government of the prudent man will be stable. As the judge of the people is, so his ministers will be; and however is the rector of the city, such will be the inhabitants of it' [Ecclesiasticus 10:1–2]. Yet it also does not deny that power is necessary, saying:

> Do not seek to be made judge unless you are equal to the strength to attack iniquities, lest perhaps you tremble before the faces of the powerful and set in readiness your own scandal. Do not sin against the multitude of citizens and so not lower yourself among the people; do not be guilty of the same sin twice, for you will not be immune even once. Do not be petty in your spirit; do not despise to pray and give alms. Do not say: 'God will consider the great number of my gifts and when they are offered by me to the Most High God, he will accept my gifts.' Do not laugh at a man in the sadness of his soul; for it is God the circumspect who humiliates and exalts.
>
> [Ecclesiasticus 7:6–12]

From this the diligent reader encounters the fact that a good will is no less necessary for a judge than is knowledge or power, since he is held at fault not only for himself but for others, and he bears the burden twice for himself and others to the extent that he will not be trusted before God on the basis of the multitude of his gifts apart from the cleanliness of his will. For this reason Plato both excellently and clearly asserts (if one would yet listen) that those who contend for holding the magistracies of the republic thereby thrash amongst themselves in exactly the way that sailors in reaction to a tempest might fight about which of them ought to be able to steer. In the reckonings of fortune, he who succeeds in a magistracy without talent or strength is either non-existent or rare, and is reckless as well. And in my own time, I have seen nothing more miserable than judges ignorant of the science of law and devoid of a good will, which their love of presents and compensation proves beyond all doubt; the power which they have is exercised in the service of greediness, ostentation, or their own flesh and blood, and they are absolved from the necessity of a sacred oath to the laws. From this it is evident that rulers that have conferred upon them ordinary jurisdiction are either ignorant or contemptuous of legal right. But, regardless of what we say about legal proficiency or the powers of execution, a judge must be an extremely religious person and one who hates all iniquity more than death itself.

Because, therefore, governors have ordinary powers to pronounce on matters of legal right, one rule is to be preserved by them and by other judges; and whatever is said of them transfers readily in its implications to the others. And so, what is first of all indicated to each by the necessity of their duties is that justice is to be served in all matters and none of the things which they are to do are to be done for a price. For what is unjust is at no time permitted; injustice is not to be done even for the price of one's temporal life. Yet what is just does not need the aid of remuneration, since it must be done for itself and it is iniquitous to offer for sale that to which one is obligated. It is iniquitous, therefore, to offer justice for sale; it is madness as well as iniquity to sell injustice. For the latter is in fact so disapproved of everywhere that it ought to exist nowhere; the former is so obligatory everywhere that it cannot be sold without the commission of a crime. For Balaam was culpable not for the reason that he had damaged the cause of the people of God when he had spoken in a way other than that which had been inspired by the Lord, but because he was so blinded by avarice that, supporting the cause of the infidels, he had been directed by malice to arrange that Israel would transgress in order that the anger of God might be provoked. He, therefore, inquired into the means by which he might justly vindicate the cause of impiety and might withdraw the grace of God from His elect by a sort of trick. Or, if he could not vindicate the opposing cause, he at least had acted in order that God would withdraw from them. For in a fight between the iniquitous, those accustomed to winning (it is said) are those who are superior in strength. You will see Balaamites who, although they refuse to make iniquitous judgements, still are so corrupted by presents that they endeavour by every trick in the book to transfer justice from one party to the other party....

BOOK SIX

Chapter 20: Who are the feet of the republic and regarding the care devoted to them

The feet are the name of those who exercise the humbler duties, by whose service all the members of the republic may walk along the earth. In this accounting may be included the peasants who always stick to the land, looking after their cultivated fields or plantings or pastures or flowers. Likewise, this category applies to the many types of weaving and the mechanical arts, which pertain to wood, iron, bronze and the various metals, and also to the servile forms of obedience and the many ways of acquiring nourishment and the sustenance of life or enlarging the dimensions of family possessions, the management of which does not pertain to the public authorities and from which the corporate community of the republic derives benefit. And there are so many of these occupations that the number of feet in the republic surpasses not only the eight-footed crab, but even the centipede; one cannot enumerate them on account of their large quantity, not since there are an infinity of them according to nature, but because there are so many varied kinds that no compiler of duties ever produced special precepts for each individual type.

None the less, in order to address generally each one and all, they are not to exceed the limits, namely, law, and are to concentrate on the public utility in all matters. For inferiors must serve superiors, who on the other hand ought to provide all necessary protection to their inferiors. For this reason, Plutarch says that what is to the advantage of the humbler people, that is, the multitude, is to be followed; for the fewer always submit to the more numerous. Therefore, magistrates were instituted for the reason that injuries might be averted from subjects and the republic itself might put shoes, as it were, on its workers. For when they are exposed to injuries it is as if the republic is barefoot; there can be nothing more ignominious for those who administer the magistracies. Indeed an afflicted people is like proof and irrefutable demonstration of the ruler's gout. The health of the whole republic will only be secure and splendid if the superior members devote themselves to the inferiors and if the inferiors respond likewise to the legal rights of their superiors, so that each individual may be likened to a part of the others reciprocally and each believes what is to his own advantage to be determined by that which he recognizes to be most useful for others.

Chapter 22: That without prudence and forethought no magistracy remains intact, nor does that republic flourish the head of which is impaired

Moreover, venerable countries, if they follow the footprints of the bees, will progress along the path of life without difficulty and most profitably. Reflect upon Maro's account of the foundations of Carthage and you can admire the comparatively happy omens for that city. For indeed you recognize that all labour was in common and no one was unoccupied and their queen worked in order that the structure of the city might rise; and if she by no means mixed her hands with the labour of her inferiors, still she watched over the work with her eyes and her whole mind was occupied with foresight. For without prudence and foresight not only does the republic not progress, but not even the least household endures. For this reason, in his commendation of Ulysses, Homer teaches that prudence, which after poetic custom he calls by the name Minerva, had been his constant companion. Also, Homer's imitator, Maro, describing a man distinguished for arms and piety and whom he supposed so worthy that he began the dynasty of the Romans, associated him with Achates in all matters rightly conducted because prudent foresight accomplishes those actions which are most suitable. The business of a circumspect man so often succeeds insofar as the deceits of the insidious never impede him and he advances along a sort of invincible path not open to everyone towards the end of his intended destination. Indeed, this is elegantly expressed, since neither military affairs nor the works of piety may be exercised effectively without forethought and prudence. Above all there is a drawing together of the faithful when prudence is associated with forethought because not only is an acute intelligence blunted by inactivity but also foresight is not beneficial unless it exerts itself upon the foundation of a rich inner disposition. 'The one demands the material assistance of and bonds together in friendship with the other' [Horace, *Ars Poetica*, ll. 410–11]. But however well any matters whatsoever begin, they do not turn out well when Minerva retreats. You may be confronted by the Mantuan poet who, under the pretext of fiction, expressed all the truths of philosophy. Heed, therefore, the diligence of the new citizens:

> It was like the bees in the new summer among the rural flowers
> performing their labours under the sun, when adult creatures
> guide the babies, or when clear honey
> and sweet nectar is squeezed from distended cells,
> or when they accept burdens from newcomers, or form a battle line
> which keep a pack of idle drones from their hives;
> work goes on, and the fragrant honey smells of thyme.
>
> [Virgil, *Aeneid* 1.445–51]

The citizens are held to their varied occupations and, in as much as the duties of each individual are practised so that provision is made for the corporate community, so long as justice is practised, the ends of all are imbued with the sweetness of honey.

Nevertheless, no republic is happy for long unless provision is made for the head of the corporate community. If you did not know this, you may learn from the example of Dido. For with how much frivolity was Aeneas admitted, how much favour was soon found for an unknown man, an exile, a fugitive, whose motives were unknown and whose person was suspect? With how much curiosity did the ruler receive into her ears the fabulous stories of a man avoiding his own blame, striving for his own glory, and chasing after that by which he could subvert the mind of his audience? Therefore, persuasive words paved the way for the man's entrance, the enticements of praise procured the favours of his hosts, a more elaborate banquet was planned for capturing the devotion of all, stories followed the banquet, which was accompanied by hunting and a multiplicity of frivolous luxuries. This engendered lewdness and led to the abandonment of the city to flames and to a perpetual reason for hostility. This is the end of the rulership of women and the effeminate because, although it may have a foundation in virtue, it could by no means devise a course towards subsequent prosperity. He was frivolously admitted who, however much by reason of the duty of piety he was not to be excluded from hospitality, should still more suitably have entered as a stranger, not like a ruler.

Chapter 24: The vices of the powerful are to be tolerated because with them rests the prospect of public safety, and because they are the dispensers of safety just as the stomach in the body of animals dispenses nourishment, and this is by the judgement of the Lord Adrian

'Go', says Solomon, 'to the ant, dull one, that you may possess foresight' [Proverbs 6:6]. Yet the philosopher sends the political man to the bees in order that he may learn from them his duties. If the Carthaginians had acceded to them, they would never have indulged in luxury and instead would have taken pleasure in the perpetual security of their nation. But because vice took root in a female lord, the effeminate citizens were led away by the neck by men of valour. Nevertheless, even if the ruler is too loose in the virtues of his office, still he has to be honoured; and, just as the bees raise up their king upon their shoulders, so subjects, whom we have said to be the feet and members, should exhibit subservience to him in every way, so long as his vices are not pernicious. For, even if he is afflicted with the vices, he is to be endured as the one with whom rests the hopes of the provincials for their security. 'If the king is safe, everyone is of a single mind; if he is lost, faith ruptures' [Virgil, *Georgics* 4.212–13].

The Illyricians and Tracians, praised for the glory of their ferocity hardened through daily practice, had terrified their neighbours, the Macedonians. The latter, beaten in battle, lay their boy-king, the progeny of their dead ruler, in a cradle and positioned him at the line of the battle, resuming the fighting more ardently as though they had been conquered because in the previous wars they lacked the foresight of their king, whereas in the future they would be victorious because by reason of either superstition or faith they were seized by the motivation to prevail. For they were guided by compassion for the infant king whose capture they would have realized if they were conquered. And so joined in battle, they routed the Illyricians with great carnage, showing their enemies that the Macedonians lacked a king, not virtue, during prior combat. Therefore, how important might be a king of advanced years and dignity, if these qualities had further promoted his value? Yet although one may be dealing with a somewhat hardened populace, still the authority of the rank and the usefulness of the office ought to soothe the spirits of the provincials.

I recall that I had cause to travel to Apulia to visit the pontiff, Lord Adrian IV, who had allowed me into closest friendship with him, and I remained with him at Benevento for nearly three months. And so since, as it is customary to do among friends, we frequently consulted together over many matters, and he inquired most intimately and diligently of me what men felt both about himself and about the Roman Church, I related openly to him the evil uses of spiritual liberty, about which I have heard in various provinces. For it was said by many that the Roman Church, which is the mother of all churches, presented itself not so much like a mother as like a stepmother of the others. Scribes and Pharisees sit within Rome, placing upon the shoulders of men insupportable burdens with which they themselves do not dirty their own fingers. They are lords over the clergy, and they do not become the models who lead the flock down the correct path of life; they accumulate valuable furnishings, they pile up gold and silver at the bank, even economizing too much in their own expenses out of avarice. For the pauper is either never or rarely allowed in, except for one who is introduced not so much because of the glory of Christ but out of his vain glory. They weaken the Church, inflame quarrels, bring into conflict the clergy and the people, have no compassion whatsoever for those afflicted by labours and miseries, delight in the plunder of churches and calculate all profits as piety. They deliver justice not for the sake of truth but for a price. For indeed everything done immediately comes with a price; but you will not obtain anything at some future date without a price either. They very frequently do harm and they imitate demons in this: they think they have done good at that time when they desist from doing harm – excepting a few who carry out the name and duties of the shepherd. But even the Roman pontiff himself is burdensome and almost intolerable to everyone, since all assert that, despite the ruins and rubble of churches (which were constructed by the devotion of the Fathers) and also the neglect of altars, he erects palaces and parades himself about not only in purple vestments but in gilded clothes. The palaces of priests glitter and in their hands the Church of Christ is demeaned. They pick clean the spoils of the provinces as if they wanted to recover the treasures of Croesus. But the Most High deals suitably with them, since they are themselves given over to the plunder of others and frequently to the most vile of men. And, as I believe, while they have thus gone astray off the path, the

46

scourge of the Lord will by no means fail Him. Indeed, the mouth of the Lord has spoken that by the judgements he has judged he will be judged, and his measure meted out to him. The Ancient of the Days acknowledges no lies.

'This,' I said, 'father, is said by the people, in as much as you desired that I should reveal to you their judgements.' 'And you,' it was responded, 'what do you judge?' 'Difficulties', I said, 'exist in all directions. For I fear lest I be associated with lies and I be infamous for flattery if I were to contradict the people on my own; but if I act otherwise, I fear lest I be accused of high treason, just as though I had opposed my mouth against heaven, thus seeming to have merited the cross. Nevertheless, because Guido Dens, the cardinal presbyter of St Potentiana, presents the testimony of the people, I do not presume to contradict him in all regards. For he asserts that within the Roman Church exists a root of duplicity and a nourishment of avarice which is the beginning and root of all evils. And this public charge was not made by him in some quiet retreat, but at meetings of the holy brothers presided over by Eugenius, when at Florence he grew angry without provocation in opposition to my own innocence.

'Yet one thing I boldly profess with conscience as my witness is that nowhere do I see more honest clerics or clerics who despise avarice more than in the Roman Church. Who does not marvel at the continence and contempt for money of Bernard of Redon, cardinal deacon of Saints Cosmas and Damian? None is alive from whom he accepts a present. Yet what was yielded rightfully by the sincere communion of brotherhood he was occasionally persuaded to accept. Who is not amazed by the Bishop of Praeneste who, fearing the scruples of conscience, abstained even from sharing in the common goods? So great is the modesty of many, so great is their dignity, that they would not be found inferior to Fabricius, whom they excel in all ways by their knowledge of the path to salvation. Therefore, because you insist, urge and command, and since it is certain that it is not permitted to lie to the Holy Spirit, I acknowledge that what you command is to be done, even though you would not be imitated in all of your works. For whoever dissents from your teaching is either a heretic or a schismatic. But, by God's favour, there are those who do not imitate all of your works. Thus, the blemish of a few stains the pure, and the universal Church will be plunged into infamy; and in my opinion a very great number of them ought to die lest they corrupt the whole of the Church. But even the good are sometimes carried off, lest they are transformed into the wicked and because corrupt Rome is perceived to be unworthy of those in the presence of God. You, therefore, have it as your duty to search for and take in the humble, those who despise vain glory and money. But I fear lest, insofar as you proceed to inquire into what you have in mind, you hear from an imprudent friend what you do not have in mind. Why is it, father, that you discuss the lives of others and investigate into yourself so little? All applaud you, you are called Father and Lord of everyone, and upon your head is poured all the oil of the sinner. If you are father,

47

therefore, why do you accept presents and payments from your children? If you are lord, why do you not arouse fear in your Romans and why do you not recall them to the faithful, suppressing their recklessness? Yet perhaps you wish to maintain the city for the Church by means of your presents. Did Pope Silvester acquire it by means of such presents? You are off the path, father, and not on the path. The city is to be maintained out of the same presents by which it was acquired. What is freely given is freely accepted. Justice is the queen of the virtues and is embarrassed to be exchanged for any amount of price. If justice is to be gracious, she is to be free of charge. She who cannot be seduced may by no means be prostituted for a price; she is entirely and forever pure. Insofar as you oppress others, you will be oppressed by even greater burdens.'

The pontiff laughed and congratulated such great candour, commanding that, whenever anything unfavourable about him made a sound in my ears, he was to be informed of this without delay. And, when he had thoroughly responded – alternately favouring himself and opposing himself – he told me a story along the following lines. He asserted: 'It happened that all the members of the whole body conspired against the stomach, as if against that which by its voraciousness exhausted the labours of all. The eye is never filled to capacity with sights nor the ear with sounds, the hands persist in their labours, the feet put on callouses by walking, and the tongue moderates usefully between speech and silence. In short, all the members keep watch over the public advantage and, in comparison to the concern and labour of all, only the stomach remains at rest, and while all share the many things which are obtained by their labour, the stomach alone devours and consumes everything. What more? They agreed that they would abstain from their labours and destroy through painful starvation this parasite and public enemy. This was suffered on the first day; on the following day it was more annoying. On the third day it was so pernicious that nearly all showed signs of faintness. And so necessity urged that the allies should gather together again as one to act with regard to their own health and the condition of the public enemy. When all were present, the eyes were feeble, the feet would not raise the bulk of the body, the arms were stiffened, and even the tongue itself, sticking to the palate and weakened, did not presume to expound the common cause of the partners. Therefore, they all yielded to the counsel of the heart and, having deliberated thereupon, reason revealed that these evils were inflicted as a result of what had previously been denounced as a public enemy. For the tribute to it was withdrawn by them and like a public provisioner it halted nourishment to everyone. And because no one can fight without a salary, the soldiers were disabled and weakened when they did not receive a salary. But the fault cannot be traced back to the provisioner, who could hardly disburse to others what he did not receive himself. And it would be far more advisable that he should be furnished with goods for his distribution than that all the members should go hungry while getting rid of him. And so it was done; persuaded by reason, the stomach was replenished, the members were revived, and the peace of all was re-established. And so they absolved the stomach, which, although it is voracious and covetous of unsuitable things, still asks not for itself but for others which are unable to be sustained by its emptiness.

'Such is the case,' he said, 'brother, if you study the matter properly, in the republic where, although the magistrates seek after a great deal, they do not accumulate it for themselves but for others. For if they are dissipated, there is nothing that they are able to bestow upon the members. For the stomach in the body and the ruler in the republic are the same office, according to Quintus Serenus:

> Those who contend the stomach is the king of the whole body,
> are seen to rest upon the truth of reason.
> For its health secures the progress of all the members,
> but by contrast its affliction weakens the whole;
> indeed rather, unless one aids it carefully, it is said to infect
> the brain and to divert the senses from their completeness.
> [Sammonicus, *Liber Medicinalia*, 300–5]

Measure neither our harshness nor that of secular rulers, but attend to the utility of all.'

Chapter 25: Of the coherence of the head and the members of the republic; and that the ruler is a sort of image of the deity, and of the crime of high treason, and of that which is to be kept in fidelity

It is indeed satisfactory to me and I am persuaded that devoted shoulders are to support the ruler; and not only do I suffer him but I suffer him gratefully, insofar as he is subject to God and follows His decrees. Otherwise, if he resists divine commandments and wills me to be a participant in his plot against God, I respond with unstrained voice that God is to be preferred to any man. In this way, therefore, inferiors cohere with their superiors, in this way all the members are to subject themselves to the head so that religion may be preserved intact. It is read that Socrates had instituted a political system and had handed down precepts which are said to emanate from that purity of wisdom which is like a sort of fount of nature. Yet these may all be condensed into the following: that the duty of the greater man in the republic is to protect most diligently those who are humbler. Reread carefully *The Instruction of Trajan*, of which mention is made above, and you will find these matters more extensively addressed. It suffices for us to have said these things about the unity of the head and members at present, to which may be added what we set out before: that a blow to the head, as we have already said, is carried back to all the members and a wound unjustly afflicted upon any member whatsoever tends to the injury of the head.

49

In another respect, any evil trick of malice planned against the head and members of the corporate community is a crime of the utmost seriousness and approaches sacrilege because, just as the latter assails God, so the former attacks the ruler, who is agreed to be a sort of deity on earth. And as a result it is called high treason because it persecutes those in the image of him who alone, as the illustrious Count Robert of Leicester (a modest proconsul administering in the region of Britain) was in the habit of saying, preserves the truth of true and noble majesty; it reckons those who attempt anything against the security of the ruler of the people, either by themselves or through another. Furthermore, in the prosecution of such a crime, everyone is on equal terms; and for the most part it happens that those with whom no one associates in life are not exonerated by benefit of death; but upon the death of the convicted party, his memory is condemned and his goods are denied to his heirs. For since he takes in hand the most vicious counsel, his mind is accordingly punished in a certain way. Once anyone has committed such a crime, it is agreed that he can neither alienate nor manumit nor can a debtor rightfully repay him.

Infamous persons, who do not have the right to accuse others, are to be admitted in these cases without hesitation, as well as soldiers, who cannot prosecute other types of cases. Indeed, those who keep watch for the peace are all the more to be heard about this accusation. Also slaves may legally accuse their lords and freemen their patrons. Yet this crime is to be regarded by judges not as an occasion for the veneration of the majesty of the ruler but as a quest for truth. For one is to look at whether the person could have done it, whether he actually did it, whether he conceived of it, and whether (before he presumed this) he was of sane mind. And no slip of the tongue is to suffer by ready punishment; for although the rash are deserving of punishment, still even they are to be spared if their transgressions are not of such a kind that either they violate the letter of the law or are to be punished according to legal precedent. Even women are to be heard in interrogation about high treason; for the woman Julia exposed the conspiracy of Sergius Catiline and she aided the consul Marcus Tullius in judging him. Also, if introduced by reason of necessity or utility, those who are believed to be at fault in the matter are to be placed under tortures when they are seen to have accepted counsel and also inspiration for the crime, so that the punishment earned can be put in place for all offending parties.

There is much, indeed, that makes up high treason, for example, if there is consideration of the death of a ruler or magistrate, or if those who oppose the country are armed, or if one flees from a public war, deserting the ruler, or if the people are solicited to struggle in revolt against the republic, or if by deceitful or evil works the enemies of the people and republic are aided with military supplies, arms, weapons, money or whatever else, or if friends of the republic become its enemies, or if by deceitful or evil works it were to occur that the pledge of a great deal of money would be given in opposition to the republic, whereby the populace of a foreign territory would be less obedient; he likewise commits high treason who releases a criminal found guilty of the act in court, on account of which he has been clamped into chains; and many other acts of this sort which it is tedious or impossible to enumerate.

But, because the formula of fidelity (or the feudal oath) should be observed above all else, from it can be most conveniently complied a few things that are not permitted. For indeed necessity is the obverse of possibility, and what ought to be done is contradicted by what is illicit. Likewise, the formula of fidelity requires what is inserted in it as necessary to faith: it enjoins what is secure, safe, honourable, useful, easy and possible. Were we bound to someone by the constraints of fidelity, we would neither injure the security of his body nor withdraw the provisions on the basis of which he is safe nor presume to undertake anything which would diminish his honour or usefulness; and it is permitted neither to make difficult what is easy nor to make impossible what is possible. Moreover, he who possesses a benefice from someone, to whom he is faithful, owes him aid and counsel in his activities; for this reason, how much is the Lord more clearly than the sun owed, if so much is owed to those to whom we are bound only by the constraints of fealty. But even the penalty for such crime is so great that I would not readily believe that anything more severe could be devised even by the lords of the islands who frequently engage in tyranny. And, lest it is supposed that the severity of the penalties have proceeded from the severity of tyranny, we may refer to the very words of the most moderate law itself....

Chapter 26: That vices are to be endured or removed and are distinguished from flagrant crimes; and certain general matters about the office of the ruler; and a brief epilogue on how much reverence is to be displayed towards him

I have taken care in the present little treatise to insert a few excerpts among many possible ones drawn from the pure core of the law. As a result of the inspection of these even men ignorant of the law may withdraw themselves at great distance from high treason, and I myself will not be accused unfairly by anyone of having presumed against the authority of the ruler. It is customarily said that it is not easy to remove the best parts from the cork tree without injuring one's fingers; but whoever separates the obedience of members from the head is injured far more equitably and rapidly. The excellence of the head must always flourish because the health of the whole body consists in it.

In the satire which is entitled *Manipean* and is about the duties of the institution of matrimony, Varro asserts: 'The vices of a spouse are to be either removed or endured. He who removes the vices is a preferable spouse; he who tolerates them makes himself a better person' [Gellius, *Attic Nights* 1.7.14]. Thus, the vices of rulers and subjects are to be either endured or removed; for in fact their confederation either equals or surpasses conjugal affection. But even the words 'to endure' and 'to remove' themselves are cleverly adapted by Varro. It appears that 'removing' is meant in the sense of correction. It is beyond doubt that his actual judgement was that what cannot be removed is to be endured. Yet a faithful interpretation of this adds that what is understood by 'vice' is what honour and religion can securely endure. For vices are more insignificant than flagrant crimes; and there are a number of acts which one is not permitted to endure or which cannot faithfully be endured. A spouse may legally be separated from a spouse by reason of fornication, and he is very often a patron of turpitude who conceals the crime of his wife. Perhaps it is for that reason said: 'He who cherishes an adulteress is both silly and impious.' Moreover, this obtains equally of any sort of physical and spiritual adultery, even though the spiritual form is the worse and is to be more carefully avoided.

Similarly, even in the connection between the members, Varro's rule about enduring and removing is to be admitted. For in fact no one questions that members ought to be cured, whether the cure for their wound proceeds from the palliative of oils or from the austere wine which the Samaritan administered. That the members are likewise to be removed is clear from that which is written: 'If your eye or your foot offend you, root it out and cast it away from you' [Matthew 18:9]. I think that this is to be observed by the ruler in regard to all of the members to the extent that not only are they to be rooted out, broken off and thrown far away, if they give offence to the faith or public security, but they are to be destroyed utterly so that the security of the corporate community may be procured by the extermination of the one member. Who will be spared, I say, by him who is commanded to do violence against even his own eyes? Indeed, neither the ears nor the tongue nor whatever else subsists within the body of the republic is safe if it revolts against the soul for whose sake the eyes themselves are gouged out. When God is offended by abuses of criminals or the Church is spurned, the well-being of the entire soul is in jeopardy. This is so foreign to the office of the ruler that, whenever these things occur in the republic, it is to be believed that the ruler either is entirely unaware or is asleep or is on a journey.

The sun shines over the whole world so that the whole world may be seen and discerned all at once; I believe the ruler to be another sun. He acts rightly above all when 'he prevents the idle swarm of drones from entering the hive' [Virgil, *Georgics* 4.168], since they pillage the beehive and whatever honey there is they gulp down or carry off. He acts rightly when he raises the Church to the apex, when he extends the practice of religion, when he humiliates the proud and exalts the humble, when he is generous to the destitute, more frugal with the wealthy, when justice walks constantly before him and sets his course on the way of prudence and all the other virtues. Truly,

In this way does one travel to the heavens, not that Mt Ossa is set upon
Mt Olympus
and that the summit of Mt Pelion touches the highest stars.
[Ovid, *Fasti* 1.307–8]

The Book of Wisdom says: 'You are not to appear glorious in the court of the king and you are not to stand in the place of the great' [Proverbs 25:6]; and this edict of the wise man pertains to the fact that whoever does not humble himself in the sight of the ruler by obscuring his merits with bewilderment is deservedly stripped of the glory which he has usurped. Indeed the ruler is the distributor of honour and, so long as he administers the government correctly, the dispensation of presents is perpetually in his hands. He administers correctly when the people rejoice in his governance and the breadth of the whole land exalts in the reign of equity. 'Perpetually', I say because, as it is written, 'the king who judges the poor according to truth secures his throne in eternity' [Proverbs 29:14]. Who, therefore, detracts from the honour of him whom one recognizes to be rewarded by God with perpetual honour? Obviously, to presume anything against the immutable image of the ruler at any time whatsoever is to be guilty of high treason and to be punished by a most painful death, just as the ancients decreed. Who, therefore, offends by the presumptuous impunity of malice against the image of God who is the ruler? Likewise, this is the greatest counsel of wise men: 'In your thought do not detract from the king and in the privacy of your bedroom do not speak ill of the powerful because the birds of the sky will convey your voice and he who has wings will pronounce your verdict' [Ecclesiasticus 10:20]. Will anything then be permitted in deed or word when even thought itself and the secrets of the bedroom and the judgements of the heart are regulated lest anything be plotted or undertaken against the ruler?

BOOK 8

Chapter 17: In what way the tyrant differs from the ruler...

The way in which a ruler differs from a tyrant, insofar as it is reviewed in the *Instruction of Trajan* authored by Plutarch, was discussed above and the duties which belong to the ruler and the members of the republic were diligently expounded. For this reason, one can more easily and in fewer words come to know those directly contrasting traits which are ascribed to the tyrant. As the philosophers have portrayed him, the tyrant is, therefore, one who oppresses the people by violent domination, just as the ruler is one who rules by the laws. Furthermore, the law is a gift of God, the likeness of equity, the norm of justice, the image of the divine will, the custodian of security, the unity and confirmation of a people, the standard of duties, the excluder and exterminator of vices, and the punishment of violence and all injuries. It is attacked either by violence or by deceit and, one might say, it is either ravaged by the savagery of the lion or overthrown by the snares of the serpent. In whatever manner this happens, the grace of God is plainly being assailed and God is in a certain fashion being challenged to a battle. The ruler fights for the laws and liberty of the people; the tyrant supposes that nothing is done unless the laws are cancelled and the people are brought into servitude. The ruler is a sort of image of divinity and the tyrant is an image of the strength of the Adversary and the depravity of Lucifer, for indeed he is imitated who desired to establish his throne to the north and to be like the Most High, yet with His goodness removed. For if he had wished to be like Him in goodness, he would never have endeavoured to snatch away the glory of His power and wisdom. Yet perhaps he aspired to be rewarded by being raised to the same level.

As the image of the deity, the ruler is to be loved, venerated and respected; the tyrant, as the image of depravity, is for the most part even to be killed. The origin of tyranny is iniquity and it sprouts forth from the poisonous and pernicious root of evil and its tree is to be cut down by an axe anywhere it grows. For unless iniquity and injustice had advanced tyranny through the extermination of charity, secure peace and perpetual calm would have dwelled among the people throughout eternity, and no one would think of advancing his borders. Just as the great father Augustine has testified, king-doms would be as calm and friendly in their enjoyment of peace as different families in orderly cities or different persons in the same family, or perhaps, what is more believable, there would be absolutely no kingdoms, for these, just as is evident from the ancient historians, were iniquitous in themselves; either they encroached upon or were extorted from God. And of course not only kings practise tyranny; many private men are tyrants, insofar as the powers which they possess promote prohibited goals. One is not to be troubled that I am appearing to have associated kings with tyranny, since, although it is said that 'king' (*rex*) is derived from the 'right' (*recte*) which is fitting for rulers, still this name incorrectly refers to tyrants. Here is one example: 'Whatever a free people would extend to one man, I have achieved, and I have lacked nothing over them except royal power' [Lucan, *Pharsalia* 2. 562–3]. And elsewhere: 'My hope of peace will be to have influenced the right hand of the tyrant' [Virgil, *Aeneid* 7.266]. And if it is permitted still to call what is against duty and the standard of living rightly a duty, then a single statement reveals all the duties, or on the contrary vices, of tyrants. This is in the mouth of Photinus (from whom tyrants could not undeservedly name themselves Photinians), the first in the monstrous house of Pelleas – that is, one among the other horrors of Egypt – distinguished by his filthiness and cruelty, who, daring to condemn Pompey to death or rather expressing the moral qualities of tyrants with his usual self-confidence, asserts:

Rights and divine law cause many, Tholomee, to be harmed.
Praiseworthy faith receives the penalty, when it sustains (it is said)
those whom fortune humbles; assent to fate and the gods,
and protect the fortunate, avoid the wretched. As stars and earth,
as fire and water, differ, so do rectitude and utility. The power of the
    sceptre is completely lost if it begins to weigh
matters of justice, and battle undermines respect for honour.
The liberty of the criminal is what protects the hateful power of
    kings,
as well as the exalted measure of the sword. Doing everything
    harshly
is not allowed to go unpunished, except when you actually do them.
    Let him exit from court who wishes to be pious; virtue and great
    power
do not do together; he is always afraid who would be ashamed of
    harsh deeds.

                         [Lucan, *Pharsalia* 8.484–95]

Therefore respect for the honourable and the just rarely or never exists in the sight of tyrants; and, whether they are ecclesiastical or earthly, they wish to have power over everything, disdaining what precedes and follows this power.

Yet I would wish that both sorts of tyrants might be persuaded that the divine judgement which was imposed upon the first humans and their children has not yet expired. It was decreed that, because they had not been willing to comply with justice when they were able, they would no longer be able to conform to justice even when they wished to do so. One is also accustomed to saying the proverb: 'Because he does not wish to act when he can, he is not able to act when he wishes.' The great Basil was the author of similar words. For it was requested of him by a common woman that he might intercede with her ruler and, approving her petition, he wrote to the ruler thus: 'This poor woman has approached me, asking me to prevail upon you; if I have influence, please show it.' And he gave the petition to the woman who, departing, gave her letter to the ruler; and reading it, the ruler wrote this back to him: 'On your account, O holy father, I would will to show pity upon this common woman, but I could not on account of the fact that she is subject to the tributes.' The holy man wrote back to him:

If indeed you could not have done what you willed, then fine, no matter how the case turns out; if you could have done what you did not will, then Christ will lead you to the chorus of the needy so that whatever you will you cannot do.

And the Truth, which is always present to the elect, by no means disregarded its instrument. For in a short time the same ruler, inciting the indignation of the emperor, was led bound into captivity, hence giving satisfaction to those unjustly oppressed by his own punishment. Yet after six days of prayer by Basil he was liberated from captivity, abandoning his imperial display just as the holy man had demanded.

And so the king is sometimes called by the name of tyrant and conversely the tyrant is sometimes called by the name of ruler, according to the maxim: 'Your rulers are faithless, associates of thieves' [Isaiah 1:23]. And elsewhere: 'The rulers of the priesthood made counsel so that they might detain Jesus by deceit and kill Him' [Matthew 26:4], who by the just judgment of the law ought to have been freed. For even among the priesthood many may be found who are driven by all their ambition and all their talents in order that they can be tyrants under the pretext of exercising their duties. For the republic of the impious has both its head and members, and it endeavours to be fashioned like the civil institutions of the legitimate republic. Its tyrannical head, therefore, is the image of the devil; its soul is formed of heretical, schismatic and sacrilegious priests and, to use the words of Plutarch, prefects of religion, assailing the laws of the Lord; the heart of impious counsellors is like a senate of iniquity; its eyes, ears, tongue and unarmed hand are unjust officials, judges and laws; its armed hand is violent soldiers, whom Cicero labels mercenaries; its feet are those among the more humble occupations who oppose the precepts of the Lord and legitimate institutions. Of course all of these can be readily controlled by their superiors....

Chapter 20: That by the authority of the divine book it is lawful and glorious to kill public tyrants, so long as the murderer is not obligated to the tyrant by fealty nor otherwise lets justice or honour slip

It would be tedious if I would wish to trace down to our own times the sequence of gentile tyrants; but this litany is beyond narration during the life span of a single man. For it escapes the mind and defeats the tongue. Yet in a book which is entitled *Of the Ends of Tyrants* one can discover more fully what I have observed about tyrants, even though I have abridged its contents with diligence so that neither the tedium of wordiness nor the obscurity of brevity are generated. But lest the authority of Roman history be impugned, since it was for the most part written by infidels and about infidels, it may be verified by the examples of divine and faithful history. For it is everywhere evident that, as Valerius asserts, the only secure power is one which imposes limits on its own strength. And surely nothing is so distinguished and so magnificent that it does not require tempering by moderation.

The first tyrant thus presented to us in the divine book is Nimrod the valiant hunter confronting the Lord (whom several histories testify is also called Ninus, even though it does not agree with the calculation of the time),

56

and he was said above to have been damned. For indeed he wished to be king and not from God, and during his rule there was an attempt to erect a tower into the heavens by a blind, scattered and bewildered human race. We may progress to him who was given command over the people by divine selection and who forfeited that gift to damnation for dominating them according to his will and not reigning royally; and Saul was so crushed that he was compelled by the burdensome distress of his afflictions to inflict death upon himself. For the correct ascension of the king is seldom or never advantageous if his following life is inconsistent with it, and the origins of a case do not concern judges, whose sentence is determined by the outcome. There is a famous history in the Books of Kings and Chronicles in which, on the authority of Jerome, it is taught that Israel had laboured under tyrants from the beginning and it is demonstrated that all the kings of Judah are to be considered as damned except for David, Josiah and Hezekiah. Yet I would readily believe that Solomon and perhaps some others in Judah would have flourished once the Lord summoned them back. And I will be easily persuaded that tyrants instead of rulers would have been deserved by a people of stiff neck and wild heart and a people who always resisted the Holy Spirit and who had provoked not only Moses, the servant of the law, but God Himself, the Lord of the law, to anger by their gentile abominations. For penitence annihilates, drives out and kills those tyrants whom sins obtain, introduce and encourage. And even before the time of their kings, just as the history of Judges narrates, the children of Israel were repeatedly enslaved under tyrants. They were afflicted at many and various times according to divine dispensation, and they were often freed by crying out loud to the Lord. And after the termination of the period of divine supervision, the death of their tyrants permitted them to remove the yokes from their necks. Not a single one of those by whose virtue a penitent and humble people was liberated is to be censured, but the memory of posterity is to recall them favourably as ministers of God....

It is also accepted by another history that it is just for public tyrants to be killed and the people to be liberated for obedience to God. Priests of the Lord themselves count their slaying as an act of piety and, if anything appears to contain an element of deceit, they call it a mystery of religion consecrated to the Lord. Thus Holofernes was laid in his grave by a woman with a sword not on account of the valour of his enemy but by his own vice, and he who was a source of terror for men was vanquished by luxury and drunkenness and was slain by a woman. And the woman would not have been accorded access to the tyrant unless she had concealed her hostile purpose in a pious deception. For that which maintains the faith and serves charity is not deceitful. And indeed it is through faith that she reproved the priests who had prescribed the time period of divine compassion on the basis of an agreement to surrender themselves and the city unless the Lord had rescued them within five days. Moreover, it was through charity that she never became afraid of the dangers as long as she might liberate her brethren and the people of God from their enemies. For these aims are also demonstrated by her departing prayer for her safety:

'Lord, bring it to pass,' she said, 'that by his own sword his pride may be cut off and that he may be captured in his own net with his eyes upon me and you will strike him by means of the charity of my lips. Grant to me a constancy in my soul so that I will despise him and strength so that I will destroy him. For it will be a monument to your name when the hand of a woman kills him off....' Thus she called her maid and, going down to her house, she removed her hair-shirt from herself and she stripped off the garments of her widowhood, and she bathed her body, and anointed herself with the best myrrh, and arranged the hair on her head, and placed a head-band on her head, and put on her most pleasing garments, binding sandals upon her feet, and she obtained bracelets and lilies and earrings and finger-rings and she adorned herself with all her ornaments. And the Lord conferred splendour upon her since all these arrangements were determined not by lust but by virtue. And so the Lord increased her beauty in order that she might appear incomparably elegant to everyone's eyes.

[Judith 9:12–15 and 10:2–4]

Arising and captivating the public enemy, therefore, Judith said this to Holofernes:

Receive the words of your slave girl since, if you follow them, God will cause things to be perfect for you. For Nebuchadnezzar, the king of the earth, lives and also alive is your strength which exists within you for the correction of all erring souls, since not only men but also the beasts in the field serve him and obey him through you. For the strength and industry of your mind is proclaimed among all peoples and it is declared to our entire generation that you alone are powerful and good among all in his kingdom and your learning is preached to all peoples.

[Judith 11:4–6]

And additionally she asserted:

Come, I will proclaim everything to you, so that I may lead you through the middle of Jerusalem and you will possess the entire people of Israel like sheep for which there is no shepherd; and not even a single dog will bark against you, since these events were related to you by the providence of God.

[Judith 11:15–19]

I ask you, could anything more insidious be devised, could anything more captivating be said, than this dispensing of mystical counsel? And so Holofernes said: 'There is nowhere else upon the earth such a woman in appearance and beauty and in the discretion of her speech' [Judith 11:19]. For his aroused heart burned with his desire. And he said: 'Drink now, and recline in pleasure, since you are finding favour in my heart' [Judith 12:17]. She who did not come to be extravagant was skilled in a false extravagance as the instrument of her faith and courage. And once he was stupefied with pleasures, she destroyed his cruelty with the weapons of charity for the liberation of her people. Therefore, she struck Holofernes on the neck and chopped off his head and she handed it to her maid so that it might be put in a bag to be brought back to the city whose safety was achieved by the hand of a woman.

The histories teach that we are to take care, however, lest anyone cause the death of a tyrant who is bound to him by the obligation of fealty or a sacred oath. For it is read that even Zedekiah was taken captive as a result of his neglect of sacred fealty; and, in another instance, a king of Judah (I do not recall whom) had his eyes plucked out because, lapsing into faithlessness, he did not keep his promise before the sight of God, to whom he swore an oath, since even the tyrant is justly to be given surety in lawsuits. And I do not read that poison was licensed by the indulgence of any legal right at any time, although I have seen that it was sometimes made use of by infidels. Not that I do not believe that tyrants are to be removed from the community, but that they are to be removed without loss to religion and honour. For even David, the best of the kings about whom I have read and one who (except for his plot against Uriah the Hittite) advanced blamelessly in all his affairs, endured the most grievous of tyrants. Although he enjoyed frequent opportunities to destroy the tyrant, David still preferred to spare him, trusting in the compassion of God who could free him without sin. He therefore decided to wait patiently to the end that the tyrant might be visited by God with a return to charity or might fall in battle or might otherwise be extinguished by the just judgement of God. For indeed his patience can be distinguished from the fact that, at the time when David had cut off his cloak in the cave and on the other occasion when, entering into camp by night, he found fault with the negligence of the guards, the king himself was compelled to admit that David acted upon the more just cause. And this method of eradicating tyrants is the most useful and the safest: those who are oppressed should humbly resort to the protection of God's clemency and, raising up pure hands to the Lord in devoted prayer, the scourge with which they are afflicted will be removed. For in fact the sins of transgressors are the strength of tyrants. For this reason, Achior, the leader of all the children of Amon, gave this most beneficial counsel to Holofernes:

> My Lord, examine if there is any iniquity of the people in the sight of
> their God, and we may surpass them, since their betrayal of God will
> deliver them to you and they will be subjugated under the yoke of your

power. Yet if there is no such offence of the people before their God, we cannot withstand them, since their God will defend them and we will be in disgrace throughout the entire earth.

[Judith 5:24–5]

4

TREATISE ON THE LAWS AND CUSTOMS OF THE KINGDOM OF ENGLAND COMMONLY CALLED GLANVILLE

INTRODUCTION

The twelfth-century revival of interest in the classical Roman model of law as a written and rationalized statute emanating from the will of a ruler or people constituted an important source for political theory. But the reception of Roman law did not occur without difficulties. Where law arose from fixed origins and in written form, such as in the case of the Church, the Romanist vision was rapidly adopted and adapted. By contrast, the legal traditions of feudal Europe, which had evolved according to a customary and localized conception of law, were less immediately receptive to the Roman model. Nevertheless, medieval authors attempted within practical limits to legitimize the pre-existing arrangement of law with reference to political ideas and legal doctrines derived from Romanist teachings.

The *Treatise on the Laws and Customs of the Kingdom of England* offers an early example of such an effort to bring the medieval and Roman approaches into line. Although attributed since the thirteenth century to the English justiciar (or chief judicial officer) Ranulf of Glanville (*c.* 1125–90), its authorship continues to be in doubt; in any case, the tract seems to be the work of one of the prominent members of the court of King Henry II. Completed about 1189, it seeks to codify the judicial procedures of English royal courts in Romanist fashion. Its author explicitly defends the claim that the common law of the kingdom, although unwritten and fragmentary, still enjoys the status of law. But he upholds this position on the basis of a conception of kingship and legislation which derives from Roman law texts. Similar hybrid marriages of the political ideals of Roman law with the legal realities of feudal Europe may be found in many other writings by lawyers and philosophers throughout the succeeding centuries.

TREATISE ON THE LAWS AND CUSTOMS OF THE KINGDOM OF ENGLAND COMMONLY CALLED GLANVILLE

Prologue

It is not merely necessary that royal power be adorned with weapons against rebels and nations rising up against the kingdom and its ruler, but it is also appropriate that it be equipped with laws for the sake of peacefully ruling subjects and peoples, so that in both times, namely, of peace and war, our glorious king may perform [his duties] so fruitfully that, by the destruction with the strong right hand of the pride of the unbridled and the untamed and by the moderation of justice for the humble and the meek by the staff of equity, he will always be victorious in subduing his enemies, just as he will constantly appear to be evenhanded (*aequalis*) in the treatment of his subjects. It would occur to no one to doubt how gracefully, how adroitly, how expertly, our most excellent king has engaged in armed battle during times of hostility in opposition to the malice of enemies, since his praise is already called out to the whole earth and his great deeds are proclaimed throughout all the far-flung lands of the world. Moreover, there is no uncertainty about how justly, how mercifully, and how discerningly this lover and author of peace has conducted himself in respect to his subjects during times of peace, since there is such equity at the court of his Highness that it may be presumed that no judge in it is so impudent or so rashly presumptuous as to stray in any way from the path of justice or to depart in any manner from the route of truth. There, indeed, the pauper is not oppressed by the power of his enemy, nor does partiality or friendship drive anyone outside the limits of just judgement. For the king refuses neither the counsel of the laws of the kingdom introduced by reason and preserved for a long time nor, what is more praiseworthy, even the counsel of such men among his subjects whose gravity of character, greatly skilled wisdom, and outstanding eloquence he knows to surpass all others in regard to knowledge of the laws and customs of the kingdom, and whom he finds with reason to be most inclined towards deciding cases through the mediating force of justice and settling lawsuits on the basis of arguments about the facts themselves, acting at one time with severity, at another with mercy, just as they may consider expedient.

Although English laws may not be written, it does not seem absurd for them to be called laws (namely, those which are accepted beyond doubt to be promulgated by decision of the Council, with the consultation of the nobility and the assenting authority of the ruler), since law itself consists in this: 'What pleases the prince has the force of law.' For if these are not considered to be laws only on account of the lack of writing, then writing would seem to bestow a greater force of authority on laws than either the equity of the legislator or the reason of their creator.

Moreover, it is certainly impossible for the laws and legal rights of the kingdom as a whole to be contained in written form, not only on account of the ignorance of scribes but also on account of the confusingly large number of such laws. Yet there are certain general and widespread principles utilized in court which it does not seem presumptuous to me to commit to writing, but instead this seems very useful and extremely necessary for the aid of the memory. I have resolved to collect together in written form at least some of these, purposefully employing the vulgar style and terminology of the courts for the sake of revealing knowledge of them to those who are less experienced in such vulgarities....

5

LETTER TO HENRY, COUNT OF CHAMPAGNE

Philip of Harvengt, Abbot of Bonne Esperance

INTRODUCTION

Philip (*c.* 1100–83) was born at Harvengt near Mons in Belgium. He received a good classical education, probably at Cambrai. A wandering preacher, Norbert of Xanten, visited Cambrai in 1119, and soon after Philip joined the order founded by Norbert in 1120 at Prémontré, near Laon, France. In 1130, Philip became the first prior at a new monastery founded by the Premonstratensian order at Bonne Esperance, in the Diocese of Tournai, Belgium.

His duties as prior were to entangle him in a controversy with Bernard of Clairvaux. In the 1140s, one of the Premonstratensian canons regular left Bonne Esperance without permission in order to join the Cistercians at Clairvaux. Bernard decided to admit him to the community despite Philip's desire to bring him back. In 1147, the dispute was brought before Pope Eugenius III. So great was Bernard's prestige (and indeed, Eugenius was a Cistercian and former disciple of Bernard) that Philip could hardly hope to win: the general chapter of Premonstratensians – Philip's own order – found him guilty of fomenting discord between the orders and he and several of his canons were exiled. However, he was exonerated not long after and returned to Bonne Esperance in 1151. In 1158, he was chosen abbot by the community.

As abbot, he encouraged intellectual activity amongst the canons and collected manuscripts for the monastery. He wrote a number of works of theology, hagiography, and commentary, including a life of St Augustine. His major work, *De Institutione Clericorum*, is a book of instruction for his canons regular and a reflection of his views on the monastic and clerical life. He resigned as abbot in 1182 in order to prepare without distractions for his passing from this life to the next. He died in April 1183.

His correspondent was Henry the Liberal, Count of Champagne (1152–81) who had a reputation as a very well-educated lay person, as this letter indicates. Son-in-law of King Louis VII of France through his marriage to the

64

king's daughter, Marie, the Count made his court a centre of learning, and, at a time when a book could be worth a king's ransom, owned at least two himself; a copy of Vegetius' *On the Art of War*, given to him by John of Salisbury, and an illuminated manuscript of Valerius Maximus. Both John of Salisbury and Nicholas of Clairvaux, Bernard of Clairvaux's former secretary, attest in letters to his learning and his generosity to scholars. Henry's early death left his wife to rule Champagne and she in turn encouraged learning and literature, particularly in French. Among the literati at her court was Chrétien de Troyes, poet of the Arthurian legend, whose works include 'Lancelot', and 'Percival, or the Holy Grail'.

LETTER TO HENRY, COUNT OF CHAMPAGNE

Your father's liberality was truly admirable and it protected him from the snares of avarice, so that his soul was ever free of that vice. He wanted you to be a worthy heir, so he decided to build you up with a worthy education. Thus by his providential care, he procured for you instruction in the liberal arts from the time you were only a boy. It was right for him to do so because while it is one's lineage that makes one noble, it is the possession of an estate that makes one wealthy, and it is the obedience of one's servants that makes one a ruler, but it is the knowledge of letters that leads one forth from the common ignorance of human beings and from the stolid torpor that characterizes the dull-witted, and renders to its pupil glorious liberty. And so the pagans rightly called the art of letters a liberal art, because this art liberates the one who studies it from the common lot of human beings enslaved to confusion; the one who obtains a mastery of letters is no longer oppressed and overwhelmed by the fetters of lethargy which bind the unlearned.

Therefore you owe your father much, for his care and earnestness secured your education. Indeed your father was so magnanimous that he gave you not only that which was his, but he also made arrangements that you should receive that which he had not been able to obtain for himself [i.e. an education]. Thus he hoped that when you come to rule the many people of the County [of Champagne], you will rule with greater perfection. He also wanted the counts of the line of Champagne to be elevated above other counts by their mastery of the art of letters. You also owe much – indeed the most – to God. Render Him thanks for your many gifts. You and your father have indeed glorified God, for you used His blessings well. Your education was a collaborative effort between you and your father which is very honourable; you were both equally diligent in applying yourselves to such an estimable endeavour. Your father offered you his thoughtfulness, guidance, admonition, and exhortation; you assisted your father by your cooperative disposition, eager study, obedience, and compliance. In this way you have pursued scholarly discipline for many years, and under the guidance of a teacher, you have acquired a knowledge of letters. Indeed, as they say nowadays, 'You are so well educated that you can hardly be ranked among the clerics, for you outdo very many of them in your erudition!'

Of course, you did not plan to become a cleric when you applied yourself to the study of letters, for your intention was to fasten a sword to your belt and fulfil your military obligations. Nevertheless, your military interests did not repel you from your studies, as though one interested in the former should necessarily find the latter a tedious burden. Rather, you persevered, and with graceful toil you acquired the commendable education you now possess. Your profit was the grace of understanding, and you are still devoted to the art of letters you loved so well. But you are also a knight, indeed, a commander of knights. You love and revere the trappings of war in a manner truly befitting a knight; and yet you love letters in a manner befitting a cleric. Not only that: you encourage others to learn letters as well. Those like yourself who strive for good causes must sometimes fight. Yet when your duties are taken care of, you free yourself from noisy outdoor matters and retire in solitude like a cleric. Then, taking up a book, you enjoy line after line of reading, in which your face shines as though in a mirror. Whether you are reading works written by pagans or Christians, you read very carefully and often re-read choice books, like the prudent reader who takes the advice of the prophet [Jeremiah 15] to separate what is precious from what is worthless. You do not find it burdensome to read with such careful reflection, since through it you learn what is right and proper for the commoner, the knight, the prince, or the prelate. You learn that whatever station in life you have been awarded is determined by Fortune, as the pagans would have it, or by the grace of God, which is what Christian authors teach. It is from this source that you have received pre-eminence over others. You also learn how your position obligates you to your superiors, equals, and subordinates. Remember that righteousness cannot take a position any-where but in its proper place, neither higher nor lower. Righteousness is averse to any wickedness and loves what ought to be loved; it guides you in character, in habits, and in authority, and it instructs you in reverence for God, neighbour, and holy religion.

To read and pore over matters of this sort in Scripture does not make you less princely; to understand what you read does not make you become any the less noble a ruler of the people; and to strive with prudence to separate what is harmful from what is helpful in your reading causes your nobility no dishonour. Rather, by doing these noble things, it is as though you refresh yourself with the water of the ancients....

Farewell. And may those who wish you well fare well also.

FURTHER READING: THE TWELFTH CENTURY

Primary sources

Peter Abelard, *The Ethics*, ed. and trans. D.E. Luscombe, Cambridge, Cambridge University Press, 1971.

Bernard of Clairvaux, *Steps of Humility*, trans. G.B. Burch, Cambridge, Mass., Harvard University Press, 1950.

Bernard of Clairvaux, *The Letters of Bernard of Clairvaux*, trans. B.S. Scott, Chicago, Henry Regnery, 1953.

Bernard of Clairvaux, *Five Books on Consideration*, trans. J.D. Anderson and K. Kennan, Kalamazoo, Mich. Cistercian Publications, 1976.

Hugh of St Victor, *On the Sacraments*, trans. R.J. Deferrari, Cambridge, Mass., Medieval Academy of America, 1951.

Hugh of St Victor, *Didascalion*, trans. J. Taylor, New York, Columbia University Press, 1961.

John of Salisbury, *Metalogicon*, trans. D.D. McGarry, Berkeley, University of California Press, 1955.

John of Salisbury, *Entheticus Major and Minor*, ed. and trans. J. van Laarhoven, 3 vols, Leiden, E.J. Brill, 1987.

John of Salisbury, *Policraticus*, ed. and trans. C.J. Nederman, Cambridge, Cambridge University Press, 1990.

[Anonymous], *Treatise on the Laws and Customs of England Commonly Called Glanvill*, ed. and trans. G.D.G. Hall, London, Thomas Nelson, 1965.

Walter Map, *Courtier's Trifles*, ed. M.R. James, C.N.L. Brooke and R.A.B. Mynors, Oxford, Clarendon Press, 1983.

Secondary sources

Benson, R.L. and G. Constable, eds, *Renaissance and Renewal in the Twelfth Century*, Cambridge, Mass., Harvard University Press, 1982.

Baldwin, J.W., *The Social Views of Peter the Chanter and His Circle*, 2 vols, Princeton, Princeton University Press, 1970.

Blumenthal, U.-R., *The Investiture Controversy: Church and Monarchy from the Ninth to the Twelfth Century*, Philadelphia, University of Pennsylvania Press, 1988.

Bynum, C.W., 'Did the Twelfth Century Discover the Individual?', *Journal of Ecclesiastical History*, 31, 1980, 1–17.

Chodorow, S., *Christian Political Theory and Church Politics in the Mid-Twelfth Century: The Ecclesiology of Gratian's Decretum*, Berkeley, University of California Press, 1972.

Duby, G., *The Three Orders: Medieval Society Imagined*, trans. A. Goldhammer, Chicago, University of Chicago Press, 1980.

Dutton, P.E., '*Illustre civitatis et populi exemplum*: Plato's *Timaeus* and the Transmission from Calcidius to the End of the Twelfth Century of a Tripartite Scheme of Society', *Mediaeval Studies*, 45, 1983, 79–119.

Evans, G.R., *The Mind of St. Bernard of Clairvaux*, Oxford, Oxford University Press, 1983.

Forhan, K.L. 'The Twelfth-Century Bureaucrat and the Life of the Mind,' *Proceedings of the PMR Conference*, 1985, 65–74.

Forhan, K.L., 'Salisburian Stakes: The Uses of "Tyranny" in the Policraticus', *History of Political Thought*, 11, 1990, 397–407.

Forhan, K.L., 'The Not-So-Divided Self: Reading Augustine in the Twelfth Century', *Augustiniana*, forthcoming.

Kennan, E., 'The *De Consideratione* of St. Bernard of Clairvaux and the Papacy in the Mid-Twelfth Century', *Traditio*, 23, 1967, 73–115.

Leibeschutz, H., *Mediaeval Humanism in the Life and Writings of John of Salisbury*, London, Warburg Institute, 1950.

Nederman, C.J. 'The Aristotelian Doctrine of the Mean and John of Salisbury's Concept of Liberty', *Vivarium*, 24, 1986, 128–42.

Nederman C.J., 'The Physiological Significance of the Organic Metaphor in John of Salisbury's *Policraticus*', *History of Political Thought*, 8, 1987, 211–23.

Nederman, C.J., 'A Duty to Kill: John of Salisbury's Theory of Tyrannicide', *Review of Politics*, 50, 1988, 365–89.

Nederman, C.J., 'Aristotelianism and the Origins of "Political Science" in the Twelfth Century', *Journal of the History of Ideas*, 52, 1991, 179–94.

Nederman, C.J. and J. Brückmann, 'Aristotelianism in John of Salisbury's *Policraticus*', *Journal of the History of Philosophy*, 21, 1983, 203–29.

Nederman, C.J. and C. Campbell, 'Priests, Kings and Tyrants: Spiritual and Temporal Power in John of Salisbury's *Policraticus*', *Speculum*, 66, 1991, 572–90.

Rouse, R.H. and M.A. Rouse, 'John of Salisbury and the Doctrine of Tyrannicide', *Speculum*, 42, 1967, 693–709.

Smalley, B., *The Study of the Bible in the Middle Ages*, Oxford, Blackwell, 1952.

Smalley, B., *The Becket Conflict and the Schools*, Oxford, Basil Blackwell, 1973.

Southern, R., *Medieval Humanism and Other Essays*, Oxford, Basil Blackwell, 1971.

Wilks, M.J., ed., *The World of John of Salisbury*, Oxford, Basil Blackwell, 1984.

Part II

THE THIRTEENTH CENTURY

6

THE BOOK OF TREASURE
Brunetto Latini

INTRODUCTION

Brunetto Latini (*c.* 1220–94) was a Florentine statesman, magistrate, notary, and scholar whose *Livre dou Tresor* provides an encyclopedia of information useful to an educated European of his day. His activity in Florence's turbulent politics led to his exile to France from 1260–66. During his exile he wrote three major works, *Tesoretto*, *Rettorica*, and, in French, *Li Livre dou Tresor*. Latini has also earned an eternal place in the history of literature via Dante's *Divine Comedy*, where Dante writes of him:

Stamped on my mind and now stabbing my heart,
The dear, benign, paternal image of you,
You living, you hourly teaching me the art
By which humans grow immortal.

(Inf. xv 82–3)

That art, for Latini, was the art of rhetoric, or 'bon parleur', as he spoke of it in the *Tresor*. Certainly this work is notable for its clarity of style and careful organization, which keep it from awkwardness despite its comprehensive subject matter.

The theme of the work is deceptively simple; Latini is providing us with 'precious jewels' of knowledge, the practical and theoretical aspects of philosophy. Book I is 'theoretical' in the medieval sense, that is, it covers theology, mathematics, and the natural sciences. Book II discusses ethics, revealing close familiarity with both Aristotle's *Nicomachean Ethics* and a number of works by Cicero. Book III, which is on rhetoric and politics, includes very practical suggestions on the process of choosing rulers, the qualities and characteristics they should have, and the negotiations that need to take place between leaders and citizens. Striking to the contemporary political theorist is the great emphasis on the contractual nature of the obligation between ruler and ruled, and the pragmatic suggestions for enforcing that obligation.

The selections included here, all from Book III, demonstrate some fascinating aspects of medieval political thought, and appear in English for the first time in this volume.

THE BOOK OF TREASURE

BOOK III

Chapter 73: On the government of cities

In the preceding first two books are described the nature and the beginning of things of the world, instruction in the vices and virtues, and the teaching of rhetoric. But in this last part, Master Brunetto Latini wishes to give his friend what he promised at the beginning of the first book, which is to define the political, that is, the governance of cities, the highest and most noble science, and the most noble office on earth, as Aristotle proves in his book.

And it has already been said that politics generally includes all the arts needed by the human community, nevertheless, the master does not discuss what does not concern him about the ruler himself and his rightful office. For from the moment that people began first to increase and multiply and the sin of the first man had rooted itself in his descendants, the world has grown worse: one covets the things of a neighbour; another, out of pride, subjects the weak to the yoke of servitude. Thus, those who wanted to live by their rights and escape the power of evil doers turned together to a single place and a single order. From there, they began to build houses, construct cities and fortresses, and surround them with walls and ditches.

Then they began to establish customs, law, and rights that were common to all the burghers of the city. This is why Tully says that a city is an assembly of people who inhabit a place and live by law. And because peoples and habitations are diverse, the laws and rights are different throughout the world, thus there are varied kinds of rule. From when Nimrod the Giant first took over the rule of the country and greed sowed war and mortal hatred among the peoples of the world, it was fitting that humans had rulers of many kinds, sometimes chosen by law and sometimes by force. And so there were some who were rulers and kings of countries, others were castellans and guardians of castles, others were dukes and leaders of armies, others were counts and companions of the king, others had other offices, and each had his land and his people to govern.

But all rulers and all officials either hold office from someone and his heirs who rule in perpetuity, as do kings, counts, castellans, and the like; or for all the days of their lives such as my lord the apostle [the Pope], the emperor of Rome, and others chosen for life; or they rule for a year, as do mayors and provosts, dignitaries, and aldermen of cities and towns; or they have a particular term, like legates, delegates, vicars, and the officials who have a more powerful ruler give them some duty or have them answer questions. But on all this the master is silent in this book. He says nothing about them nor about the rule of those who do not govern their cities for a term of one year. These are of two kinds, first, those which are in France and other countries, which are subject to the rule of kings and other hereditary princes, who sell the office and protect those who buy it (in his own interest, not for the benefit of the citizens).

The other is in Italy, where the citizens and the burghers and the population of the city choose the authorities and the ruler they believe to be most beneficial to the common good of the city and its subjects. And it is of this kind that the master speaks, for the other is not suitable for him or to his friend. Nevertheless, all rulers, whatever kind of rule they have, can acquire a lot of good information.

Chapter 74: On rule and its foundation

All rule and all rank is given us by the sovereign Father, who in the healthy establishment of things of the world desires the government of cities to be founded on three pillars: justice, reverence, and love. Justice must be established so firmly in the heart of the ruler, that he gives to each his due, and does not 'incline either to the right or to the left'. For Solomon said, 'No evil will befall the just king.' His burghers and his subjects owe him reverence, for it is the only thing in the world that is less than the merits of faith, and which is better than any sacrifice. On which the Apostle said, 'Honoured be our Lord.' They ought to love one another, for rulers ought to love their subjects heartily and with pure faith, and watch over them day and night for the common good of the city and of all people. All others must love their ruler with all their heart and true intention and give him help and counsel in the maintenance of his office, for nothing can be accomplished alone.

Chapter 75: Who should be chosen to rule and govern

The ruler is like the head of the citizens. Since everyone desires to have a healthy head, and because when the head is unhealthy all the members [of the body] are ill, above all, they must aim to have a governor who will lead them to a good end, according to law and to justice. He should not be chosen by lots nor by the luck of fortune, but by the great foresight of a wise council, and they ought to consider twelve things.

The first is that Aristotle said that by long experience of many things people become wise, and one cannot have long experience without having had a long life. Thus it seems that a young person cannot be wise, although he can have a good mind. Because of this, Solomon said, 'Unfortunate is the land with a young king.' Nevertheless, one can be of great age and have little sense, for one can be young in sense as well as in age. For this reason the burghers ought to choose a ruler who is young in neither one nor the other, but better that he be 'old' in each. It is not for nothing that in law no one can hold office before the twenty-fifth year (although the laws of the Church name the twentieth year).

The second is that they not look at his power or that of his ancestors, but the nobility of his heart and the honourableness of his morals, his life, and the virtuous works that he should do on his estate and his other lands; for the house ought to honoured by a good ruler and not the ruler by a good house. If he is noble in heart and in lineage, certainly he is worth a great deal in everything.

The third is that he be just, for as Tully said, 'sense without justice is not sense but malice; nothing has value without justice.'

The fourth is that he have a good mind and subtle understanding to know all the truths of things, to understand and know with agility what is suitable, and to perceive the reason for things; for it is an ugly thing to be deceived by poverty of understanding.

The fifth is that he be strong and steadfast in intention but not from evil and vainglory, and that he not believe too quickly what everyone says. There was once a city where no one could be ruler if he were not the best and so long as this was the custom, there was no evil fortune nor poverty in this country. He can do as much as possible, if he does not believe in himself more than he should. Nor is one held worthy because of his rank, but because of his deeds, for the wise person prefers to be a ruler rather than to seem to be.

The sixth is that he not be greedy for money nor other goods. For these are two things which will quickly destroy the person. It is a most dishonourable thing when he who does not let himself be deflected by fear is corrupted by money, thereby being defeated not by great difficulty, but by his own will. But most of all, a person ought not to desire honours excessively, for many times it is better to let them go than to accept them.

The seventh is that he speak well, because the ruler is expected to speak better than others, for everyone thinks one wiser when something is wisely said, even by a young man. But in all things it is suitable that he not speak too much, for those who do not speak too much commit no sins. Just as one string alone makes a cithera out of harmony, so with one bad word, one can be dishonoured and undone.

The eighth is that he not be immoderate in spending or using things, for all who do so are capable of falling into theft and rapine. Nevertheless, he must not avoid these vices in such a way that he seems stingy or greedy, for that is something most vilely shameful against the person of the ruler.

The ninth is that he not be too quick to anger and that his wrath not last, for anger that lingers in ruling is susceptible to explosion and does not allow true knowledge nor right judgement to judge.

The tenth is that he be rich and powerful, for if he has the other virtues, it appears that he has not been corrupted by money. None the less, I praise the good poor rather than the evil rich.

The eleventh is that he has no other rule, for it is not credible that any person is capable of two things of such weight as is the governing of people.

The twelfth is the sum of all the others: that he have a right faith in God and man, for without faith and loyalty, justice is never kept.

Good citizens ought to look for these and the other virtues before they choose their ruler, in such a way that he has as many good points as possible. For many do not examine morals, giving the position because of his power, because of his lineage, or because of his desire, or for friendship with the city from which he comes. But they will be disappointed in him in this, for in this, war and hatred have so multiplied among the Italians in times past, and among the peoples of many lands, that there is division in all cities and enmity amongst the burghers. Indeed, whoever has the support of one party will have the enmity of the other. Furthermore, if this civil officer is not very wise, he will fall into the contempt and ill will even of those who chose him. In this manner, where each had hoped to find his good, each finds his ruin.

Chapter 76: How and in what manner rulers ought to be chosen

When the wise people of the city who are concerned with the election are in agreement on any person of integrity, next they ought to look at the customs, law, and constitution of the city, and ought to choose their ruler accordingly, and not to one who gives honours or goods. Next a wise and well-written letter must be written, to inform the worthy individual how he was chosen and to stipulate the conditions of rule and public office for the following year in their land, and to summarize all his responsibility, and make everything clear at the beginning so that no mistake will be made. The day ought to be specified when he must be physically within the city and give his oath to the constitution of the republic; that he ought to bring with him judges, notaries, and other officials to do these and related things; what days will be convenient for him to stay after the end of his term to render his accounts (in case anyone has a claim against him); what pay he ought to have and how it should be paid; what horses he must bring and how; that all risk to him and to his things is on him; the contracts and other things concerning business – everything ought to be announced in letter according to the custom and law of the city. But one thing ought not be forgotten, and it ought to be clearly written; that he accept or refuse the office within two or three days, more or less, according to the custom of the city, and if he does not do this, the election is void.

Where they have [the custom] that the council requests from my lord the Apostle [the Pope] and from the emperor to be sent one good ruler each year, all the agreements must be so clear that there is no subject for anger. When these letters are written and sealed, they must be carried to the worthy person with polite messengers who explain the circumstances and who will carry the letters giving his answer. On the first visit, they ought not to send very eminent men nor serious business, because he might not accept the position, and this would bring great shame to them and their city. Nevertheless, if he accepts it, he can then send honourable messengers to accompany them, although it could raise suspicions if in that way they become acquainted with the ruler and his domain more than is their business. The ruler should not be deprived of his companions for two reasons; first, so that his dignity not be lowered, and secondly, because of the suspicions that the people might have of him and his staff.

Chapter 77: Which shows more clearly the form of the letter

In order to make this teaching clearer and more appropriate in this part, the master prefers to write a little example of the letter to the one who is chosen to be governor and ruler:

'To a man of great worthiness and renown, my lord Charles, Count of Ango and of Provence, governor of Rome and all its consulates, greetings and may your honours increase. Although all human people commonly desire the liberty that nature first gave them, and willingly avoid the yoke of servitude, nevertheless, because of evil desires and the faculty of sin, those who are not virtuous turn to endanger humans and to destroy human society. Concern for justice raised over the people various kinds of rule to govern them, in order both to enhance the renown of the good and to confound the malice of the wicked. And so, it is appropriate from necessity as well as from nature that people be under justice and that liberty obey judgement. Because of desires which are now even more corrupt and because of perversities which increase in our time, nothing can be more profitable to a people and to a community to have a just ruler and wise governor. Together we have reflected on a man to lead us for the next year who will come and take care of the community, maintaining what is private and belongs to others, and protecting the goods and the persons of all, in such a way that justice does not diminish in our city. It has thus come to us by divine demonstration that in all one hears from the wise and the worthy about such a high thing as rule over people, you were acclaimed the best. Because of this, Sire, by the common consent of the city, we have established you to be ruler and governor of Rome, beginning the next feast of All Saints [Nov. 1] for a term of one year.

'And we have no doubt, and everyone proclaims it, that you understand and desire to give judgement in the nation, measured justice, and to strike the sword of justice in vengeance against evil doers. And to this, Sire, all of us, both great and humble, hold themselves bound, so we beg you and request in good faith, from all our hearts, that you take and receive the rule that we offer to you more willingly than any other; with a salary of 1,010 livres of provisions, with the agreements that you see in the notarized charter and chapters of the Roman constitution enclosed with this letter. And know that you must bring with you ten judges and twelve honest and praiseworthy notaries to accompany you and reside with all your household, at your expense and at your own financial and corporal risk. Come to Rome the day of Our Lady in September [Sept. 8]. As soon as you arrive, before going to your residence, you will take the oath of your office upon the book of the constitution, closed and sealed. It shall be done this way for you and for all others in office within the Capitol of Rome. But know one thing, that within three days of receipt of these letters, you must accept them or refuse to rule, and if this is not done, all will be void, and the election futile.'

Chapter 78: How the ruler ought to take counsel on whether to accept or reject rule

Whether in this form or another, wise authors prefer the letters to be sent to rulers with all the charters of covenant, and the messengers should deliver them courteously and privately without outcry and noise. And the ruler ought to accept them in a wise manner, and going quietly to a private place, he should break the seal, read the letters and know what is in them, and think carefully in his heart if doing this would be suitable for him. He ought to seek the advice of his good friends and see if it is suitable to follow. Tully said, 'Do not desire to be a judge over the people if you are not one whose virtues could vanquish iniquity.' None the less, he ought not to lose hope even if he is greedy; these things ought to balance each other in his heart, the counsels of his friends, honour and shame, good and evil; for it is better to reflect at the beginning than to repent at the end. And even if he refuses, he should certainly honour the messenger according to his rank, giving his answer in beautiful and courteous words.

Just as earlier the writer gave an example of the greeting in fair words, now we have the response:

'Because the dignity of authority is higher than all the honours of the world, no city or people can give greater reverence to a man than to choose him from among others and submit themselves in good faith to his rule. It is a sign of very great love and of sure faith. It is the glory that enhances his name and that of the nation forever. We recognize the grace and honour that you have given us, which is all the larger and greater given that the rule of you and your city is the most honourable in the world. And although we are not able to accept this honourable grace, none the less, we thank you with all our heart and all our desire, as one who will always be obliged to you and your community. But because we are now embroiled in many things which require our presence, we pray and request the gift of grace that you pardon us, noble sirs, from accepting your government, for the need that detains us is so great that it is fitting to remain here.'

Chapter 79: The things that the ruler ought to do when he accepts the office

But if his council advises him to accept the office that is offered, he considers deeply in his heart that he is accepting a high office and undertaking a heavy burden. And he ought to foresee a lot of preparation for this, since the proper reward for the service of rule is to know that he must have the care of the city, maintain its honours and dignities, keep the law, and do justice – and that everything is promised on his faith. Next, he ought to honour the messenger as if they owed fealty to each other, and clarify all the covenants with him (if he has the power), in such a way as to avoid any kind of question with good charters.

And when this is done, he delivers the letters to him with the salutation first, and then as follows:

'The truth is that nature made all equal, but, to restrain the iniquity caused, not by vice of nature but by evil deeds, one man has rule over others, not because of their nature but because of their vices. Without doubt, only he is worthy of such a very honourable thing who knows how to advance others according to their merits and their virtues. This one person alone should be charged with ruling, whose goodness makes him worthy of the position and the honour, and whose shoulders are not too feeble for such heavy burdens. For although ruling is a great honour, none the less in itself it is risky and burdensome. Only the capabilities of Jesus Christ make a man capable of this office, not by his faith in himself alone, nor by the goodness that is in us. In the name of the Sovereign Father, by the common counsel of all our friends, we take and accept the honour and the office of your government, according to the conditions of your letters. We faithfully believe that the intelligence and knowledge of the knights and the people, and the strength and loyalty of all the citizens, will help us to carry part of our burdens and lighten our obligations by true obedience.'

And when he has sent the letters and the messenger back, next he begins his preparations. He seeks out good and trustworthy horses and equipment, but above all, he searches for a wise, discreet and experienced judge and assessor. He fears God, speaks well, is not dishonourable, is chaste with women, not proud, nor wrathful, nor fearful, speaks two languages, and who is neither too harsh nor lenient, but is strong and upright, just and of good faith and religious towards God and the Holy Church. For in law, it is the judges who are called holy at the beginning of the Digest, where it says, 'You are worthily called priests'. The code of judgement, the code of the sacraments, and many other places, have the law that the judge is consecrated in the presence of God, and he is like God on earth. But if he does not find one with all these qualities, just as all birds are not swans, let him be at least loyal and stable, incorruptible, trustworthy and not too naive, nor enmeshed in evil vices. The ruler is careful that he does not allow the good judge to be found where the money is, for it is written, 'Unfortunate is he who goes alone, for if he falls there is no one to catch him'. Which is why I say that the ruler who rules in order to acquire honour is better than one who rules out of greed for money. Certainly, he ought to supervise those by whom the law will be applied. As the ship is governed by the tiller, cities are guided by the knowledge of the judge.

Also he ought to have very good notaries, wise in the law, who know how to speak and read well, and write charters and letters well, and who know good authors, and who are chaste in their persons; because many times a good clerk amends and compensates for the defects of the judge, and carries a large burden of the entire office. Also he ought to bring into his company wise and well-taught knights, who love the honour of their master; seneschals; valets; and sergeants. The whole household ought to be wise and moderate, without pride and without wickedness, and should be willingly obedient to him and to his staff.

Next they need to make new robes for him and for his companion, to dress the household in livery, to refurbish the armour, his pennants, and the other things that are suitable to his needs. And then when the time is near, he should send his seneschal to the city to furnish the residence with whatever is needed, for the wise say that it is better to see in advance than to look for advice after the fact.

Chapter 80: What the ruler ought to do while on route

It sometimes happens that at the time when the ruler ought to go on his way, the population of the city sends honourable citizens from the city to his residence to escort him on the way or to persuade the people of his own city that he leave them to go to his office, or for other reasons. But however that may be, he should honour them, give marvellous feasts, send great presents and go to see them at their residence. But he should be careful not to speak to any of them privately, for this often gives birth to evil suspicions. For this reason, while this once was the custom, now few cities send such ambassadors to meet him.

And when the ruler has prepared for his journey, he sets out in the name of the true God, and he goes straight to his office, always enquiring and examining the customs and conditions of the city, and the nature of the people, so that he knows early what he is about to undertake. And when he is only one day from the city, he ought to send ahead his seneschal and all those who manage his household and his residence, and also he should inform the city of his arrival.

And on the morning that he is supposed to enter into the city, he ought to hear mass and the service of our Lord without fail. Moreover, his predecessor, that is, he who ruled the city before, once he receives the word of arrival from the new ruler, has it announced throughout the city, so that every knight and burgher from the city sees his entry, and he even ought to meet him with the bishop of the city (if there is one and if he desires to go). And indeed, the new ruler and his predecessor ought to honour each other at their encounter to allay any suspicions, and they ought to greet the people affably. In this way, he ought to go directly to the main church, kneel before the altar, pray to God humbly with all his heart and faith, put his offering on the altar honourably, and then use and go where he must.

Chapter 81: On the diversity of cities

At this point there are many variations. There are cities where the custom is for the ruler to go to his residence, where the statute books of the city are delivered, and then he takes his oath. In this is a great advantage, for one can better provide for the chapters that are against him. There are others which have the custom that, now that the ruler is in the city, and he has been before the altar, he is brought to the council of the city, or before the community of people where they are assembled, then he takes the oath, followed by his staff, and then the statute books are shown and delivered to him or to his judge. But before he puts his hand on the seals, the wise ruler would require the community to give him an arbiter in case of mistakes, not only for his own advantage, but for the benefit of the city and the disadvantage of malefactors. If he should confirm it, it is good, and if not, he should request that any malicious chapter opposing him, the honour of the people, or the Holy Church, can be rectified by the counsellors of the city. And if they do it, it is good to have it written in a notarized charter. If not, he takes the oath according to what has been devised in the name of the community. The form of oath is this:

'My lord A _____, [do you] swear on the saints to govern the goods and the needs of this city as is suitable to your office; to guide, conduct, maintain, and benefit the city and all the countryside and all men and women, great and humble, knight and burgher; and to maintain their law, defend and keep it; and to do what the common law and the constitution order; to see that it is kept, and guarded for all people, even orphans, widowed women, and other humble people, and to all men who come to plead their cause before you and yours?

'And, [do you swear] to protect, maintain, and defend churches, temples, hospitals and all religious houses, roads, pilgrims and merchants; and to do whatever is written in the statutes of this city? To which you swear with a good and loyal conscience so that love and hate, esteem, recompense and all malice be put aside, according to your true intention, from this All Saints Day, for one year, until next All Saints Day.'

In this manner, the ruler shall take his oath, unless he wants something to be removed from the oath, and it should be removed before he places his hand on the seals. And when he has sworn, his judges, knights and notaries, standing around him also ought to swear, standing near around him, to fill their office well and faithfully, to give good counsel to their ruler, and to keep confidential that which must be private.

Chapter 82: What the ruler ought to do when he has come to the city

At this point there are many variations. There are cities which have the custom that after the ruler has taken his oath, he addresses the people of the city. In others, he never says a word, but goes straight to his residence, even if the city is not at peace. And there are other variants: when the city is at war against its neighbours, or if there is conflict internally amongst the burghers, or it is at peace internally and externally. This is why I say that rulers should follow the usages of the country, for if it is the custom required by the city, he will be able to speak well and courteously without commanding anything. For just like his predecessors in ruling he can entreat and advise the people well without commanding or ordering them at all.

And if the land is at peace he can speak in this way: 'At the beginning of my words, I call upon the name of Jesus Christ, the all powerful King who gives all wealth and all power, the glorious Virgin Mary, and my lord Saint John, who is patron and guide of this city, that by their holy compassion they will give me the grace and power that I beseech today, and for as long as I will be in your service, I will say and do everything for the honour and glory of his Majesty, the reverend and honourable Ruler, Apostle and Emperor of the Holy Church and the Roman Empire. Honour and reward be to my Lord A____ who was your ruler and is still; and increase improvement, and happiness to your estates, and the city, and to all your friends.

'I desire to base my speech on the praise of this very noble city, and enumerate the honour, the intelligence, the power, and other works of you and your ancestors. Indeed, I could not come to the end of my speech there is so much to recount about the high chivalry and the free people of this city. Because of this I will cease speaking soon. About my Lord A_____himself, about the good works that he has accomplished this year in ruling you, and about the governing of the people and all these things, I will say nothing, for their splendour around the world is as bright as the sun. He has seen that you have chosen me, and given me power and rule over you, and although I am not worthy because of my merits or for my goodness, with faith in Jesus Christ and the good people of this city, I accept the honour that you offer me. So I dedicate myself, my heart and intention, to you and yours, despite the risks to my body and detriment of my goods. And because you have given me the greatest honour that people can give in this living world, that is, to make me your guide and ruler out of your own good will, I hope and truly believe that you will be steadfast and obedient to my authority and my commands, for the benefit and governance of you and yours. And, know that to all those who do so, I will love and give great honours, but those who defy my honour, do wrong, or are unreasonable to anyone, no matter how great or humble, I will convict them and punish them severely in their bodies and their possessions.

'And I did not come out of greed to make money, but to acquire praise, reward, and honour, for me and for all of my staff. And for this, I will be centred in law and justice, in such a way that I lean neither to the right nor the left, for this I know well and each must know it: that cities are to be governed according to right and truth, so that each has his due. The evil doer is to be either exiled or punished. Indeed, the people and their belongings ought to increase and multiply in good peace and in its honour and that of its friends. Which is why I return where I began: it is God, the all-powerful, who gives to you, me, and to all citizens, and to the judges of this city, those here and elsewhere, the grace and the power to do and say what brings honour to the city, and glory to us, and to the people of the city and to all those who love us with full heart.'

In this way the new dignitary gives his inaugural speech, but the wise speaker ought carefully to observe the usage, estate, and the condition of the city, so that he can mute his words and find others according to the place and time. If the city has internal conflict (because of discord within it), it is appropriate for the ruler to speak on this matter, and then he will be able to follow the speech given above. If he sees that it would be better, he can remember in his speech how our Lord commanded that peace and goodwill be among people, and how he would be pleased with them. It is very important to a ruler that his subjects be at peace with each other, and if they are not he must change them. And he should say how concord enhances cities and enriches the merchants, while war destroys them, and to remember Rome and other good cities which, because of internal war, were weakened and went awry. Civil war unleashes evil hands to rob temples and roads, to burn houses, to murder, to rob and to steal, and to lose God and the world.

The ruler will say these and other words on his arrival, entreating and advising people to do well, to make peace and to relinquish hatred. He says how they will have a council of integrity, and establish the necessity well and honourably.

When the city is at war against any other city, on his arrival the ruler can certainly follow the process as shown above. If he thinks it would be better, he can add these words:

'It is true, everyone knows, that because evil and wrongdoing ought not and could not be allowed any longer, war has come between you and your enemies which is a great injustice and disloyalty on their part. And, while much is required, nevertheless, I will not speak of that now, for it is fitting to be more gentle in words than in deeds. But if there is in this world a situation when one can exercise his strength, power, and acquire great fame for one's quality, I say that it is this war, above all. It takes a person strong in arms, frank in spirit, vigorous, full of virtue, strong at labour, watchful at rest, subtle and ingenious in everything. Examine yourself! Be armoured with strong armour and good horses for these things give desire to one in combat, and victory follows, and give your enemies fear of loss, and the desire to flee. Be of one heart and one will! Be steadfast together, and do not leave without permission. Remember your ancestors and their victorious battles! And I have so much confidence in your valour and goodness and that of your people, and in the right which you have against your enemies, that you will have the victory and honour that you desire.'

These and other words (which the wise rhetor will know how to find on the subject) ought to be spoken before the citizens, in such a way that he sees what is most agreeable and finishes his speech. And when he is seated, his predecessor, if he is present, ought to rise and give his speech well and wisely, answering what others have said, praising him and his intelligence, his accomplishments and his lineage, and giving him graceful thanks for what he said in his speech. At the end of his talk, he ought to ask everyone to obey the new ruler, and to put into action his ideas. When he has done this, he takes leave of the people and each goes to his house.

Sometimes it happens that well-born people from his own city came with the new ruler to the community. They speak at this time, bringing greetings and describing the love between the two communities, praising the city and its citizens, and the former governor and his good rule. Also they praise the new ruler, his lineage, his accomplishments, and they show how the whole of their city holds the [new] ruler in great honour and affection. And they say that the ruler and the people [of their city] have commanded him on the peril of their bodies and their resources that he must rule for the honour and benefit of the city. They entreat the people of the city to obey him and give him aid and counsel, so that he can honourably complete his office. And when this has been said, the former governor must give an agreeable answer in his speech, responding to the new ruler as was described before, or in another manner as is appropriate.

Chapter 83: What the ruler ought to do after he has taken his oath

After the oaths and speeches, the ruler should go to his residence and open the books of statutes and charters for the city. His judges and notaries ought to read and study them, night and day, from front to back, and note what is appropriate to do. For it is very valuable for judges and notaries to read and reread often, in such a way that they learn it all by heart, and that they know the points and places that concern them. Yet the ruler himself promised to study them well, even parallel points, and to remember them always.

After they have carefully examined them, they ought to note the form of oath and the instructions which must be sworn to by all the judges and they should be proclaimed in each parish, and then make them take the oath with hand raised, put their names in writing, and accept them as notaries. Then he ought to choose his council according to the law of the city, but he ought to search for counsellors who are good, wise, and of good age, because from good people comes good advice. Then he should choose other good and loyal officials and sergeants of the court, that they can help him carry the [burden] of office. During this time, if the ruler is at his residence making these and other arrangements before he goes to the official residence, or is at his own estate, he ought to consult often and closely with the worthy people of the city about things that will bring honour to him and the city. And if the city is in conflict either from within or without, he ought to work hard to have peace, but not in such a way that the citizens do not want him to meddle, for the ruler should carefully guard against falling into the hatred or suspicion of his people.

Chapter 84: What the ruler ought to do when he first enters into his rule

When the day comes that he ought begin his office, he should go early in the morning to church to hear the service and pray to God and his saints. Next he goes to the official residence, and takes office. Because it has become customary that one leaves to the governor the precaution of establishing penalties, even for small offences, the ruler, in consultation with the wise, ought to establish his orders and rules to be in accord with the good customs of the city, but not so they contradict the promises he made the first day. And the first feast day to arrive, he assembles all the people of the city in the customary place, and speaks before them, loudly enough so that each one hears his voice, and he says in his speech the same things as he did the first day, except that he should now speak more plainly, to command, order, threaten, plead, or warn as he thinks appropriate as ruler. And when he has finished his address, his notaries should read the ordinances loudly and clearly. The ruler should allow anyone in the city to rise and say anything at the assembly, for if one is stopped, another would say it again, and this would be a serious obstacle, especially if there are two parties in the city.

Chapter 85: How the ruler ought to encourage his officials

After this, the ruler ought to assemble his judges, notaries, his companions, and the other officials of his household, to request and encourage them to do well and fairly all they can, and after asking, command that they guard and maintain his honour and that of the community, and that each of them examine and study his office, and that they render to each his due, that they resolve quarrels as quickly as they can, safeguarding the order of reason. They should keep themselves from vice and the blame of the people, they should not be wrathful with the people, nor go to taverns, nor impose on anyone for food or drink, and they should deprive no one of anything, but keep themselves from being corrupted by money, by women, or by anything else.

And if they do otherwise, I say that they ought to be punished more severely than others, for 'the gravest penalty falls on us, and on those who must enforce our laws'.

Chapter 86: How the ruler ought to honour his predecessor

Among the other things which are appropriate to the ruler is that he calm the mind of his predecessor, giving him honour and respect when he can. And when he has to turn over his office, do not allow him to be shamed or wronged, for he took an oath to restrain the iniquities of the evil. 'As he behaves to his father, so will his sons treat him', for it is written that we ought to act towards our fathers as we want our sons to act towards us.

Chapter 87: How the ruler ought to assemble the city council

When the ruler has come to his office and his rule, he ought to think day and night about the things concerning his government. And although he is head and guardian of the community, nevertheless, in great need and uncertainty he ought to assemble the counsellors of the city, telling them the situation and asking their counsel on what would be best for the good of the city, and listening to what they say.

If the need is serious, he ought to consult them one, two, three, or more or as many times as is necessary, either the privy council or the great council. He should add to the council other persons of integrity: judges, scholars, and other worthy people, for it is written, 'from a large council come large solutions'. And to tell the truth, the ruler can surely follow the decisions of the council, for as Solomon said, 'Do everything with counsel, and then once done, you will not be sorry'.

But the ruler is careful that any proposition that he makes before the counsellors be brief, and is written in only a few chapters, for a multitude of things becomes an impediment, obscures the mind, and weakens the best common sense, for the mind thinking of many things is master of none.

When the notary has placed the proposals before the counsellors, the ruler rises and recounts what the need is and in what direction it is going. But he is careful of what he says and that his conduct is clear and simple, in such a way that no one can tell what is his preference. I do not say that the ruler can never reveal it, but so that it does not engender suspicion, for there are many people who out of envy or hate speak more against the ruler than for the common good. And when the ruler has made the proposal he ought then to order no one to say anything further on this subject, and no one busy himself in praising it to him or his staff, but that they listen to those who speak. Then he ought to order his notaries to write down carefully the words of the speakers; not all that they say, but all that concerns the point before the council. And do not allow too many people to rise to speak.

And when they have spoken on one side or the other, the ruler rises to separate the ideas of one side from the other. If there is agreement, the greater part of the people who are assembled in council ought to be firm and stable, and everything should be written down, and the needs described so as to clarify the necessity better. He can then write down for the counsellors whether he agrees with one counsel or another. And when all is well and carefully done, the ruler excuses them and, 'as the need requires, so he commands'. Those who do not follow through ought to be condemned as traitors. Among other things, the ruler ought to honour the people of his council greatly, for they are as members [of the body] and what they institute ought to be without reward for them, but be done specifically for the improvement of the community. But one should not assemble the council for everything but only if there is a real need.

Chapter 88: How the ruler ought to honour delegates and foreign ambassadors

When ambassadors of a foreign land come to him for any need that concerns either one land or the other, certainly the ruler ought willingly to see, honour, and receive them courteously. Before he assembles the council, he ought to try to know the reason why they come, if he can, because it could be something for which he does not need to assemble the council at all, or maybe only the privy council, or perhaps the full council, or even the whole population of the city. But if they are legates from my lord the Apostle [the Pope], or the Emperor of Rome, or from their powerful vassals, he ought not to refuse counsel, and he ought to go to greet them, and accompany them, and honour them with all his might. When they have spoken to the council, the ruler ought to answer well and courteously, telling them that they are free to come and go, and that the wise people of the city will think over what would be suitable. And when the ambassadors have come out of the council, the ruler should hear the will of the councillors, their suggestions about what they should do and what their answer ought to be.

Chapter 89: How the ruler ought to send his ambassadors

When he has anything for which one ought to send messengers or ambassadors out of the city, certainly if the need is not of great weight, he should choose by lots among the counsellors of the city, or otherwise according to the custom of the city. But if they must be sent to the Pope or the Emperor, or somewhere that requires great solemnity, I believe that the ruler himself should choose the best in the city, if that is the will of the council.

Chapter 90: How the ruler ought to hear cases and advocates

In order to hear the desires of the people and to appease the clamour of citizens, the authority is confided in him to hear extraordinary disputes often, to ease and to alleviate the judicial process for all the people, for it is a great good that the ruler constrain his subjects within the framework of the law, and that he not bring them to discord, for fires that are not put out sometimes attain great strength. But if they have some strong point on which he has doubts, I counsel him to bring in his judge and follow his advice or that he adjourn until he has been counselled on it. But the best and most honest thing in the ruler, as he sits in court, is to listen calmly to each of them, even the advocates and investigators of the case, because they reveal the strength of the pleas and manifest the nature of the question, which is why the law says that their office is honourably right and necessary to human life, as much or more than if they fought with sword or blade for their people and for their country. For we do not believe, as in *The Deeds of the Emperors*, that only those who use the buckler and halberc are knights, but advocates and investigators of cases are chivalrous also. Thus as a part of his office the ruler ought to provide so that no poor person or any other has to plead before him who cannot have an advocate, whether because of his weakness or the strength of his adversary. He ought to retain some good advocate to aid him and counsel him on his rights and on his speech.

After the ruler hears the parties, he should consider how he will respond. He must not say anything foolish but speak wisely and thoughtfully, and all that he orders and institutes should be with advice and be carried out, so that he seems just and wise in his deeds and in his speech. Otherwise his words would be a mockery, and everyone would hold them worthless. Which is why I say that if sometimes he goes against that which is good, either in his words or his orders, he should not be ashamed to amend them, since it is a great virtue to correct one's error and turn to the better. Thus must the ruler do, according to the law's command.

Chapter 91: That the ruler ought to act on offences

Everything that the powerful do ought to be so that the city that is under his governance is in good estate, without tumult and without crime. And this cannot be if he does not do enough so that the countryside is invaded and mocked by thieves and murderers and all kinds of malefactors, for the law commands that the ruler purge the countryside of evil people and this is why there is rule over both foreigners and inhabitants who commit crimes in his jurisdiction. Nevertheless, he should not give over to punishment those who are not guilty, for it is a more holy thing to acquit the evil doer than to convict the person who does no evil, and it is an ugly thing if you take away the name of the innocent out of hatred for the guilty.

On crime the ruler and his officials ought to follow the custom of the country and the order of reason, in this way: first, the accused must swear on the saints to tell the truth in accusation and in defence, and that he is not bringing any false testimony to his hearing. Then he gives his accusation or denunciation in writing, or if not, the notary must write it down word-for-word as he gives it, and then question him carefully, to see that it is accurate. The ruler or the judges themselves will believe that which appears to be fact, the truth of the thing, and then afterwards summon him who is accused of the crime. When he comes make him swear and assure the court of his pledge, then put down in writing his confession or denial as he gives it, and if he gives no pledge, or if the crime is too grave, he must be put under guard. Then the ruler or the judge ought to judge and hear the witnesses who are willing to come, and compel those who do not come, and examine everything well and wisely, and put their decision in writing. And when the testimony has all been received, the judges and the notaries ought to summon the parties before them, and when they are there, they should open and make public the words of the witnesses and give them to them so they can confer and show their reasons.

Now sometimes in serious crimes, one cannot be sure or prove with certainty, but one finds against the accused information or strong arguments for suspicion against the accused. At this point, one can put him to torture to make him confess his crime, otherwise not. And if he confesses under torture, the judge must not ask if 'John did the murder', but should ask more generally 'who did it?'

Chapter 92: How the ruler ought to convict or acquit the accused

One ought to receive the accused and the proofs of crimes in this way: when the two parties have made their case, then the ruler ought to go without delay with the judges and notaries into one of the rooms of his residence and see, hear, and carefully examine the entire case, from top to bottom, until they know the truth according to what has been shown them. And if they are certain of the crime because either the criminal has confessed of his own will without torture, or because of testimony, or because of the battle of a champion, or because of his contumacy, they ought to punish him either in his body or in his goods, depending on the crime and according to the law and custom. But the ruler should ensure that it is not more severe or more lenient than the nature of the thing requires, in order to avoid a reputation either for severity or leniency. And although serious penalties are appropriate for serious crimes, none the less the ruler ought to have some moderation out of compassion. (But in our time there are those who do not do so, but punish and torture as harshly as they can.) Those who are not guilty must be acquitted. The notary puts it all in writing, the convicted on one page and the acquitted on the other.

Afterwards, the ruler ought to assemble the council according to the custom of the country, and order that no one make any outcry. If he wishes he can first address them and caution the people to avoid misdeeds, saying that if no one pays attention to small penalties that he now places on some of the criminals, the next time he will make them more severe, so they will increase until the end of his term of office.

Then he ought to address those who are to be given corporal punishment. They should now be in his presence to hear their sentence so that a sentence of corporal punishment is not given against anyone who is not present. Next the notary rises and reads the sentences aloud – the acquitted first and the convicted after. When it has all been read, the ruler confirms it; he commands that corporal punishment be given immediately, and that the others pay their fines on the day named; and then he gives the evidence to the public officials and dismisses the people.

Chapter 93: How the ruler ought to guard the wealth of the community

If the day passes by which the convicted are supposed to pay, and they have not paid, the ruler should force them to pay, for it is worth little to convict them and not make them pay. On the other hand, he ought to ensure that public officials are well supplied with money for both large and small expenses which are incurred by the community. But he ought to examine the public officials' accounts, often and carefully, both income and expenses, and take care that the wealth of the community is not spent immoderately. For just as he ought to keep himself from too great expenditures, certainly he ought to conserve all the more the community's wealth, for it is an ugly thing to be miserly with one's own money, but generous with that of someone else. And despite his own heavy expenses, he ought to be guardian of the community, and save and maintain the rights of the community, the debts, justices, lordships, castles, cities, houses, persons, officials, places, streets, roads, and everything that belongs to the community of the city, in such a way that the estates and profits of the community do not decrease, but grow and increase during his time. Also the ruler ought to guard and defend the city inside and out, even at night, from theft and other serious crimes.

Chapter 94: How the ruler ought to take care of the wealth of his own estate and that of his staff

Within his residence, the ruler ought to establish his household well and wisely, each person in his place and in his office, correcting one with words, another with a switch. He ought to advise his seneschal to be moderate in expenses, not in such a way that he is blamed for avarice, but so that he maintains his goods and that he meet the needs of his staff, so that nothing is lacking, because a lack of necessities can bring them to villainous thoughts.

Chapter 95: How the ruler ought to consult with the wise

He ought to honour and love all those of his household, and amuse and divert himself sometimes with them, but above all he ought to love and honour the judges and notaries of his staff, because he has put into their hands the greater part of his honour and his worth. Because of this, the powerful ought to bring the wise together often and carefully, even feast days and evenings in winter time, in his chamber or elsewhere, and enquire about what they are doing, what cases they have before them, the nature of the pleas, and he ought to consult with them on what they must do. For it is a very sensible thing to remind oneself what is going on, establish the present, and provide for the future. He ought to require them and counsel them to be the scale that weighs rights and wrongs according to God and to justice, that they take care that justice is not sold either for money, for love, for hate, or for any living thing, but remind them what our Lord commanded: 'love justice, you who judge the earth'. But on this the master is silent and turns to other things.

Chapter 96: On the argument about whether it is preferable to be feared or loved

In this section, the master says that between the governors of cities there is a difference; that one prefers to be feared rather than loved, and the other desires more to be loved than feared. Those who prefer to be feared desire to have renown for their great severity. Those who would seem fierce and cruel give very severe punishments and harsh torments in the belief that this makes them more feared and thus the city more easily kept peaceful. And they prove this by quoting from Seneca that lack of punishment corrupts cities, and an abundance of sinners brings the habit of sin. He who is severely punished loses the boldness of malice. The tolerant prince confirms the vices, and the gentle ruler eliminates the shame of the evil doer. The more dreaded the punishment that is instituted by his ruler, and the more the torment, the more it is profitable as an example – everyone fears the fierce and the bold, and the punishment frightens many.

By contrast those who prefer to be loved rather than feared say that love can never be without fear, but fear can be without love. Tully said, 'There is no more sure defence in the world than to be loved, but nothing more frightening than to be feared.' For everyone hates that which he fears, and he who is hated by all may as well be dead for no riches can counter the hate of many. Long-lasting fear is a poor guard; cruelty is the enemy of nature. It is fitting that everyone fear him or those by whom he would be feared, for power that comes from fear will not last long.

All punishment must be given without cruelty and not inflicted by the ruler except for the good of the community. No punishment should be greater than the crime; no one should be convicted of the crimes of another; and all government should be without folly and laziness. Tully said, 'Take care that you do nothing for which you cannot show a reason'. And Seneca said, 'He does wrong who would please his fame more than his conscience.' Cruelty is nothing more than fierceness of spirit in great punishment, which is why I say that he is cruel who does not moderate a sentence when he has the opportunity. Plato said that no one wise punishes the one who committed a crime as much as the one who planned it in advance.

What is the difference between a king and tyrant? They are the same in fortune and in power but the tyrant commits acts of cruelty by desire, while a king does not do them without necessity. One is loved and the other is feared. He is called a bad father who always severely beats and frightens his child. The most sure defence in the world is the love of citizens because it results in the most beautiful thing in this world: that everyone desires you to live!

Through this discussion, one can well understand the argument, because clemency, which is the opposite of cruelty, is moderation of mind about the penalty that it can establish. Tully said that the most beautiful thing in ruling is clemency and pity, if it is joined with justice, without which the city cannot be governed. Seneca said,

> When I am in charge of care of the city I find so many vices among so many people, that to cure the worst in each, it is fitting that one be healed by anguish, another by exile, another by pilgrimage, some by suffering, some by poverty and others by cruelty; all are suitable for those who have been convicted. I will not go in fury nor in cruelty but will go along the path of the law, by deeds, by wisdom without pride, by judgement without anger. With such spirits the evil are similar to serpents and other venomous animals.

It is not fitting that the ruler be too cruel nor too full of clemency, for it is cruel to pardon all, just as it is to pardon none, but it is the highest clemency to confound the evil by pardoning them. But I say that no one should pardon the evil doer, for the judge is condemned when the guilty is pardoned. Also, he ought not to be too cruel, because no punishment ought to be greater than the misdeed or fall upon the innocent. In the case of homicide, punishment of the body; a crime against money, it is fitting that it be repaid.

Chapter 97: The things that the ruler ought to consider during his rule

Remember then, you who govern the city, the oath that you swore when you took the office of ruler. Remember the law and His commandments and do not forget God and His saints but go often to church and pray to God for yourself and your subjects. For David the prophet said, 'If God did not guard the city, those who guard it work for naught.' Honour the shepherds of the

Holy Church, for God said from his own mouth, 'Who receives you, receives me.' Be religious and show upright faith. For there is nothing more beautiful than a prince of the land who has an upright faith and true belief. And it is written: 'When the just king is seated on his throne, nothing evil can befall him.' Thus, take care of the churches, the houses of God, take care of widows and orphans, for it is written, 'be a defender of orphans and widows' (that is, you defend their rights against the misdeeds of the powerful, but not in such a way that the powerful lose their rights because of the tears of the weak), since the powerful, the humble, and those in between are all in your care. Thus from the beginning it is fitting that you take office with a clean heart and a pure intention, and that for God and the law your hands be clean from all profit outside of the salary from the community, and that you defend the things of the community and give to each his due, and that you provide within your power so that there is no hate nor discord between subjects, and that if there is, that you do not favour one or the other, neither for money, nor women, or anything else, and that you listen carefully to pleas and complaints, and that you see that all is written in the statute books of the city. See that you maintain the works and buildings of the community, that you make arrangements for highways, bridges, gates, walls, ditches and other things. Do not allow criminals to escape without punishment, and see that no one hides them in the countryside. You ought to punish murderers, traitors, and those who rape young women and who do other crimes severely, according to the law and custom of the country. Demand of your officials that they do no wrong or injury. Have such counsellors around you as are good, wise, and loyal to you and to reason. See that you seem terrible to the bad and kind to the good. In sum, look at the second part of this book, there where the subject is the vices and the virtues, and take care that you are clothed in the virtues and naked of the vices.

Chapter 98: The things of which the ruler ought to take care for his own good

Now, the master says that in this last part, he does not wish to name the assurances with which the ruler ought to be provided, for he has spoken of that at length in Book II, and so he has said enough. Nevertheless, he will say something of the vices from which the ruler ought fiercely to guard himself, both in him and in his advisors. For without doubt, he ought most to take care of those things of which he commands that others to take care, according to what the Apostle [Paul] says, 'I chastise myself, my body and subdue it, so that I not be condemned in chastising others.' Cato said that being master is an ugly thing when the guilt returns to him. But better to say what is praiseworthy if he does it, because to speak well and do badly is nothing else than to damn oneself by one's own words. He must keep himself from drunkenness, pride, wrath, cruelty, greed, envy, and lechery, because each of these sins is a mortal offence to God and to human beings, and makes the prince fall from his throne. But most of all, he ought to keep himself from speaking too much, for with few and good words one is believed to be wiser, and to speak much is not without sin. Also he ought to keep from too much laughter, for it is written that laughter is in the mouth of fools. Nevertheless, he can laugh and play and divert himself sometimes, but not in the manner of children nor of women; nor should he laugh falsely or arrogantly. And if he is good to others, he will be feared if he frowns, even when he is seated hearing cases. Also he ought not praise himself, in order that he be praised by the good, and he should not be concerned if he is not praised by the evil. He should be careful of jongleurs who praise him in his presence. He should believe more in himself than in others and also be as sad when he is praised by the evil as if he were praised for evil works. Also he must guard himself from spies and neither say nor do anything which if it became known, he will be blamed for. Also take care that justice not be sold for money, for the law says that he would deserve to be condemned as a thief. Also he should take care not to be intimate with his subjects so that he not fall into contempt and suspicion. He should also take care not to receive any present from anyone under his governance, because anyone who receives a gift or service because his judgement is for sale is as obligated as if it were a debt. He should also take care that he not confer with anyone from the city privately, nor ride with anyone, nor see anyone for dinner and for anything at his house, for this engenders suspicions about him among the citizens.

Chapter 99: The things the ruler ought to take care of for the good of the community

The ruler ought to be careful that he make no pact or association with the other cities and towns of the countryside in the name of the community in his care. If such an alliance is suitable, than it ought to be done by the council of the city and by the common assent of the people. In these things, he must think and rethink at length so that he avoids the necessity of later breaking his promise, or if he does not break it, it is dangerous to him. He should also be careful that during his term, no charter of sale, nor debt, nor alliance of the community be made that is not for the manifest benefit of the city and by the common establishment of the council.

Chapter 100: What the ruler ought to do in time of war

In this part, the master says that in ruling there are two seasons: peace and war. And because he has already said enough of both in Book II, the one on vices and virtues, in the chapter on magnificence, he will not now say anything. Indeed, if when he desires to govern the city, the ruler finds it at peace, he ought to be very happy and content, and take care that he not begin a war during his term if he can, for in war is destruction.

If it is necessary to begin one, it must be by the common consent of the citizens, the wise people of the city, and by decree of the council. If the war was started in the time of his predecessor, I believe that he should pursue peace, or at least a truce. If he does not, he ought often to seek the advice of the wise and examine the power of his side and that of the enemy, and ensure that the city is well guarded from within and without, and that its castles and estates are under his protection. And he must have around him a group of wise and worthy men from the city, who are in his counsels, who know how to fight battles and who are also leaders and captains of war. And he should search out all the friends, companions and subjects of the city, some by letter, others by word of mouth, and others by messengers so that they will be armed and prepared for battle.

After this he ought to assemble the people of the city at the central square of the city, or in another customary place, and speak to them words of war, reminding them of the wrongs of the enemy and the rights of the citizens, describing the powers and valour of their ancestors and their virtuous battles, inciting the people to war and encouraging them to battle, and commanding that each of them provide a large amount of equipment, horses, tents and all the other things that are needed in war. These and other words the ruler ought to say to encourage the spirits of the people as much as he can, but take care that he not sound feeble, and that his face is fierce and wrathful, and seem terrible, his voice menacing, his horse neighing and striking the earth with its hoofs many times throughout his speech. The tumult and the cries excite the citizens, as they do in battle. Nevertheless, he must consider what kind of war to fight, whether it is suitable to be fought between the upper-classes, or between equals, or between the humble [in each city].

After his discourse, his notary should read in a clear and understandable voice the ordinances and charters on war, and perhaps, if he can, he can arbitrate the misdeeds of the army, and when all is done, he ought to carry in his own hands the pennants and banners according to the custom of the city. Thus, before the war, the ruler himself and his subjects should prepare without ceasing in such a way that nothing is lacking the army or the battle at the right moment.

But how he should command the army, where to camp, how to care for the army's surroundings night and day, how he ought to situate the troops, how he must be here, there, and everywhere, and how to guard his own person, that he not fight if it is not out of necessity, how he must watch over his city if it is besieged, of many other things concerning war, the master says nothing more, but leaves it to the foresight of the ruler and his council.

Chapter 101: The general training of public officials

From the teaching of this book one can see how to rule a city correctly in time of peace and in war, with the help of God and with good counsel. And although this is enough instruction, there are so many kinds of rule that no living person could write nor tell by word of mouth about all of them. In sum, he ought follow the common law and custom of the city in good faith and conduct his office according to the usage of the country. For as the city dwellers say: 'when you are in Rome, live like the Romans, for it is their country.' For misdeeds he ought to follow the style of the doctor, who for little illnesses has small medicines, and for greater ones uses greater and stronger medicines, and for the most serious he uses fire and iron. In just this way, he ought to convict malefactors according to the kind of crime, without pardoning those who are guilty, but without punishing those who are not.

Chapter 102: How the new ruler ought to be chosen

And when the time comes to think of a new ruler for the following year, according to the law of the city, the ruler must assemble the city council and find those of integrity, and if needed, change the statutes of the city. And when he has found them, and they have sworn their oath, they ought to be secluded in one place, while they complete what is suitable to their office. And once the accounts are put in order, the book should be closed and sealed and guarded until the new ruler arrives. And when everything is properly completed and put in order, they ought to choose the new ruler according to the process that the master described at the beginning of this book. But if the citizens wish you to be ruler for the year to come, I counsel you not to do it, for trouble can come at the end of the second term.

Chapter 103: How the ruler ought to provide for the end of his rule

After this, you ought to assemble the judges and the notaries and your other officials, demanding and advising them that all cases and pleas before them be decided according to right judgement, and that they leave nothing to be amended by another. In the same way, you should consult with them and examine in your heart whether you have burdened anyone more or less than justice demands. And if you have left something to do on the city's books, now reflect in what manner you can change it or fulfil it in whatever way you can, whether by yourself or by establishment of the council, because wise rulers prepare themselves from the beginning (whether from those who change the constitution or from the counsellors themselves) and thus discharge themselves of everything.

In addition, if necessary during your term, you should find ambassadors from the community to accompany you to your residence and to bring greetings, thanks, and good testimony about you and your deeds to the population of your [own] city. Also with the advice of the city, provide a house for yourself where you will be living at the end of the term while you render your accounts. Do not forget, eight or ten days before the end, to have proclaimed that anyone owed anything by you or your staff should come to be paid so that everyone receives what is due. Also take care that you retain the copy of all the charters and statutes of the council concerning you and your oath, in such a way that you can help yourself if anyone challenges you.

Chapter 104: How you ought to speak to and assemble the people on the last day of office

And when the last day of your office comes, you ought to assemble the people of the city, and in powerful and agreeable words, in order to acquire the love and good wishes of the citizens, recount the good works, the honours, and benefits to the city that came during your tenure. Thank them for the love and the honour which they have given you and yours, and offer yourself and all your strength in their service for your life. And so as better to attract the spirits of the people you can say that if anyone has harmed them against this oath, that you pardon him (if he is not a murderer or thief or other malefactor or convicted by the city). Nevertheless, retain all your authority until midnight when you commit it to the new official. After this speech, that same day or the next, according to the usage of the country, you ought to render to the new ruler all the books and other things which you have from the community, and then go to the residence where you will live while you render your accounts.

Chapter 105: How you ought to reside in the city to render your accounts

When you have come to this situation, it is appropriate to be finished and to render the accounts of your office for yourself and your household. If there is someone who complains of you, you must open the book at his request, and take counsel with your advisors, and respond as they advise you. In this fashion, you ought to stay in the city until the day established when you took over office. Then if God pleases, you will be absolved honourably and will take leave of the council and the population of the city, and you will be covered in glory and honour. Amen.

7

ON KINGSHIP, SUMMARY OF THEOLOGY AND COMMENTARY ON ARISTOTLE'S POLITICS

Thomas Aquinas

INTRODUCTION

Without question, Thomas Aquinas (*c.* 1225–74) was the towering figure of thirteenth-century philosophy. A man of prodigious learning, he turned his pen with equal vigour to virtually every branch of knowledge under discussion in his time, including political theory. Born into a minor aristocratic family in the south-central Italian town of Aquino, he received an excellent education from an early age, first at the Abbey of Monte Cassino, later at the University of Naples. Over the strenuous objections of his family, Thomas entered the Dominican Order and continued his education at two of the centres of learning in Northern Europe, Paris and Cologne. His teachers, most notably the Dominican Albert the Great, furthered his introduction to the vast body of Aristotelian writings which had gradually re-entered the West during the course of the previous century. Aquinas was to emerge thereafter as the leading exponent of the idea that the teachings of the pagan Aristotle were consistent with the tenets of the Christian faith. Hence, he upheld the capacity of reason unilluminated by divine revelation to grasp truths about nature (and even some about God); yet he remained committed to the view that certain truths (indeed, the higher insights into the mysteries of divinity) were accessible only by way of direct experience of God as found in Scripture. This position placed him in conflict both with more traditional Christian thinkers (such as St Bonaventure, of whom he was an exact contemporary) and with those advocates of a more radical and thorough-going Aristotelianism who abounded at the University of Paris.

Thomas' academic career proceeded more or less according to the standard path set out for scholars trained within the newly emerged universities of thirteenth-century Europe. Between 1252 and 1256, he wrote commentaries and lectured on the Scriptures and on the standard theological textbook of the Middle Ages, Peter Lombard's *Sentences*. Thereafter, he earned the right to teach as a Master of the University of Paris, but only remained in

France until 1259. During the following decade, he taught at several Italian universities and also apparently busied himself with political activities related to his family's affairs. He returned to Paris in 1269 for a further three-year period of teaching, only to be called back to Italy on ecclesiastical business. Throughout his French and Italian sojourns, he continued to write voluminously on a vast range of topics. Controversies surrounding his ideas did not abate with his death. In 1277, the bishop of Paris condemned 219 'Aristotelian' propositions supposedly derived from Thomist writings. Thomas' canonization in 1323 brought his thought more into the mainstream of Roman Christianity, but it was not until the Counter-Reformation of the sixteenth century that he achieved his semi-official status as the pre-eminent philosopher and theologian of the Catholic Church.

Aquinas made use of several of the major medieval genres of political writing, namely, the advice-book (or 'mirror of princes'), the commentary, and the theological treatise. His *On Kingship* (sometimes also known as *On the Governance of Rulers*), supposedly written at the behest of the King of Cyprus, seems to have been the earliest of his political works. Thomas started to compose it about 1266, but abandoned the project early in Book 2; it was completed posthumously by his student, Ptolemy of Lucca. (Some scholars have lately questioned whether any part of it derives from Aquinas' hand, but the weight of evidence and tradition supports the current attribution.) *On Kingship* is in many ways a conventional 'mirror' work: drawing heavily on Aristotelian categories, it asserts the naturalness of the political community, while arguing for the superiority of monarchy over other forms of govern-ment, explaining how and why kings differ from tyrants, and setting out the duties incumbent on good rulers.

Also left unfinished was Thomas' *Commentary on the Politics of Aristotle*, which he undertook sometime during his last stay in Paris. The composition of line-by-line exegesis of scriptural and classical texts was a common literary format, derived from the method of lecturing favoured by medieval school-men. Between 1269 and 1272, Aquinas wrote a set of commentaries on most of Aristotle's major works. He only managed to complete his analysis of the *Politics* up to the middle of Book 3, however; the rest of the commentary was executed by another pupil, Peter of Auvergne. Although his commentary on the *Politics* adheres closely to Aristotle's text, and contains mainly simple clarifications and amplifications, it reveals a great deal about how classical political doctrines were disseminated by medieval teachers and assimilated by their students.

By far the most extensive and fruitful source for Thomas' political thought is his massive *Summary of Theology*. Written between 1266 and 1273, the *Summary* represents perhaps the single greatest monument of medieval scholasticism. Arranged in three parts (with the second part itself subdivided into two sections), the *Summary* purports to be an introductory exposition of the major problems facing the student of Christian theology. The parts are divided into 'questions', each of which ordinarily contains several articles. The articles commence with a number of statements contrary to the doctrine Thomas wishes to uphold, followed by an extended articulation of his own position (the 'body' of the article), and concluding with a refutation of the earlier objections to it. In constructing the *Summary* in this fashion, Thomas adapts some of the standard techniques of scholastic disputation to the formalized presentation of systematic thought. There is no single section of the *Summary* which encapsulates the whole of his political ideas. Rather, he touches on various questions pertaining to politics in the midst of relevant theological discussions. Thus, Aquinas' presentation of the modes of law occurs in the context of his account of God's relation to the realm of creation, while his treatment of property arises from his review of the forms of human sinfulness. Therefore, we should look upon the *Summary* not as a cohesive statement of Thomas' political teachings but as an indication of how political theory for him could never properly be detached from its broader theological framework.

ON KINGSHIP

BOOK I

Chapter 1: That it is necessary for humans living together to be ruled diligently by someone

At the start of our undertaking here, it is necessary to set forth what is meant by the title of 'king'. In all things which are ordered towards some end, in which matters may proceed one way or another, some directive principle is necessary through which the due end is reached by the most direct route. A ship, for example, which is moved in different directions according to the impulse of opposite winds, would never reach the aim of its destination if it were not brought to port through the skill of its navigator. And now human beings have an end to which their entire life and actions are ordered, since they are acting with reference to intelligence, of which it is clearly a part to work towards an end. Humans, however, adopt different methods to proceed towards their intended end, just as the diversity of human interests and actions itself demonstrates. Therefore, humans need some directive principle to guide them towards their end. Moreover, all human beings are naturally endowed with the light of reason, by which they are directed in their actions towards an end. And indeed, if human beings were suited to living alone, as many animals do, they would require no other guide to their end, but each individual would be a king unto himself, although under God, the highest king, inasmuch as he would direct himself in his actions by the light of reason given to him by God. However, it is natural for a human to be a social and political animal, to live in a multitude, even more than all other animals, as the necessity of his nature demonstrates. For other animals, nature has prepared food, a covering of hair, teeth, horns, and claws as a means of defence, or failing that, speed in flight. Humanity, on the other hand, was created without any such natural provisions, but instead of these it was endowed with reason, through which one could prepare these things for oneself by the service of one's hands. But one person alone is not able to prepare them all for oneself. It is, therefore, natural for human beings that they should live in the company of many others. Furthermore, other animals have an inborn, natural instinct towards everything which is useful or harmful, just as the sheep naturally regards the wolf as his enemy. Some animals even recognize, out of natural instinct, certain medicinal herbs and other things necessary for their life. But human beings have a natural knowledge of things which are necessary only in general terms for this life, inasmuch as they have the power to attain the knowledge of particular matters necessary for human life by reasoning from universal principles. But it is not possible that one human being could attain knowledge of all these things by individual reason. It is, therefore, necessary for human beings, because they should live in a multitude, that each one is to be assisted by the others, and different people may be occupied in seeking different discoveries by their reason, one, for example, in medicine, one in this and another in that. This is, further, most clearly evidenced by the fact that the use of speech is more closely related to humanity, through which one person is able to express conceptions to others. Other animals, it is true, express their feelings to one another in a general way, as when a dog expresses anger by barking, and other animals demonstrate their feelings in like fashion. So human beings communicate with their own kind at a higher level than any other animal which is known to be gregarious, such as the crane, the ant, and the bee. Therefore, Solomon says in Ecclesiastes 4:9: 'It is better to be two than one. For they have the advantages of mutual company.' If, therefore, it is natural for human beings to live in the society of many, it is necessary that there exist among them some means by which the common people may be governed. For where there are many people together, and each one is looking out for his own interests, the multitude would be scattered and broken apart unless there was also someone from its number to take care of what extends to the good of the multitude; in like manner, the body of a human being or any other animal would disintegrate unless there were some general regulating force within the body which would extend to the common good of all the members. With this in mind, Solomon says (Proverbs 11:14): 'When there is no governor, the people shall be scattered.' Indeed, it is reasonable that this happen: for what is one's own and what is common are not identical. Things differ according to their individuality, but are united according to what they have in common. For different things have different causes. Accordingly, it is proper for something to exist which promotes the common good of the many, as well as that which promotes the private good of each individual.

For this reason, also, in all things that are governed according to a single end, something is found which rules the rest. In the corporeal universe, for example, other bodies are regulated according to a certain order of divine providence by the first body, namely, a celestial body, and all bodies are controlled by a rational creature. Likewise, in the individual human being, the soul rules over the body, and among the parts of the soul, the passions and desires are ruled by reason. And thus also, among the members of the body, one is principal and moves all the others, such as the heart or head. Therefore, in every multitude it is proper to have some governing power.

However, it happens that certain matters in which we are ordered towards an end may proceed in a correct way and also in an incorrect way. And so, too, in the government of a multitude, both a right way and a wrong way may be discovered. Now, anything is properly directed when it is guided towards an appropriate end, but wrongly directed when it is guided towards an inappropriate end. Moreover, the appropriate end of a multitude of free persons is different from that of a multitude of slaves. For the free person is one who is his own cause; but the slave owes himself to another. If, therefore, a multitude of free persons is governed by their ruler for the common good, the government will be right and just, such as is proper for the free person. If, however, the government is arranged not for the common good of the multitude but for the private advantage of the ruler, then it will be an unjust and even perverse government, for which reason such rulers are threatened by the Lord, who speaking through Ezekiel (34:2) says: 'Woe to the shepherds who were feeding themselves' (as though seeking their own interests); 'should not the flocks be fed by the shepherds?' Indeed, shepherds ought to seek the good of their flocks and any ruler ought to seek the good of the multitude subject to him. If, therefore, an unjust government is exercised by only one person who seeks his own advantage from his rule, and not the good of the multitude subject to him, such a ruler is called a tyrant, a name derived from 'strength', because he clearly oppresses through power, and does not rule by justice; and thus among the ancients, all powerful men were called tyrants. If, however, the unjust government should arise not from one but through many, especially by a select few, it is called an oligarchy, that is, the rule of a few. This happens when a few – differing from the tyrant only because they are more than one – oppress the people by means of their wealth. Moreover, if bad government is conducted by the multitude itself, it is called a democracy, that is, control by the people. This occurs when the plebian populace by force of numbers oppresses the wealthy. In this way, the whole people becomes virtually a single tyrant. And similarly, we must discern between just governments. For if it is administered by some multitude, the name of the community is called a polity, as, for instance, when a group of warriors exercises lordship over a city or province. If, however, it is administered by a few people (although virtuous), this kind of government is called an aristocracy, that is, the political power of the best or rule by the best individuals, who for this reason are called the nobility. But if a just government is extended to one person alone, he is properly called king; for this reason, the Lord says through Ezekiel (37:24): 'My servant, David, will be king over all, and all of them will have one shepherd.' From this it is clearly shown that, concerning the idea of the king, he will be one who excels and he will be a shepherd, seeking the common good of the multitude and not his own advantage. Still, since human beings must live in a multitude because, if they remain solitary, they would not in themselves be sufficient with regard to the necessities of life, it follows that the society of a multitude will be more perfect to the extent that it is more sufficient in itself with regard to the necessities of life. Of course, some sufficiency of life exists in one family of one household, namely, insofar as this relates to the natural acts of nutrition and begetting offspring and other matters of that kind; and in a single village, it pertains to those things with regard to one trade; however, it exists in a city, which is a perfect community, with regard to all the necessities of life, but still more in one province, because of the need to fight together and to help one another mutually against enemies. Thus, he who rules the perfect community, that is, a city or province, is called a king; but he who rules a home is called head of household, not king. Nevertheless, he has a certain resemblance to a king, on account of which kings are sometimes called the fathers of the people.

It is plain from what is said, therefore, that a king is one who rules the multitude of a city or province, and rules on account of the common good. For this reason, Solomon says in Ecclesiastes 5:8: 'The king rules over all the land subject to him.'

Chapter 2: That it is more useful that a multitude of human beings living together be ruled by one person rather than by many

And having set forth these issues, it is proper to enquire what is more advantageous for a province or city: whether to be ruled by one person or by many. Now, this can be considered on the basis of the very purpose of government. For the aim of any ruler should be directed so that he secures the welfare of those whose government he undertakes. The task of a pilot, for instance, is to protect his ship against the dangers of the sea, and to bring it to port safely. Now, the welfare and safety of a multitude formed into a society are that its unity, which is called peace, may be preserved, since if unity is removed, the advantage of social life is lost and moreover the multitude, disputing within itself, becomes a burden to itself. Therefore, the ruler of a multitude ought to uphold the most important concern, so that he should attend to the unity of peace. It is not legitimate that a ruler should deliberate whether or not to administer peace to a multitude subject to him, just as a physician does not deliberate whether he should cure the sick person entrusted to him. For no one should deliberate about an end which one ought to uphold, but only about the means to attaining those ends. Therefore, the Apostle [Paul], having commended the unity of the faithful people, says (Ephesians 4:3): 'Be careful to protect the unity of the spirit in the bond of peace.' Accordingly, the more effective the government is with regard to protecting the unity of peace, the more useful it will be. For that which leads better to the end we call 'useful'. And now it is clear that what is itself singular is more able to bring about unity than several things, just as the most effective cause of heat is that which is hot in itself. Therefore, the rule of one person is more useful than the rule of many.

Furthermore, it is evident that several people would by no means keep a group safe if they totally disagreed. For a certain union is required among them if they are able to rule in some fashion: for instance, many men could not pull a ship in one direction unless joined together in some manner. Now, many are said to be united by approximating oneness. One person, therefore, rules better than many who approximate one.

Once again, that which is in accord with nature is best: for all things function by nature in the best way; thus, every government by nature is by one man. Indeed, in the multitude of bodily members, there is one which moves them all, namely, the heart; and among the parts of the soul, one power commands them in chief, namely, reason. Even among bees there is one king, and in the whole universe there is one God, Creator and Ruler of all. And this is reasonable. For every multitude is derived from unity. For this reason, natural things are imitated by a work of art, and since a work of art is better insofar as it attains a closer likeness to what is in nature, it necessarily follows that in a human multitude it is best to be ruled by one person.

This is also evident from experience. For provinces or cities which are not ruled by one person are troubled with differences of opinion and waver without peace, so that the lament of the Lord, speaking through the Prophet (Jeremiah 12:10), is fulfilled: 'Many shepherds have destroyed my vineyard.' But, by contrast, provinces and cities which are ruled under one king enjoy peace, flourish in justice, and rejoice in abundance. Hence, the Lord, by his prophets, promises to his people that as a great reward he will place them under one head and that one ruler will be in the midst of them.

Chapter 3: That just as the lordship of one person is best, so its opposite is worst, and this is proved by many reasons and arguments

Just as the government of a king is best, so the government of a tyrant is worst. Now, a democracy is the opposite of a polity, for either is a government conducted by many persons, as is evident from what has been said; moreover, oligarchy is the opposite of aristocracy, because either is conducted by a few people, and kingship is the opposite of tyranny, since either is conducted by one man. And it has already been shown that monarchy is the best government. If, therefore, the worst is opposed to the best, then it follows that tyranny is the worst kind of government. Furthermore, a unified force is more effective in producing its effect than a force scattered about or divided. For many people acting together can pull a load which could not be pulled by each one taking his part separately. Therefore, just as it is more useful for a force operating for the good to be more united, in order that it may perform the good more effectively, so it is more beneficial for a force operating for evil to be one than to be divided. Now, the strength of the unjust ruler functions to the detriment of the people, since he transforms the common good of the multitude into his own personal advantage. Therefore, for the same reason as in a just government, the government is more useful when the ruling power is one – so that monarchy is better than aristocracy, and aristocracy is better than polity – so the converse will be true in an unjust government, namely, the ruling power will be more harmful in proportion as it is more united. Accordingly, tyranny is more harmful than oligarchy, and oligarchy more harmful than democracy.

Moreover, a government becomes unjust by the fact that, rejecting the common good of the multitude, it seeks the personal advantage of the ruler. For this reason, the more the ruler departs from the common good, the more unjust the government will be; yet there is a greater departure from the common good in an oligarchy, in which the advantage of a few is sought, than in a democracy, in which the advantage of many is sought; and there is a still greater departure from the common good in a tyranny, in which the advantage of only one person is sought: for a great number is closer to the entire totality than a small number, and a small number closer than only one. Therefore, the government of a tyrant is most unjust. And a similar point is made clear to those who consider the order of divine providence, which arranges everything for the best. For in all things, good comes from one perfect cause, as if all the conditions are able to help the production of the good, while evil separately results from singular defects. For there is no beauty in a body unless all of its members have been properly disposed; but ugliness results when any member conducts itself improperly. And thus, ugliness appears in different ways from many causes, but beauty from one perfect cause in one way: and it is so with all good and evil, inasmuch as God, providing that good which arises from one cause, is stronger, while evil, arising from many causes, is weaker. It is expedient, therefore, that a just government be ruled by one man alone, so that it may be stronger. But if the government deviates into an unjust one, it is more expedient that it be a government of many, so that it may be weaker, and its parts may mutually hinder each other. Therefore, among unjust governments, democracy is more tolerable, but the worst is tyranny.

The same conclusion is most apparent if one considers the evils which come from tyrants, because, since a tyrant, despising the common good, seeks his private advantage, it follows that he would oppress his subjects in different ways, according to what different passions sway him to acquire certain goods. For one who is held down by the passion of desire seizes the goods of his subjects, for which reason Solomon says (Proverbs 29:4): 'A just king builds up the land, a covetous man will destroy it.' If, indeed, he is swayed by the passion of anger, he sheds blood needlessly, as is said by Ezekiel 22:27: 'Her rulers in the midst of her are like wolves ravaging the prey in order to shed blood.' Therefore, this kind of government is to be avoided, just as the wise man advises, saying (Wisdom 9:18): 'Keep yourself far from the man who has the power to slay, because evidently he kills not for the sake of justice, but through his power, for the desire of his will.' Thus, there will be no safety, but everything is doubtful when there is a departure from justice, nor is anything able to be strengthened when it depends upon the will of another, much less his desire. Nor does he only oppress his subjects in corporeal matters, but he also hinders their spiritual good, since those who try to be in charge rather than to be beneficial prevent all progress of their subjects, suspecting all excellence on the part of their subjects to be pre-judicial to their harmful lordship. Good people have been suspected more by tyrants than evil ones, and virtue in others is always more terrifying to them. Therefore, these tyrants attempt to prevent those among their subjects who have become virtuous from evolving a spirit of magnanimity and refusing to tolerate their harmful lordship; they attempt to prevent the establishment of a pact of friendship among their subjects and their enjoyment of peace amongst themselves, in order that, as long as no one trusts another, nothing can be attempted against their lordship. Consequently, they sow discord among them, foster disagreement, and prevent whatever tends to ally people, such as weddings, banquets, and other such events through which familiarity and confidence among men are normally produced. They also attempt to prevent them from becoming rich or powerful because, sus-pecting their subjects in full awareness of their own malice, they fear that the power and wealth of their subjects will be harmful to them, just as their own power and wealth is used to work harm. For this reason, Job (15:21) says of the tyrant, 'The sound of terror is always in his ears, and when there is peace', that is, when no one is attempting to harm him, 'he is always suspicious of treason'. So it follows from this that, when such rulers, who ought to lead their subjects towards virtue, are wretchedly envious of the virtue of their subjects and hinder it as much as they can, few virtuous people can be found under tyrants. For, according to the opinion of the Philosopher [Aristotle], the brave are found among those whom all the bravest people honour, and as Tully [Cicero] says, 'The things which are despised by everybody always languish and flourish but little' [*Tusculan Disputations* 1.2.4]. For it is natural that human beings brought up in fear should fall into a servile spirit and become discouraged in regard to any strenuous and virile deeds: this is clear by experience in the provinces, which have for a long time been under tyrants. For this reason, the Apostle says (Colossians 3:21): 'Fathers, do not provoke your children to indignation, lest they be discouraged.' Likewise, considering the evil effects of tyranny, King Solomon (Proverbs 28:12) says: 'When the wicked reign, men are ruined', because, evidently, through the wickedness of tyrants, subjects fall away from the perfection of virtue; and again he says (Proverbs 29:2): 'When the wicked shall bear rule the people shall mourn, as though led into slavery'; and again (Proverbs 28:28): 'When the wicked rise up, men shall hide themselves', so that they may escape the cruelty of tyrants. This is no wonder, because a person governing without reason according to the desires of his soul differs in no way from a beast, for which reason Solomon says (Proverbs 28:15): 'As a roaring lion and a hungry bear, is a wicked ruler over the poor people'; and, since people hide from tyrants as from cruel beasts, it seems that to be subject to a tyrant is the same as to be beneath a raging beast.

Chapter 4: How the government among the Romans has varied and that among them the republic was sometimes better advanced by the lordship of the many

Because both the best and the worst are found in monarchy, that is, the government of one person, the royal dignity is rendered hateful to many people on account of the malice of tyrants. In fact, while some who desire the rule of a king fall under the cruelty of tyrants, too many rulers exercise tyranny under the pretence of royal dignity. Now, a clear example of this is found in the Roman Republic. For when the kings had been driven out by the Roman people, because they were no longer able to bear the royal – or rather, tyrannical – arrogance, they established for themselves consuls and magistrates by whom they began to be ruled and guided, wishing to change the monarchy into an aristocracy and, as Sallust relates, 'It is incredible to recall to what extent the Roman state increased in a short time, once it had gained its freedom' [Sallust, *On the Catalinean Conspiracy*, Chapter 7]. For it often happens that people living under a king seek the common good more slowly, inasmuch as they hold that what they devote to the common good they do not contribute to themselves, but to others, under whose power they see the common good to be. But when they do not see a single person in charge of the community, they do not attend to the common good as if it belonged to another, but each attends to it as his own: for this reason, it is realized from experience that one city administered by annual rulers is sometimes able to do more than some kings, if they have three or four cities: and small services extracted by kings weigh more heavily than great burdens if they are imposed by the community of citizens – a fact which has been observed about the development of the Roman Republic. For the common people were enlisted in the army, and when the common treasury was not sufficient for paying wages, private wealth came to the aid for public uses to such an extent that, except for individual gold rings and individual gold studs, which were an insignia of dignity, even the Senate left itself with nothing made of gold. But when they were worn down by continual dissension, which grew all the way into civil wars, through which the freedom for which they had greatly striven was snatched out of their hands, they began to be under the power of emperors who were at first unwilling to be called kings because the royal name had been hateful to the Romans. Now, some of these emperors faithfully attended to the common good in a kingly manner, and by their enthusiasm the Roman Republic was increased and preserved. But most of them were in fact tyrants to their subjects, yet indolent and pacifistic towards their enemies, and brought the Roman Republic back to nothing. Likewise, a similar process occurred among the Hebrew people. For, at first, while they were ruled by judges, they were ravaged by their enemies on all sides, for each one was doing what was in his own eyes good. But on their own insistence they received the divine gift of kings, and on account of the wickedness of the kings they departed from the worship of one God and they were finally led into captivity. Therefore, danger threatens from either side: either when tyranny is feared, the best rule of a king is shunned, or when this rule is contemplated, royal power is changed into tyrannical power.

Chapter 8: Here the Learned Teacher declares what the true end of the king is, which ought to cause him to rule well

Therefore, because worldly honour and human glory are not a sufficient reward for royal responsibilities, it remains to inquire about what kind of reward is sufficient. Now, it is appropriate that a king should look to God for a reward. For a servant looks to his master for a reward for his services; a king, however, is a minister of God in governing his people, as the Apostle says (Romans 13:1, 4): 'All power is from the Lord God', and 'God's minister is an avenger to execute punishment upon whoever does evil'; and in the book of Wisdom kings are described as being ministers of God. Therefore, kings ought to look for a reward from God in return for their ruling. Now, God occasionally rewards kings for their service with temporal goods, but such rewards are common to both the good and the wicked; for this reason, the Lord says (Ezekiel 29:18): 'Nebuchadnezzar, the king of Babylon, has made his army undergo hard service against Tyre, and neither he nor his army have been rendered any reward in connection with Tyre for the service that he rendered to me against it', namely, for that service in which power, according to the Apostle, is the minister of God and the avenger to execute punishment upon whoever does evil; and afterwards, concerning the rewards, he added [Ezekiel 29:19]: 'Therefore, the Lord God says: I shall send Nebuchadnezzar, the king of Babylon, into the land of Egypt and he will ravage its spoils and it will be wages for his army.' If, therefore, wicked kings who fight against the enemies of God, although not with the intention of serving God, but to execute their own hatred and desires, are repaid by God with such great rewards, so that He gives them victory over their enemies, subjects kingdoms and offers them spoils to ravage, what will He do for good kings, who rule the people of God and attack His enemies with a pious motive? He promises them not an earthly reward, but an everlasting one in none other than Himself, as Peter says to the shepherds of the people of God (1 Peter 5): 'Feed the flocks of God which are among you, and when the prince of pastors appears', that is, the King of kings, Christ, 'you will receive a never fading crown of glory'; concerning this Isaiah says (28:5): 'The Lord will be a wreath of exultation and a crown of glory to his people.'

This is also clearly shown by reason. For it is placed in the minds of all who have the use of reason that the reward of virtue is happiness. In fact, the virtue of anything whatsoever is described as that which makes its possessor good and renders his work good. Towards this, then, everyone strives by working well to attain what is most deeply implanted in desire, namely, to be happy, which no one is not able to will. It is appropriate, therefore, to expect as a reward for virtue that which makes human beings happy. But if to work well is a deed of virtue, then the work of a king is to rule his subjects well, and that which makes him happy will also be the reward of the king. But what that is has to be considered. Indeed, we say that happiness is the ultimate end of our desires. Now, the movement of desire does not go all the way to infinity; for natural desire would be in vain, since infinity cannot be traversed. Since, then, the desire of an intellectual nature is for the universal good, the only good which will be able to make it truly happy is that which, once attained, leaves no further good to be desired: for this reason, happiness is called the perfect good; for those who have riches desire to have more and, likewise, it is clear for other things. And if they do not seek more, still they desire that those things which they already have should last or others should follow in their place. For nothing permanent is found in earthly things and, therefore, there is nothing earthly that can quiet desire. And so nothing earthly is able to make a person happy, so that it can be an appropriate reward for a king.

Again, the final perfection and perfect good of anything depends on something higher, and even bodily entities are made better by the addition of the better things, but worse by being mixed with baser things. For if gold is mixed with silver, the silver is made better, while by an admixture of lead it is made impure. Now, it is true that all earthly things are beneath the human mind; however, happiness is the final perfection and perfect good of human beings, which all humans desire to reach: therefore, there is no earthly thing which is able to make human beings happy; nor is any earthly thing a sufficient reward for a king; for, as Augustine says, we do not call certain Christian rulers happy merely because they have ruled for a long time, or because after a peaceful death they have left their sons to rule, or because they have conquered enemies of the republic, or because they were able to guard against and suppress citizens who stood up against them; but we call them happy if they rule justly, if they prefer to rule their passions rather than any nations, if they do all things not on account of the flame of empty glory but out of the love of eternal happiness. We say such Christian rulers are happy, now in hope, afterwards in the very fact, that what we await shall come in the future. But there is not any other created thing which would make a person happy and could be set up as the reward for a king. For the desire of each thing tends to its origin, which is the cause of its being. But the cause of the human soul is no other than God, who made it in his own image. Therefore, it is God alone who can pacify human desires and make them happy and be the fitting reward for a king.

Furthermore, the human mind knows universal good through understanding and desires it through will: but universal goods are not found except in God. Therefore, there is nothing which is able to make a person happy, satisfying his every desire, except God, of whom it is said in Psalm 103:5: 'It is Him who satisfies your desire with good things'; in this, therefore, the king ought to determine his reward. Accordingly, King David, considering this, said (Psalm 72:25): 'What have I in heaven? And besides you what do I desire on earth?' And afterwards, replying to this question he adds: 'It is good for me to adhere to my God and to put my hope in the Lord God.' For it is he who gives salvation to kings, not only temporal salvation by which he saves beasts and humans alike, but also that salvation of which he says through Isaiah 51:6: 'But my salvation shall be forever'; by which he saves human beings, bringing them to the level of angels. Therefore, it can thus be verified that the rewards of a king are honour and glory. For what worldly and frail honour can be likened to this honour, so that a person can be made a citizen and member of the household of God, numbered among the children of God, and can obtain the inheritance of the heavenly kingdom along with Christ? This is the honour of which King David said in desire and wonder (Psalms 139:17): 'Your friends, God, are exceedingly honoured.' In addition, what glory of human praise can be compared to this, which is not spoken from the deceptive tongue of flatterers nor the fallacious opinion of human beings, but is brought forth from the witness of our innermost conscience and is confirmed by the testimony of God, who promises to those who profess Him that He will profess them in the glory of the Father before the Angels of God? Yet those who seek this glory both will find it and will have arrived at the human glory which they did not seek, as in the instance of Solomon, who not only received the wisdom which he sought from God, but who was made glorious above other kings.

Chapter 10: That the king and ruler ought to be eager for good rule on account of his own good, and the utility which follows from it, the opposite of which follows from tyrannical rule

Since so great a reward in heavenly blessedness is offered to kings if they have acted well in ruling, they ought to keep careful charge over themselves not to turn to tyranny. For nothing should be more unacceptable to them than to be transferred from the royal honour, from which they are raised up on earth into the glory of the heavenly kingdom. But tyrants err when they desert justice for a few earthly advantages; for they are deprived of the great reward which they are able to obtain by ruling justly. That it is foolish, however, to squander eternal goods for trifling and temporal goods is clear to everyone except a fool or an unbeliever. It is to be added further that these temporal advantages, for which tyrants abandon justice, are provided for the greater profit of kings when they serve justice. Thus, first among all worldly things, there is nothing that would seem to be preferable to friendship. For it is precisely this which unites good men and preserves and promotes virtue. It is that which all people, regardless of the occupation in which they are engaged, need; it is that which does not advance itself inappropriately in prosperity and does not desert in adversity. It is what brings with it the greatest delights, to such an extent that all delights are changed to boredom without friends. For love makes all difficult things easy and nearly insignificant; there is no tyrant so cruel that friendship does not bring pleasure. When Dionysius, a certain tyrant of Sicily, wanted to slay one of two friends, Damon and Pythias, the one who was to be killed asked leave to go home, so that he could set his affairs in order; the other friend, indeed, surrendered himself to the tyrant as a guarantee for his return. When the appointed day was approaching, and he had not yet returned, everyone accused him of being a fool. But he proclaimed that he had no fear concerning his friend's loyalty. Now, at the very hour that he was to be put to death, his friend returned. But the tyrant, admiring the courage of both, remitted the execution on account of the loyalty of their friendship, asking in addition that they should receive him as a third member in their bond of friendship. But although tyrants desire this bond of friendship, they are nevertheless not able to obtain it. For when they do not seek the common good, but their own, there becomes little or nothing in common between them and their subjects. Yet all friendship is established through some common bond. For we notice that those who, through a common natural origin, or through a similarity of character, or who share any common alliance, unite in friendship. Therefore, there can be little, or rather no, friendship between tyrants and their subjects; and likewise, when subjects are oppressed by tyrannical injustice, and they do not feel loved but despised, they by no means love their rulers. Nor have tyrants any reason to complain of their subjects if they are not loved by them, because they do not act in such a fashion that they deserve to be loved by them. But good kings, when they show that they love their subjects, are loved by many, being enthusiastically intent on the public good, and their subjects realize that they gain many benefits from their devoted care: for the majority of people could not be so malicious as to have hatred for their friends and return evil for good to their benefactors. And out of this love it results that the government of good kings is stable, because their subjects do not refuse to expose themselves to any dangers whatsoever on their behalf; an example of this is evident in the case of Julius Caesar, of whom Suetonius relates that he loved his soldiers to such an extent that when he heard that some of them had been murdered, he cut neither his hair nor his beard until he avenged them: by those means, he made his soldiers most loyal to him and most vigorous, so that when many of them were captured, they refused life offered to them on the condition that they would serve as soldiers and fight against Caesar. Octavius Augustus also, who had used his imperial power very moderately, was loved by his subjects so much that, when he was dying, many people ordered the sacrifices which they had saved for themselves to be burnt instead for him, so that they gave up their preservation for him.

It is not easy, therefore, to shake the government of a ruler whom the people so harmoniously love: because of this, Solomon says (Proverbs 29:14): 'The king who judges the poor in truth shall have his throne established forever.' Yet the government of tyrants is not able to last for a long time because it is hateful to the multitude. For what is against the wishes of the many cannot long be preserved. It is indeed difficult for people to pass through the present life without undergoing some adversities. However, in the time of adversity, there can be no lack of occasion to rise against the tyrant; and when this occasion is present, there will not be lacking some sort of opportunity for one or many to use it. For the people will favour the insurgent; and what is attempted with the support of the multitude will not easily be deflected from its result. Therefore, it will scarcely ever come to pass that a government of a tyrant endures for a long time.

This becomes still more clear if we consider how tyrannical government is preserved. It is not upheld by love, since there is little or no friendship between the subject multitude and the tyrant, as is clear from what we have said. For such great virtue is seldom found among human beings that they will be restrained by the virtue of fidelity from throwing off the yoke of undue servitude, if they are able to do so. According to the opinion of many people, it would perhaps not be contrary to loyalty if any means whatsoever are adopted to frustrate tyrannical wickedness. It remains, then, that the government of tyrants is sustained by fear alone, and for this reason they strive with all their effort to be feared by their subjects. Fear, however, is a frail foundation. For those who are subjected to fear will rise against their rulers – if the opportunity occurs when they can hope to do it safely – all the more passionately the more that they have been held against their will by fear alone, just as water confined under pressure flows with greater impetus

111

when it finds an outlet. But that very fear itself is not without danger, because many people become desperate out of excessive fear. And despair of safety precipitates human boldness to consider any solution. The government of a tyrant, therefore, cannot be of long duration.

This appears also from examples no less than from reason. For if we consider the history of antiquity and events in modern times, it is difficult to find the government of a single tyrant which has lasted for a long time. For this reason, Aristotle in his *Politics*, having described many tyrants, shows that all their governments were of short duration, although some of them reigned for a fairly long time because they were not excessively tyrannical, but in many ways they imitated the moderation of a king.

In addition, this becomes more evident upon consideration of divine judgement. For it is said in Job 34:30: 'He makes a man who is a hypocrite reign for the sins of the people.' No one, indeed, can be more truly called a hypocrite than the person who assumes the office of a king and displays himself as a tyrant. For it is said that a hypocrite is one who depicts himself as another personage, as is done on the stage. So, therefore, God permits tyrants to achieve power for the sake of punishing the sins of subjects. In the Holy Scriptures, it is customary to call such punishment the anger of God. Thus, in Hosea 13:11, the Lord says: 'I will give you a king in my anger.' But unhappy is the king who is given to the people in the anger of God. For his lordship cannot be stable, because God will not forget to show mercy and he does not confine his mercies in his anger. On the contrary, it is said in Joel 2:13 that 'he is patient and rich in mercy and ready to forgive the malice'. Therefore, God does not permit tyrants to rule for a long time, but after the storm brought upon the people through his own actions, he restores tranquility through their eviction. As is said in Ecclesiasticus 10:17: 'God has overturned the throne of proud leaders, and he has set up the meek in their stead.'

It is even more clear from experience that kings obtain greater riches through justice than tyrants do through robbery. Because the government of tyrants is displeasing to the multitude subject to it, therefore tyrants have many bodyguards who are paid to protect them against their subjects, and on whom it is necessary to spend more than they can rob from their subjects. However, the government of kings, since it is pleasing to their subjects, has all the subjects for its protection instead of bodyguards, for which they demand no pay; but occasionally, in times of need, they voluntarily give more to their kings than tyrants can steal and thus what Solomon says is fulfilled (Proverbs 11:24): 'Some' – namely kings – 'distribute their own goods to their subjects and grow richer. Others' – namely, tyrants – 'take away what is not their own and are always in want.' But in the same way it happens by the just judgement of God that those who unjustly heap up riches uselessly scatter them or are justly deprived of them. For as Solomon says (Ecclesiasticus 5:9): 'A covetous man shall not be satisfied with money, and he who loves riches shall reap no fruit from them'; and again as Proverbs

15:27 says: 'He who is greedy for gain troubles his own house.' But to kings who seek justice, God gives wealth, as he did to Solomon, who, when he sought wisdom to make judgement, received a promise of an abundance of wealth. Indeed, it seems superfluous to speak about fame. For who can doubt that good kings live not only in this life, but in a way more after their death, in the praises of human beings, and they are regarded in love; but the name of wicked kings immediately vanishes, or if they have been excessive in their wickedness, they are remembered with execration. Thus, Solomon says (Proverbs 10:7): 'The memory of the just is with praises, and the name of the wicked shall rot', either because it falls or remains with a stench.

Chapter 12: He proceeds to show the duty of a king, wherein in accordance with the path of nature, he demonstrates the king to be in the kingdom just as the soul is in the body, and in the same manner as God is in the universe

The next point to be considered is what constitutes the nature of the royal office and what sort of person the king should be. Now, because that which accords with art imitates that which accords with nature, from which we conclude that we ought to work in accordance with reason, it seems that the best royal duty to accept is formed under the guidance of nature. However, in affairs of nature, there is found both a universal and a particular government. It is universal because everything is contained under the rulership of God, who governs the universe under his providence. But the particular rulership, which is found in humans, is in fact most like the divine rulership; on account of this, the human being is called a smaller world, since in him there is found the form of universal rulership. For just as the universe of corporeal creatures and all spiritual powers are contained under the divine government, so in this way are the members of the body and other powers of the soul ruled by reason; thus, in a certain manner, reason is in human beings in just the same way as God is in the world. But because human beings are by nature social animals living in a multitude, as we have shown above, a likeness to the divine rulership is found among human beings not only insofar as one person is ruled by reason, but also inasmuch as a multitude is governed through the reason of a single person: this is what most pertains to the duty of the king, although among certain animals which live socially, a similarity to their rulership is found, just as among ants, among which it is said that there are queens – not that among them rulership is controlled by reason but through the natural instinct given to them by the great ruler, who is the originator of nature. Therefore, the king ought to recognize that such is the duty he undertakes that he exists in his kingdom in just the same way as the soul exists in the body and God exists in the world. If he carefully reflects upon this, from one side, a zeal for justice will be kindled in him, when he considers that he has been appointed to this position in place of God to exercise judgement in his kingdom; and from another, he will acquire the gentleness of mildness and clemency, when he considers those individuals who are subject to his government to be just like his own members.

Chapter 15: That just as a king disposes his own subjects to live virtuously in order to attain their ultimate end, so he must do the same to attain the intermediate end. And here is set out that which disposes one towards a good life, and that which hinders one, and also the remedy that the king ought to apply in connection with the said hindrances

However, just as the life by which human beings live well is ordained as a means to the end of that blessed life which they hope for in heaven, so, too, whatever particular goods are administered by human beings, whether wealth, profit, health, eloquence, or education, are ordained as a means to the end of the common good. If, therefore, as it has been said, the person who has care of the ultimate end ought to be over those who have care of the things ordained towards that end, and to direct them by his rule, it clearly follows from what is said that the king, just as he should be subject to the lordship and government which is administered by the office of the priest-hood, ought to preside over all human offices and to regulate them by the command of his government. However, anyone who is inclined towards something that is ordained to another thing as to its end ought to pay attention that his work is agreeable to that end. For example, the artisan fashions the sword so that it is suitable for fighting, and the architect so designs the house that it is suitable for habitation. Therefore, since the happiness of heaven is the end of that good life which we live at present, it pertains to the duty of the king to promote the good life of the multitude in line with reason, according to which it is suitable for the attainment of heavenly happiness, it is correct to say that he should command those things which lead to the happiness of heaven and, as far as possible, forbid the contrary. Yet one learns the road to true happiness, and what hinders it, from the divine law, the teaching of which pertains to the office of the priest, according to Malachi 2:7: 'The lips of the priest shall guard knowledge and they shall seek knowledge from his mouth.' And therefore in Deuteronomy 17:18–19, the Lord instructs:

> But after he is raised to the throne of his kingdom, the king shall copy out for himself the Deuteronomy of this law in a volume, following the copy of the priests of the tribe of Levi, and he shall have it with him and he shall read it all the days of his life, that he may learn to fear the Lord his God, and keep his words and ceremonies, which are commanded in the law.

114

Therefore, the king, having been instructed in the law of God, should aim as his principal concern at the means by which the multitude subject to him may live well. This concern is divided into three: first, to establish the good life in the multitude subject to him; second, to preserve it once it is established; and third, to extend its greater perfection.

For the good of an individual, two things are necessary: the first and foremost is to operate according to virtue (for virtue is that by which one lives well); the other, which is secondary and almost instrumental, is a sufficiency of those bodily goods the use of which is necessary for any act of virtue. Nevertheless, human unity is caused by nature, while the unity of a multitude, which is called peace, must be administered through the effort of a ruler. Therefore, to establish the good life of the community, three things are necessary. First of all, the multitude must be established in the unity of peace. Second, the multitude thus united in the bond of peace is to be directed towards good deeds. For just as a human being is able to do nothing well unless a unity within his members is presupposed, so a multitude of human beings who are without the unity of peace is hindered from virtuous action, since it fights within itself. In the third place, it is necessary that there be present an adequate supply of the things required for proper living, through the efforts of the king. If, therefore, the good life is established in the multitude by the service of the king, it remains for him to direct its preservation.

Now, there are three things which do not allow for the permanence of the public good, and one of these arises from nature. For the good of the multitude should not only be established for the moment, but should be in a sense perpetual. Human beings are not, however, able to endure forever, since they are mortal. Even while they are alive they do not always have the same vigour, for human life is subject to many changes, and so humans are not always suited to accomplish the same duties throughout their entire life. However, another impediment to the preservation of the public good comes from within, consisting in the perversity of the will, inasmuch as people either are too lazy to do what the republic requires or, moreover, are harmful to the peace of the multitude, since by passing over justice they disturb the peace of others. The third hindrance to the preservation of the republic is caused from outside, when peace is destroyed through the invasion of enemies, and occasionally the kingdom or city is entirely demolished. Therefore, in respect to these three dangers, a triple charge will loom over the king. First, he must take charge of the appointment of persons to succeed or replace those in charge of the various offices, just as is provided in the case of divine rule over corruptible things, since they are not able to last forever the same, so that they are succeeded by other generations in their place; just as the integrity of the universe is preserved in this way, so the good of the multitude subject to the king will be maintained by his devotion if he diligently attends to appoint successors in the place of those who are failing.

In the second place, by his laws and orders, punishments and rewards, he should limit the wickedness of the people subject to him and should lead them to virtuous works, learning from the example of God, who gave His law to humankind and who rewards those who observe it and punishes those who transgress it. The third care of the king is to keep the multitude subject to him safe from the enemy. For there is no point in avoiding internal dangers if the multitude cannot be defended against external dangers.

So, therefore, for the proper arrangement of the multitude there remains a third matter which pertains to the duty of the king, that he be concerned with its improvement, which is achieved when, in each of the things mentioned above, he corrects what is out of order and, if anything can be done better, he tries to execute it. And for this reason, the Apostle admonishes the faithful that they should always strive after better gifts of the Holy Spirit.

These, then, are what pertains to the duty of the king, about each of which there ought to be more diligent discussion.

SUMMARY OF THEOLOGY

THE FIRST PART OF THE SECOND PART

Question 90: On the essence of law

Article 2: Whether law is always ordained for the common good

1. It seems that law is not always ordained towards the common good as its end. For law pertains to prescription and prohibition. But these precepts are ordained for the sake of some individual good. Therefore, the end of the law is not always the common good.

2. Besides, the law directs human beings towards actions. But human actions relate to particular matters. Therefore, law is also ordained for the sake of some particular good.

3. Besides, Isidore says, 'If law is founded on reason, then every law will be in accord with what reason will establish' [*Etymologies* 2.10 and 5.3]. But reason establishes not only what is ordained for the sake of the common good, but also what is ordained for the sake of the singular private good. Therefore, law is not ordained solely for the sake of the common good, but also for the sake of singular private goods.

But on the contrary, it is the case that Isidore says that 'law is not drawn up for private benefit, but for the common utility of citizens' [*Etymologies* 5.21].

Response: It may be stated that, as was said, law pertains to that which is a principle of human acts, of which it is a rule and measure. For just as the principle of human action exists in reason, so also there is in reason itself something which is a principle in respect to everything else: hence, it is primarily and chiefly on account of this that law must be applied. The first principle of action, insofar as it stems from practical reason, is the ultimate end. The ultimate end of human action is the happy or blessed life, as is maintained above. For this reason, it is necessary that law chiefly attends to an order which aims for blessedness.

Once again, since all parts are ordained towards the whole just as the imperfect is ordered towards the perfect, and one human being is part of the perfect community, it is necessary that law itself attends to an order for the sake of the common happiness. For this reason, the Philosopher, setting forth the definition of 'lawful', makes mention of political happiness and sharing: for he says in *Nicomachean Ethics* 5[.1] that 'we call those acts legally just that produce and preserve happiness and its elements in the political collectivity'; for the perfect community is the city, as it said in *Politics* 1.

To speak of a 'chiefly' in any class of things connotes a principle of otherness, and other things are spoken of according to an order in relation to it, just as fire, which is chiefly hot, is the cause of heat in mixed bodies, which are called 'hot' insofar as they participate in fire. It is for this reason necessary, since law is spoken of chiefly according to an order related to the common good, that any other precept regarding particular activities will not have the cause of law unless it accords with an order related to the common good.

And therefore, every law is ordained for the sake of the common good.

1. As to the first statement, therefore, a precept involves an application to the matters which laws regulate. The order related to the common good, which pertains to law, is applicable to individual ends. And in accordance with this, precepts are given with regard to particular matters.

2. As to the second statement that activities relate to particular matters, these particulars can be referred to the common good – yet not 'common' according to genus or species, but the final cause of the community, on account of which the common good is called the common end.

3. As to the third statement, just as nothing is firmly established according to speculative reason except by its resolution into indemonstrable first principles, so nothing is firmly established by means of practical reason except by ordering towards the ultimate end, which is the common good. Whatever reason establishes in this manner has the character of law.

Article 3: Whether law may be made by anyone's reason

1. It seems that law may be made by anyone's reason. For the Apostle says that 'when the Gentiles, who do not have the law, do naturally that which is in the law, they are the law in and of themselves' [Romans 2:14]. He says this generally of everyone. Therefore, anyone can make law for oneself.

2. Moreover, as the Philosopher says, 'A legislator's aim is that human beings may be led towards virtue' [*Nicomachean Ethics* 2.1]. But any human being can lead others towards virtue. Therefore, any human reason whatsoever is a maker of law.

3. Further, just as the ruler of a city is the governor of a city, so any head of a household is the governor of the household. But the ruler of a city can

make law for the city. Therefore any head of household can make law for his household.

But on the contrary, it is the case that Isidore says in book 5[.10] of the *Etymologies* (and it is maintained in [Gratian's] *Decretum* [1.2.1]), 'Law is a constitution of the people, according to which persons of high birth enact something in just the same way as the masses.' Therefore, making law does not pertain to anyone at all.

Response: It may be said that law itself primarily and mainly attends to an order for the sake of the common good. Ordering something for the common good pertains either to the whole multitude or to some vice-regent of the whole multitude. And therefore, creating law either pertains to the whole multitude or it pertains to public persons who have care of the whole multitude, because here as elsewhere, ordering towards an end pertains to whomever that end is appropriate.

1. As to the first statement, as is said above, law exists not only in the person of the regulator, but also in partnership with the regulated. And in this manner, each person is himself a law insofar as he participates in the order by which everyone is ruled; for this reason the same Apostle speaks afterwards of 'those who reveal the works of law written on their hearts' [Romans 2:15].

2. As to the second statement, a private person cannot effectively lead towards virtue: for one can only instruct; but if one's admonition is not heeded, one does not have the power of coercion, which the law must have in order that it may effectively lead people towards virtue, as the Philosopher says. This coercive strength is possessed by the multitude, or the public person, to whom it pertains to inflict penalties, as will be said below, and therefore to whom it alone pertains to make laws.

3. As to the third statement, just as a human being is part of a household, so a household is part of the city; for the city is the perfect community, as is stated in *Politics* 1. And therefore, just as the good of a single human being is not the ultimate end, but is ordered in relation to the common good, so also the common good of one household is ordered towards the single common good of the city which is the perfect community. For this reason, that person who governs some family can to some extent make certain precepts or statutes, yet not those which properly possess the character of law.

Article 4: Whether promulgation pertains to the character of law

1. It would seem that promulgation does not pertain to the character of law. For natural law has the chief characteristics of law. But natural law does not require promulgation. Therefore, it does not pertain to the character of law that it is to be promulgated.

2. In addition, it properly pertains to law to obligate for the sake of doing or not doing something. But not only are those in whose presence the law is promulgated obligated to carry out that law, but also others. Therefore, promulgation does not pertain to the character of law.

3. Besides, the obligation of law also extends into the future, because 'laws impose a necessity on future business', as the Laws say [*Codex*, 1.14.7]. But promulgation is to those who are present. Therefore, promulgation is not of necessity for law.

But on the contrary, it is the case that it is said in the *Decretum* [1.4] that 'laws are instituted when they are promulgated'.

Response: It may be stated that, as was said, law is imposed upon others in the manner of rules and measures. A rule and measure is imposed in such a manner that it is applied to those who are ruled and measured. Hence, in order that law may obtain the force of an obligation, which is appropriate to law, it is necessary for it to be applied to human beings who ought to be regulated in accordance with it. Such application occurs inasmuch as it is drawn to their notice by means of promulgation itself. For this reason, promulgation itself is necessary in order that law may have its force.

And thus, on the basis of the four preceding articles, a definition of law can be assembled, according to which it is nothing other than a certain ordinance of reason for the sake of the common good promulgated by those who have care for the community.

1. As to the first statement, the promulgation of natural law occurs inasmuch as God places it in the human mind in the manner of a natural form of knowledge.

2. As to the second statement, those who are not present at the promulgation of law are still obligated to the observance of law, insofar as the act of promulgation is drawn, or can be drawn, to their notice by others.

3. As to the third statement, promulgation in the present extends to the future through the stability of writing, in which manner it is always promulgated. hence, Isidore says that 'law (*lex*) derives its name from reading (*legendo*), because it is written' [*Etymologies* 2.10].

Question 91: On the diversity of law

Article 1: Whether there is some eternal law

1. It seems that there is no eternal law. For all law is imposed on someone. But no one exists from eternity upon whom law could be imposed; for only God exists from eternity. Therefore, there is no eternal law.

2. Moreover, promulgation is a characteristic of law. But promulgation cannot be from eternity, because there would not have been anyone to whom it would have been promulgated. Therefore, law can never be eternal.

But on the contrary, it is the case that Augustine says, 'The law which is called the supreme reason cannot be understood as other than immutable and eternal' [*On the Freedom of the Will* 1.6].

3. Besides, law leads to an ordering for the sake of an end. But nothing that is ordered towards an end is eternal: for only the ultimate end is eternal. Therefore, no law is eternal.

Response: It may be stated that, just as was said above, law is nothing other than a dictate of the practical reason of a ruler who governs some perfect community. Supposing that the world is ruled by divine providence, as was maintained in Part One, it is apparent that the whole community of the universe is governed by divine reason. And thus that reason governing reality, existing in God in the manner of a ruler of the universe, has the character of law. And because divine reason conceives of nothing in time, but has eternal concepts, as is said by Proverbs [8:23], therefore it is the case that one ought to call such laws eternal.

1. As to the first statement, those things which do not exist in themselves still exist in the presence of God, insofar as they are known and preordained by him 'who summons that which does not exist just the same as that which does exist', according to Romans [4:17]. Therefore, the eternal concept of divine law has the character of eternal law, on account of which it is ordained by God for the sake of the governance of reality by means of his fore-knowledge.

2. As to the second statement, promulgation may be both verbal and written; and eternal law receives promulgation in both ways in connection with God's promulgating of it, because the divine Word is eternal and also because the written book of life is eternal. But in relation to the creatures hearing or reading it, promulgation cannot be eternal.

3. As to the third statement, law leads to an ordering for the sake of an active end, namely, certain things are ordered towards an end through it; but law is not ordered towards an end in a passive sense, except by accident in the case of a governor whose end is outside of himself, towards which it is necessary that his law is ordained. But the end of divine governance is God himself, and his law is nothing else than himself: for this reason eternal law is not ordered in relation to another end.

Article 2: Whether there is some natural law within us

1. It seems that there is not some natural law within us. For humanity is sufficiently governed by means of the eternal law. For Augustine says that 'eternal law is what is just inasmuch as everything is best ordered thereby' [*On the Freedom of the Will* 1.6]. But nature does not abound in things which are superfluous just as it is not deficient in things which are necessary. Therefore, there is not some natural law in human beings.

2. Furthermore, humanity is ordered in its actions towards ends by means of law, as was maintained above. But the ordering of human actions towards an end is not through nature, as occurs in the case of irrational creatures, which act according to an end only on account of a natural appetite, but the human being acts according to an end through reason and will. Therefore, there is not some natural law for humanity.

3. In addition, to the extent that someone is freer, one is less under law. But humanity is freer than all other animals on account of freedom of the will,

which places it before other animals. Therefore, since other animals are not placed under natural law, neither is humanity placed under any natural law.

But on the contrary, it is the case that, in regard to the text cited above, 'When the Gentiles, who do not have the law, do naturally that which is in the law' [Romans 2:14], a gloss says that 'if they do not have written law, still they have natural law, which each understands and through which one is self-conscious about what is good and what is bad' [Peter Lombard, *Gloss on Romans*].

Response: It may be stated that, just as was said above, law, since it is a rule and measure, can exist in something in two ways: in one manner, as in the ruler and measurer; in the other manner, as in that which is ruled and measured, because insofar as something participates in rule or measurement, it may be ruled or measured. For this reason, since everything which is placed under divine providence may be ruled or measured by divine law, as is evident from what was stated, it is clear that everything participates equally in eternal law, namely, inasmuch as they have inclinations towards their own acts and ends from its impression.

Among the various created beings which fall under divine providence, rational creatures are the most pre-eminent, insofar as they are participants in providence itself by providing for themselves and others. For this reason, too, they participate in eternal reason itself through which they have natural inclinations towards due acts and ends. And such participation in eternal law by rational creatures is called 'natural law'.

For this reason, when the Psalmist has said, 'Offer the sacrifice of justice', as though speaking to those who ask what the works of justice are, he adds, 'Many say, Who show goodness towards us?' Responding to this question, he says, 'The light of your countenance, Lord, is signed upon us' [Psalms 4:6]; it is as though the light of natural reason, by which we discern what is good and what is bad, which pertains to natural law, is nothing other than the impression of the divine light upon us.

For this reason, it is clear that natural law is nothing other than the participation of eternal law in rational creatures.

1. As to the first statement, that reasoning would follow if natural law were quite distinct from divine law. Yet it is nothing except a participation in it, as was said in the body of the article.

2. As to the second statement, all activity of reason and will in us is derived from that which is according to nature, as was maintained above. For all reasoning is derived from naturally known principles, and all appetites for those things which exist for the sake of an end are derived from a natural appetite for the ultimate end; and thus it is also necessary that the primary direction of our actions towards ends occurs by means of natural law.

3. As to the third statement, even irrational creatures participate in the eternal reason in their own manner, just like rational creatures. But because rational creatures participate in it intellectually and rationally, therefore the

participation of rational creatures in eternal law is called 'law' properly speaking: for law pertains to reason, as was said above. In an irrational creature, there will be no rational participation: for this reason, one cannot call it law except figuratively.

Article 3: Whether there is any human law

1. It would seem that there is no human law. For natural law is a participation in eternal law, as was said. But through eternal law, 'everything is best ordered', as Augustine says [*On the Freedom of the Will* 1.6]. Therefore, natural law suffices for the sake of ordering all human affairs. It is not, therefore, necessary that there exists any human law.

2. Additionally, law embraces the measure of reason, as was said. But human reason is not a measure of reality, but rather the reverse is true, as is stated in [Aristotle's] *Metaphysics* [9.9]. Therefore, law can never proceed from human reason.

3. Once again, a measure ought to be extremely reliable, as is said in the *Metaphysics* [9.9]. But the dictates of human reason regarding matters of conduct are unreliable, since according to Wisdom [9:14], 'The thoughts of mortal creatures are fearful, and our prudence is unreliable.' Therefore, law can never proceed from human reason.

But on the contrary, it is the case that Augustine [*On the Freedom of the Will* 1.15] posits two laws, one eternal, and the other temporal, which he says is human.

Response: It may be stated that, just as was said above, law is a sort of dictate of practical reason. It is known that the procedures of practical and speculative reason are similar: for both proceed from certain principles to a certain conclusion, as was maintained before. According to this, therefore, it may be stated that just as in speculative reason, the conclusions of the different branches of knowledge are produced out of naturally known indemonstrable principles, yet these conclusions themselves are not known by us through natural endowment but through the industry of rational invention, so also it is necessary that human reason proceeds from the precepts of natural law, as though from certain common and indemonstrable principles, to certain more specific matters to be disposed.

And these particular dispositions arrived at according to human reason are called 'human laws', insofar as they comply with the other conditions which pertain to the character of law, as was stated above. For this reason, Tully says in his *Rhetoric* [*On Invention* 2.53] that 'the beginning of justice is advanced by nature; thereafter certain things pass into custom by reason of utility; later the things advanced by nature and approved by custom are sanctioned by fear of and reverence for law'.

1. As to the first statement, human reason cannot participate completely in the dictates of divine reason, but only in its own way and imperfectly. And therefore, just as in the case of speculative reason there is within us knowl-

edge of a certain common principle by means of a natural participation in the divine wisdom, although not knowledge properly speaking of each and every truth as it is contained in divine wisdom, so also in the case of practical wisdom humanity naturally participates in the eternal law according to a certain common principle, although not according to particular individual directives, which are nevertheless contained in eternal law. And therefore, it is necessary that human reason proceed further on to certain particular sanctions of law.

2. As to the second statement, human reason is not on its own account a measure of things, but the principles with which it is naturally endowed are rules of a general sort and measures for all those things which are done by human beings, of whom natural reason is the rule and measure, although it is not the measure of those things which derive from nature.

3. As to the third statement, practical reason is concerned with works to be done, which are individual and contingent, and is not concerned with necessary matters like speculative reason. And therefore human laws could not have that infallibility which the conclusions of the demonstrative branches of knowledge enjoy. Nor is it necessary that every measure be entirely infallible and certain, but merely that is should be appropriate to its genus.

Question 93: On eternal law

Article 3: Whether all law is derived from eternal law

1. It seems that not every law is derived from eternal law. For there is a certain law of passion, as was stated above. This does not derive from divine law, which is eternal law, for it pertains to matters of carnal prudence, regarding which the Apostle says that 'the law of God cannot be subjected' [Romans 8:7]. Therefore, not all law proceeds from eternal law.

2. Besides, nothing iniquitous can proceed from eternal law, because, as is stated, 'eternal law is what is just inasmuch as everything is best ordered thereby' [Augustine, *On the Freedom of the Will* 1.6]. But certain laws are iniquitous, according to Isaiah [10:1], 'Woe to those who create iniquitous laws!' Therefore, not all law proceeds from eternal law.

3. Once again, Augustine says that 'law which is written for the rule of the people rightly permits many things which are to be avenged by divine providence' [*On the Freedom of the Will* 1.5]. But the expression of divine providence is eternal law, as was said. Therefore, not every law proceeds aright from eternal law.

But on the contrary, it is the case that Proverbs [8:15] says of divine Wisdom, 'Through me kings reign, and the creators of law discern justice.' Yet the expression of divine Wisdom is eternal law, as was said above. Therefore, all laws proceed from eternal law.

Response: It may be stated that, as was said above, law involves the rational direction of certain human actions towards an end. In all ordered movements, it is necessary that the energy of the secondary mover is derived from the strength of the primary mover, because the secondary mover does not move except insofar as it is moved by the primary. For this reason, we see the same thing in everything which is governed, because the governing reason is derived from the primary governor by the secondary one, just as those plans which are enacted in a city are derived from the king through his precepts by inferior administrations, and also in construction the master plan of the building derives from the architect by the inferior craftsmen who work with their hands.

Therefore, since the eternal law is the governing plan in the supreme government, it is necessary that every governing plan by which inferiors are governed derives from eternal law. Such plans for the governance of inferiors are still in some other way laws apart from the eternal law. Thus, all laws insofar as they participate in right reason are to that extent derived from eternal law; and on account of this, Augustine says that 'nothing is just and legitimate in temporal law that human beings have not derived for themselves from eternal law' [*On the Freedom of the Will* 1.6].

1. As to the first statement, therefore, passion in human beings has the character of law insofar as it is a penalty resulting from divine justice; and in accordance with this, it is evident that it is derived from eternal law. Yet insofar as it inclines towards sin, it is contrary to God's law, and it does not have the character of law, as is clear from remarks above.

2. As to the second statement, human law has the character of law insofar as it is in accordance with right reason; and accordingly, it is evident that it is derived from eternal law. Yet insofar as it recedes from reason, it is to that extent called iniquitous law; and it does not have the character of law, but rather is a violence against law. And nevertheless iniquitous law maintains something of a similarity to law, on account of the ordering power by which it is made law, as a result of which it is also derived from eternal law. 'For all power is from the Lord God', as is said in Romans [13:1].

3. As to the third statement, human law is said to permit certain things not by virtue of approving them but by virtue of not being able to direct them. For many things are directed by divine law which cannot be directed by human law: for more matters are subject to higher authority than to lower. For this reason the fact that human law is not to introduce itself into those affairs which it cannot direct comes from the order of eternal law. The case would be otherwise if it were to approve that which eternal law reproves. Thus, it should be concluded from this not that human law is not derived from eternal law, but that human law cannot obtain its perfection.

Question 95: On human law in itself

Article 1: Whether it may be useful for any laws to be set down by human beings

1. It does seem that it would not be useful for any laws to be set down by human beings. For the aim of every law is that by it human beings will become good, as was said above. But human beings are better led towards a good will by instruction than by coercion through laws. Therefore, it would not be necessary to lay down laws.

2. Moreover, as the Philosopher says in the *Ethics* [5.4], 'Human beings have resort to a judge as a sort of animate justice'. But animate justice is better than the inanimate justice which is contained in laws. Therefore, it would be better that the execution of justice is undertaken by the will of a judge than that some law is erected on top of this.

3. Further, all law is a direction for human actions, as is evident from previous statements. But since human acts consist in individuated events, which are infinite, those things which pertain to the direction of human actions cannot be adequately considered except by some wise person who examines individual matters. Therefore, it would be better for human acts to be directed by the will of wise people than by any imposed law. Therefore, it would not be necessary to impose human laws.

But on the contrary, it is the case that Isidore says, 'Laws are made so that human pride may be limited by their threat, and the innocent may be safeguarded against the wicked, and the ability of the wicked to do harm may be restrained by the terror of punishment.' But such things are especially necessary among the human race. Therefore, it is necessary to set down human laws.

Response: It may be said, as is evident from previous statements, that humanity naturally has an inclination towards virtue; but it is necessary for perfect virtue that human beings achieve it by some instruction. Also, just as we see that by some industry human beings are supplied with their necessities, such as food and clothing, which have their origin (although not their completion) in nature, namely, reason and the hands, so nature gives other animals adequate covering and nourishment. In regard to learning, someone who is self-sufficient is not easy to find, because perfect virtue consists especially in the human refusal of undue pleasures, to which human beings are especially prone, most particularly young people, with regard to whom instruction is more effective. And therefore it is necessary that such instruction is shared by human beings with others, by means of which they will arrive at virtue.

And in regard to those young people who are prone to acts of virtue by a good disposition whether of nature or of habit, or rather by a divine gift, paternal discipline by admonition is sufficient. But because some of them are found to be brash and prone to vice, which cannot easily be altered by words, it is necessary that they are held back from vice through fear or force, in order that they at minimum desist from their evil acts and that perhaps even by means of such persistent effort in this regard they are induced to do voluntarily that which they first carried out from fear, and thus they become virtuous. Such instruction through fear of compelling punishment is the instruction of law.

For this reason, it is necessary for the sake of human peace and virtue that laws are laid down, because, as the Philosopher says in the *Politics* 1[.1], 'Just as man, if he has perfect virtue, is the best animal, so if he is separated from law and justice, he is the worst of all', because humanity possesses the weapon of reason for the expulsion of passion and savagery, something which other animals do not possess.

1. As to the first statement, human beings are better led to be well disposed by voluntary admonition to virtue than by coercion; but those who are ill disposed do not arrive at virtue unless they are coerced.

2. As to the second statement, as the Philosopher says in the *Rhetoric* 1[.1], 'It is better for all matters to be ordained by law rather than to be undertaken by the will of judges'; and this is the case in three ways. First, it is easier to find a few wise people who suffice for the imposition of rightful laws than to locate the many wise people who would be necessary for the sake of the correct judgement of individual cases. Second, those who impose the laws reflect for a long time on what is to be proposed by the law; but judgements regarding individual suits arise out of the sudden action of cases. A person can more easily see what is right by considering many cases than by considering only the facts of a single case. Third, legislators judge in general and with regard to the future; by presiding, human judges judge with regard to what lies before them, in connection with which they may be influenced by love or hate or some such desire; and this may distract their judgement.

Therefore, because animate justice is not found in many judges, and because it is flexible, it is hence necessary that, to the extent that it is possible, law is to determine matters of judgement, and the human will is to undertake the fewest matters.

3. As to the third statement, regarding specific matters which cannot be covered by the law, it is necessary for judges to undertake these, as the Philosopher says in the previously-cited work, for example, in regard to what is or is not factual, and other such problems.

Article 2: Whether all law imposed by humanity is derived from natural law

1. It would seem that not every law set down by humanity is derived from natural law. For the Philosopher says in the *Ethics* [5.7] that 'what is legally just is that principle which is a matter of indifference'. But those things which originate from natural law are not matters of indifference. Therefore, those

things which are established by human law are not always derived from the law of nature.

2. In addition, positive right is separate from natural right, as is shown by Isidore and by the Philosopher. But whatever is derived from the general principles of natural law in the manner of a conclusion pertains to natural law, as was stated above. Therefore, whatever belongs to human law is not derived from the law of nature.

3. Besides, the law of nature is the same among everyone: for the Philosopher says in the *Ethics* 5[:7] that 'natural right is that which has the same potency everywhere'. Therefore, if human laws would be derived from natural laws, it would follow that the former would also be the same among everyone, which appears to be false.

4. Once again, those things which are derived from natural law can be assigned some rationale. But not everything which is established by the laws can be granted a rationale, as the Jurist says. Therefore, not all human laws are derived from natural law.

But on the contrary, it is the case that Tully says in his *Rhetoric* [*On Invention* 2.53], 'The things advanced by nature and approved by custom are sanctioned by fear of and reverence for the law.'

Response: It may be said that, as Augustine observes in *On the Freedom of the Will* 1[.5], 'There does not seem to be a law which is not just': for this reason, insofar as it possesses justice it has the force of law. In human affairs, something is said to be just inasmuch as it is right according to the rule of reason. Yet the primary rule of reason is natural law, as is evident from earlier statements.

For this reason, to the extent that all established human law issues from the law of reason, it derives from natural law. And if it is in any way discordant with natural law, it will not be law, but a corruption of law.

But it is to be realized that things can be derived from natural law in two ways: in one way, as conclusions from principles, in the other way, as sorts of determinations regarding certain general matters. The first way is like that of the sciences in which conclusions are drawn demonstratively from premises. The second way is like that of the arts in which a general form will set the boundaries to special conditions, as in the case in which the general form of a house is necessary for its builder to determine the particular style of the house.

Therefore, certain things are derived from the general principles of natural law in the manner of a conclusion: so it is the case that 'do not commit murder' is a conclusion that can be derived from 'never do evil actions'; yet certain things have the character of determinations, as when natural law maintains that he who sins is to be punished; yet because it does not specify a particular punishment, this is a sort of natural law determination.

Therefore, both things are to be found in established human law. But those things which belong to the first mode are included in human law not merely insofar as they are laid down as law, but they also have a certain force from natural law. But those things which belong to the second mode have their force from human law alone.

1. As to the first statement, the Philosopher is speaking of those cases in which laws are laid down by the determination or specification of the precepts of the law of nature.

2. As to the second statement, that argument proceeds from those cases in which things are derived from the law of nature in the manner of conclusions.

3. As to the third statement, the general principles of the law of nature cannot be applied in the same way everywhere on account of the great variety of human affairs; and this results in a diversity of positive laws among diverse peoples.

4. As to the fourth statement, this remark of the Jurist is to be understood in regard to those things which are introduced by superiors on the order of particular determinations of natural law; in regard to such determinations, expert and prudent persons enjoy judgement on the basis of a certain principle, namely, that they see at once whether a particular determination is congruent with natural law. For this reason, the Philosopher says in the *Ethics* [6.11] that 'in such matters it is necessary to pay attention to the judgements of expert and older or prudent persons in regard to their demonstrable statements and opinions no less than to their demonstrations'.

Question 96: On the power of human law

Article 5: Whether everyone is subject to the law

1. It seems that not everyone is subject to the law. For only those are subject to the law for whom the law is laid down. For the Apostle says in 1 Timothy [1:9] that 'the law is not laid down for the just'. Therefore, the just are not subject to human law.

2. Furthermore, Pope Urban II said, it is maintained in the *Decretum* [2.19.2], 'He who is led by private law is for no reason to be restrained by public law.' Yet the private law of the Holy Spirit leads all spiritual men, who are the sons of God; according to Romans [8:14], 'Those who are roused by the Spirit of God are the sons of God.' Therefore, not every person is subjected to human law.

3. Moreover, the Jurist says that 'the ruler is unrestrained by laws' [*Digest* 1.3.31]. But those who are unrestrained by law are not subject to law. Therefore, not all people are not subject to the law.

But on the contrary, it is the case that the Apostle says in Romans [13:1], 'All souls are to be subject to the higher powers.' But one does not seem to be subject to a power who is not subject to the laws which that power makes. Therefore, all human beings ought to be subjected to law.

Response: It may be stated, as is evident from foregoing comments, that law in itself has a dual character: first, it is a rule for human action; second, it possesses coercive force. Therefore, a person can be subjected to law in two ways.

In the first way, all of those who are subject to a power are subject to the laws which that power makes. It could occur that someone is not subject for two reasons. One reason is that he is absolved pure and simple from his subjection – for which reason, he who lives in one city or kingdom is not subject to the laws of a ruler of another city or kingdom, since this is not his lord. The other reason is that he is ruled by a superior law: for example, if someone subject to a proconsul ought to be ruled by his mandate, yet he is not ruled in those matters in which he is relieved by the emperor, for to that extent one is not bound by the mandate of an inferior when one is directed by the mandate of a superior. And according to this, it happens that someone who is subjected to law pure and simple may not be bound to a certain law on account of the fact that he is ruled by a superior law.

The other way someone is said to be subject to law is as coercive constraint; and in this way, virtuous and just human beings are not subject to the law, but only bad people. For what is coerced and enforced is what is contrary to the will. Yet a good will is consonant with the law, while a bad will conflicts with law; and therefore according to this, the good are not under law, but only the bad.

1. As to the first statement, therefore, that argument proceeds from subjection which falls within the sense of coercion. For the just are not under the law in this way, because 'they are a law unto themselves, insofar as they reveal that the work of the law to be written on their hearts', as the Apostle says in Romans [2:14]. For this reason, the law has no coercive power over them, as it has over the unjust.

2. As to the second statement, the law of the Holy Spirit is superior to all law laid down by humanity; and therefore spiritual people who are led in accordance with the law of the Holy Spirit are not subject to law to the extent that it is incompatible with the leadership of the Holy Spirit. But nevertheless spiritual people are subject to those human laws which arise from the leadership of the Holy Spirit, according to 1 Peter [2:13], 'You are to be subject on account of God to all human creations.'

3. As to the third statement, a ruler is said to be unrestrained by law in regard to the coercive force of law, for no one is properly compelled by himself; and law does not have coercive force except by means of the power of the ruler. Therefore, the prince is said to be unrestrained by law in this way, because no one can impose a sentence of judgement upon him if he acts contrary to law. For this reason, in regard to the Psalm which says, 'I have only sinned against you', a gloss says that 'the king has no man who may judge his deeds' [Peter Lombard, *Gloss on Psalms* 50:6].

But in regard to the directive force of the law, the ruler is subject to law by his own will, in accordance with what is said in the *Decretals* [of Pope Gregory IX, 1.2.6], 'Whoever establishes law for another ought to practice the same law himself.' And a wise source says, 'Subject yourself to the way which you make' [Pseudo-Ausonius, *Seven Wise Thoughts* 2.5]. Also, there is disapproval by the Lord of 'those who speak and do not act', and who 'impose heavy burdens on others, and do not allow themselves to move even a finger', as Matthew [23:3–4] says.

For this reason, in regard to the judgement of God, the ruler is not unrestrained by law in the sense of its direct force, but he ought to carry out law voluntarily, not under constraint. Yet the ruler is above law insofar as he can alter the law if it would be expedient, and he can grant exemption from it on account of circumstance of time and place.

THE SECOND PART OF THE SECOND PART

Question 66: Theft and robbery

Article 1: Whether it is natural for human beings to possess external things

1. It would not seem to be natural for humans to possess external things, because no one ought to attribute to oneself what belongs to God. Rule over all creation belongs to God, as the Psalm indicates, 'The earth is the Lord's', etc. Therefore, the possession of external things is not natural to human beings.

2. Moreover, Basil explains the words of the rich man found in Luke, 'I will store all my inheritance and my goods', as follows, 'Tell me, what is yours, and where did you get them from to bring them into your life?' But what a person possesses naturally, he could justifiably call his own. Therefore humans do not naturally possess external goods.

3. Moreover, Ambrose says 'Rule denotes power.' But humans have no power over external things, since they cannot change their nature.

On the contrary, we are told in the Psalm, 'You have set all things under his feet', i.e. human feet.

Response: We can consider external things in two ways. One way is to look at their nature, which is not subject to human power, but only to God's power, which everything obeys at His pleasure. Another way is to look at their use and management, and in this humans have a natural dominion over external things, for a person has a mind and a will with which to turn them to his own use. They seem to be made for him insofar as imperfect things are for the sake of the more perfect, as was discussed earlier. And this is the reason the Philosopher [Aristotle] uses to prove that the possession of external things is natural to human beings. Furthermore, this rule over the rest of creation, which is natural to a person as a creature possessed of the reason in which the image of God consists, is manifested in the very creation of the human being; Genesis says 'Let us make a human being in our image and likeness; and let them have rule over the fish of the sea', etc.

1. God has pre-eminent lordship over all things, and in his providence he ordered certain things for human material support. This is why it is natural

for humans to have rule over things in the sense of having the power to use them.

2. The rich man in question was criticized for thinking that external goods were his without qualification, as if he had not first received them from another, namely God.

3. The argument turns on rule being taken in the sense of lordship over the very nature of external things, and this, of course, as we have already said, belongs to God alone.

Article 2: Whether it is legitimate for individuals to possess anything as their own

1. It would seem not to be legitimate, because all that is against natural law is wrong. According to natural law everything is common to all, and this is contradicted by the individual holding of possessions. Therefore it is wrong for any individual to appropriate any material thing.

2. Moreover, Basil says in the commentary on the rich man's statement quoted already, 'Rich people who regard common property as their own simply because they have been the first to occupy it are like those who prevent others from coming to the public games by arriving at the arena first and so appropriating what is meant for common use.' But it is not legitimate to preclude others from using common property. Therefore it is illegitimate to appropriate any common property for oneself.

3. Moreover, Ambrose states what is confirmed in the *Decretum*, 'Let no one say that what is common is his own.' But it is material things that he calls common property, as is clear from the context. It would therefore seem to be illegitimate for somebody to appropriate any material thing to himself.

On the contrary, this is what Augustine says, 'Those called "apostolic" arrogantly claimed this title for themselves because they refused to admit married people or property owners to their fellowship, arguing from the model of the many monks and clerics in the Catholic Church.' But such people are heretics because they cut themselves off from the Church by alleging that those who, unlike themselves, marry and own property have no hope of salvation.

Response. Human beings have a double competence in relation to material things. The first is the title to care for and distribute the earth's resources. It is therefore not merely legitimate for a person to possess things as his own, it is even necessary for human life, for three reasons. First, because each person takes more trouble to care for something that is his sole responsibility than what is held in common or by many, because in such a case each individual avoids the work and leaves the responsibility to somebody else, which is what happens when too many officials are involved. Second, because human affairs are more efficiently organized if each person has a separate responsibility to discharge; otherwise there would be confusion if everybody cared for everything. Third, because humans live together in greater peace where everyone is content with his own responsibility. We do, in fact, notice that quarrels often break out amongst those who hold things in common without distinction.

The other competence of human beings is to use and manage the world's resources. Now in regard to this, no one is entitled to manage things merely for himself, he must do so in the interests of all, so that he is ready to share them with others in case of necessity. This is why Paul writes to Timothy [1 Timothy 6:17–18], 'As for the rich of this world, tell them to be generous and willing to share.'

1. Community of goods is said to be part of the natural law not because it requires everything to be held in common and nothing to be appropriated to individual possession, but because the distribution of property is a matter not for natural law but, rather, human agreement, which is what positive law is about, as was said before. The holding of possessions individually is not, therefore, contrary to the natural law; it is what rational beings agree to as an addition to the natural law.

2. A person who arrives at the public games first in order to get things ready for others is not acting wrongly, but only if he stopped them from getting in. And, similarly, a rich person who takes prior possession of something that was previously common is not doing anything wrong pro- vided he is ready to share; he sins only if he unreasonably prevents others from using it. This is why Basil, in the same passage, says, 'What point is there in your enjoying plenty when another person is a beggar except for you to gain the merit of managing your wealth well and for him to win the crown of patience?'

3. When Ambrose says, 'Let no one say that what is common is his own', he is talking about the use and management of property in the common interest. That is why he goes on to say, 'To charge more than what meets the expenses is expropriation with violence.'

Article 7: Whether theft is justifiable in cases of necessity

1. We have seen that necessity does not seem to justify stealing. Penalties are imposed only on sinners. But the law states that 'any person who steals food, clothes, or cattle when he is starving or naked must do three weeks' penance.' Necessity does not, therefore, justify stealing.

2. The Philosopher says in the *Ethics* that the very words for certain acts imply malice, and he includes theft. But what is evil cannot become good just because of some good end. Therefore, one may not steal to provide basic necessities.

3. A person must love his neighbour as himself. But, as Augustine says, no one is entitled to steal in order to give to a neighbour. Therefore, no one is entitled to steal in order to provide basic necessities.

On the contrary, in the case of necessity everything is common. There-fore a person who takes someone else's property which necessity has rendered common does not commit a sin.

Response: The dictates of human law cannot derogate from natural or divine law. The natural order instituted by divine providence is, however, such that lower things are meant to enable a person to supply his needs. A person's needs ought to be met out of the world's goods even though a certain division and apportionment of them is determined by law. And this is why according to natural law goods that are held in surplus by some people should be used for the maintenance of the poor. As Ambrose says and is repeated in the *Decretum*, 'It is the bread of the poor which you are holding back; it is the clothes of the naked that you stockpile; it is the relief and liberation of the wretched which you are thwarting by burying your money in the ground.' At the same time there are so many poor people and they cannot all be supplied out of one supply, and this is why it is left to each individual to decide how to manage his property in such a way as to supply the needs of the suffering. Nevertheless, if there is so urgent and obvious a necessity that the immediate needs must be met out of whatever is available, as when a person is in imminent danger and he cannot be helped in any other way, then a person may legitimately supply his own needs out of another's property, whether he does so secretly or openly. And in this case there is strictly speaking no theft or robbery.

1. The decretal in question is not dealing with a case of urgent necessity.

2. If one is to speak quite strictly, it is improper to say that using someone else's property taken out of extreme necessity is theft. For such necessity renders what a person takes to support his life his own.

3. A person is even entitled to take someone else's property by stealth in order to help another where that other is also in extreme need.

Question 104: Obedience

Article 5: Whether subjects are obligated to obey their superiors

1. It appears that subjects must obey their superiors in everything. 'Children obey your parents in all things', St Paul says [Ephesians 6:1]; and later on, 'Servants, obey in all things your masters according to the flesh' [Ephesians 6:5]. Therefore, then, the obedience of other subordinates must be universal.

2. Furthermore, the statement, 'I was the mediator and stood between the Lord and you at that time to show you his words' [Deuteronomy 5:5] indicates that superiors are mediators between God and their subjects. To go from one end to another involves passing through the middle. Therefore, the precepts of a superior are to be counted as precepts from God. This point is made by St Paul, 'You received me as an angel of God even as Christ Jesus' [Galatians 4:14]; and, 'When you had received of us the word of the hearing of God, you received it, not as the word of human beings, but, as it is indeed, the word of God' [1 Thessalonians 2:3]. Therefore, just as a person ought to obey God in all things, so also superiors are to be obeyed.

3. Furthermore, just as members of religious orders take vows of chastity and poverty, so also obedience. Just as they are obligated to observe chastity and poverty in all cases, they ought to obey also.

On the contrary, 'We ought to obey God rather than human beings' [Acts 5:29], and at times the commands of superiors are against those of God. Therefore superiors are not to be obeyed without exception.

Response: As has been said, by the demands of moral rightness one who obeys is under the influence of a superior's command in a way similar to the sub-rational creature being by force of nature under the influence of the power of its mover. There are two ways in which it can happen that some sub-rational being is not moved by its mover. The first is interference coming from the stronger power of another moving force; for example, wood is not burned by fire when stronger water-power intervenes. The second comes from a lack of complete subjection in a recipient to its moving force, i.e. there is subjection in some respect but not in all; for example, moisture may receive the action of heat to the point of being warmed, but not of being dried up or evaporated.

Similarly, there are two ways it can happen that a subordinate is not obligated to obey a superior in everything. The first is because of the precept of a higher superior; a gloss on Romans, 'He that resists the power, resists the ordinance of God', asks,

> Should a commissioner issue an order, are you to comply if it is contrary to the bidding of a proconsul? Again, if the proconsul commands one thing and the emperor another, would you hesitate to disregard the first and observe the second? Therefore if the emperor orders one thing and God another, it is God who is to be obeyed.

The second way is for a command to be given in a matter where no subjection to the superior exists. As Seneca says, 'He is mistaken who supposes that slavery takes in the whole person. It does not touch the better part; the body may be subject and assigned to an owner, but thoughts have their own law.' Thus we are not obliged to obey humans but only God in what pertains to the inner life of the will.

Those matters in which one person is obligated to obey another are outward actions involving the body. Even so, one is not obligated to obey humans but God alone with respect to natural life, since in these matters all persons are equal: for example in what concerns taking food and begetting children. There is no obligation to obey that slaves have towards their master or that children have towards their parents with respect to contracting marriage, vowing virginity, or the like. In human conduct and affairs, a subject is obligated to obey his superiors within the limits of the authority in question – a soldier, his commander in military matters; a slave, his master in carrying out the labours of his service; a child, its parents in what concerns upbringing, running the household, and so on.

1. The Apostle's words mean 'all' within the limits of a parent's or master's right to command.

2. A person is subject to God completely and in everything, internal and external; thus he is bound to obedience in everything. But subjects are not under their superiors in all respects, but only within fixed limits; here superiors are mediators between God and the subject. In other things, subjects are under the direct authority of God, whose instrument is law, both natural and written.

3. Members of religious orders vow obedience with regard to the observances of their community, and on this basis are subject to their superiors. The obedience to which they are obligated and which is necessary for their salvation, therefore, bears only upon matters affecting their manner of life. Should they wish to extend their obedience to other matters, this would involve an extra degree of perfection, so long as nothing forbidden by God or by their rule were done, for then obedience would be wrong. From this we see three kinds of obedience: one sufficient for salvation, extending namely to matters of obligation; a second, perfect obedience, embracing all that is permissible; a third, indiscriminate obedience, going even beyond what is lawful.

Article 6: Whether Christians must obey civil authority

1. There seems to be no good reason why Christians should be obligated to obey secular authority. On Matthew, 'Then the children are free', the Gloss says, 'If in any kingdom the children of the ruling monarch are free, then, wherever they are, the children of that king whose rule is over all, must be free.' And the text, 'He gave them power to be made the children of God', shows that by faith in Christ Christians become children of God. Consequently, they are not bound to obey the secular arm.

2. Furthermore, as it says in Romans with respect to the law of the Old Testament: 'You are become dead to the law by the body of Christ.' But human law, by which people are subjected to civil authority, is less than the divine Old Testament law. Thus by becoming members of the body of Christ, people are freed from the laws binding them to the secular power.

3. Furthermore, we have no obligation to obey thieves accosting us, and Augustine has it: 'Where there is no justice, what is the regime but a band of thieves?' Since the regime of secular rulers is often marked by injustice, or else they have unjustly usurped power, it seems that Christians should not obey them.

On the contrary, in the letter to Titus [3:1], it says, 'Admonish them to be subject to princes and powers.' In 1 Peter [2:13–14]: 'Every human creature be subject for God's sake, whether to kings as superiors or to governors as sent by him.'

Response: Faith in Christ is the source and support of all righteousness: according to Romans [3:22], 'The justice of God by faith of Jesus Christ', thus through the faith of Christ, the order of justice is not abolished but strengthened. Now the order of justice calls for inferiors to obey their superiors; otherwise it would be impossible to maintain stability in human affairs. Thus, their faith in Christ does not exempt the faithful from the duty to obey civil authority.

1. As said above, the subjection whereby one person is under another's power applies to the body not the soul, which remains free. In this life we are free through Christ's grace from ills of soul but not from those of the body, as is clear from the Apostle who said about himself in Romans that his mind served the law of God, but his body the law of sin. Therefore, those who through grace have been made children of God are free from the spiritual slavery of sin, but not from the bodily service where they are said to be bound to temporal rulers, as the Gloss says on 1 Timothy: 'Whosoever are servants under the yoke', etc.

2. The old law, as the symbol of the New Testament, had to pass away with the coming of the reality it prefigured. This is not the same for human laws that subject a person to the authority of others. Note also that it is from divine law itself that one person is held to obey another.

3. The obligation to obey secular authority is measured by what the order of justice requires. For this reason when any regime holds its power not by right but by usurpation, or commands what is wrong, subjects have no duty to obey, except for such extraneous reasons as avoidance of scandal or danger. Where scandal or danger would be involved, subjects are still not held to obey, since unjust commands have no moral standing; rather subjects should observe charity, a higher justice or some other virtue to restain themselves from outright disobedience.

COMMENTARY ON ARISTOTLE'S POLITICS

PROLOGUE

1. Just as the Philosopher teaches in Book 2 of the *Physics*, art imitates nature. The reason for this is that just as principles amongst themselves stand in proportionate relation to one another, so do operations and effects. Now, the principle of those things which come into being through art is the human intellect, which is derived in compliance with a certain similarity from the divine intellect, which is the principle of natural things. For this reason, it is necessary that the operations of art should imitate the operations of nature; and the things which exist through art should imitate the things which exist in nature. For if an instructor of some art were to accomplish a work of art, it is proper that the disciple who receives the art from the teacher pay attention to that work so that the student might perform in the same way. And likewise, the human intellect, the light of whose intelligence is derived from the divine intellect, must be informed by the examination of things which are made through nature, so that it should operate similarly.

2. And from the foregoing, the Philosopher says that if art were to create the works of nature, it would operate the same as nature: and conversely, if nature were to create works of art, it would make them in the same way that art does. But nature, indeed, does not accomplish works of art, but only prepares certain principles and, in a way, supplies artists with a model by which they may operate. Although art is able to inspect the works of nature, and use them in order that its own work be perfected, still it cannot be perfect. From this it is clear that human reason is only able to know the things that exist through nature: however, it both knows and creates the things which exist according to art. For this reason, it is necessary that the branches of human knowledge which concern natural things be speculative, whereas those sciences which concern the things made by humans are practical or operative on account of the imitation of nature.

3. Now nature in its own operation proceeds from the simple to the compound, so that in the things which come into being through the operation of nature, that which is of the greatest complexity is perfect and complete and the end of other things, just as is apparent in every totality with respect to its own parts. For this reason, human reason, operating from the simple to the compound, proceeds in this manner from the imperfect to perfect.

4. However, since human reason has to arrange not only the things which come into the use of human beings but also humans themselves, who are ruled by reason, it proceeds in either instance from the simple to the complex: in the case of things which enter into the use of human beings, as when someone constructs a ship out of wood and a house out of wood and stone; and in the case of human beings themselves, as when it orders many people into a certain single community. Indeed, among communities, since there are different degrees and orderings, the highest community is the city, which is ordered to the satisfaction of the needs of human life. For this reason, among all human communities, the city is most perfect. And because the things which come into the use of humans are ordered to humans as to their end, it is therefore necessary that the whole which constitutes the city is the principle of all other wholes which can be known and constituted by human reason.

5. From what has been said about the political teachings which Aristotle delivers in this book, we are able to understand four points.

The first is the necessity of this branch of knowledge. For to be able to know all that is rational, it is necessary to teach something about the perfection of human wisdom, which is called philosophy. Since, then, that whole which constitutes the city is subject to certain judgements of reason, it has been necessary for the completion of philosophy to institute learning with regard to the city, which is called 'politics' or 'civil science'.

6. Second, we can perceive the genus of this branch of knowledge. For, since practical knowledge is distinguished from speculative knowledge, in that speculative fields of knowledge are ordered only to the knowledge of truth, whereas practical fields are ordered to some work, so it is necessary

that this branch of knowledge be included within the realm of practical philosophy, since the city is a certain whole, which is not only known by human reason but is also produced thereby.

And furthermore, reason is engaged with certain things by way of making, in which the operation crosses over into external matter, which pertains properly to the arts which are called 'mechanical', analogous to that of the craftsman and the ship builder and the like; by contrast, other things should be performed by way of an action in which the operation remains within the persons who acts, just as when one deliberates, chooses, wills and attends to the other acts pertaining to moral science. It is clear that political science, which is concerned with the ordering of human beings, is not included under the science of making, which encompasses the mechanical arts, but under the science of action, which comprises the moral sciences.

7. Third, we can perceive the dignity and order of political science in relation to all other practical sciences. For the city is the most important of the things which can be constituted by human reason. For all forms of human community are directed to it.

Furthermore, all the wholes which are constituted by the mechanical arts out of the things that come into human use are ordered to people as to their end. If, therefore, the most important branch of knowledge is the one that is concerned with what is most noble and perfect, it is necessary that of all the practical fields of knowledge, political science is the most important and the architectonic of all the branches of learning, inasmuch as it is concerned with the highest and perfect good in human affairs. And on account of this the Philosopher says at the end of Book 10 of the *Nicomachean Ethics* that the philosophy which pertains to human affairs is perfected in politics.

8. Fourth, from what has been said, we can learn the mode and order of this branch of knowledge. For just as the speculative fields of knowledge, which examine some whole, bring about a knowledge of the whole out of consideration of its parts and its principles by revealing all its properties and operations, so that science which examines the principles and parts of the city passes on a knowledge of the city by revealing its parts and properties and operations; and because it is a practical science, it reveals in addition how each thing is able to be accomplished, which is necessary in every practical branch of knowledge.

BOOK 1, LESSON 1

11. ...A community is a certain whole but in all wholes is found an order such that the whole which includes within itself another whole be the highest whole; for example, a wall is a whole, and because it is included in that whole which is a house, it is clear that the house is the highest whole. And similarly, the community which includes other communities is the higher one. Now, it is clear that the city includes all other communities. For

households and villages are both united under the city, and so political community itself is the highest community. Therefore, it seeks the highest goods among all human goods: for it is directed towards the common good, which is better and more divine than the good of one individual, as is stated at the beginning of the *Ethics*.

12. He compares the city to these other societies, in which respect he makes three points. First, he lays out the false opinion of certain individuals. Second, he shows how the falsity of the stated opinion can become known. Third, according to the method indicated, he lays out the true relationship between the city and other communities.

13. Concerning the first point, it should be considered that there are two forms of community known to all, namely, the city and the household.

Now, the city is governed by a two-fold rule, namely, the political and the royal. For there is royal rule when the one who presides over the city has full power. However, there is political rule when the one who presides over the city has power restricted according to certain laws of the city.

Similarly, the household has a two-fold rule, namely, the domestic and the despotic. For everyone who has slaves is called a despot. But the procurator or superintendent of any family is called a domestic head. For this reason, despotic rule is that by which a master commands slaves, but domestic rule is that by which one dispenses the things that pertain to the whole family, in which are contained not only slaves but also many free people. Therefore, some people have maintained – but not correctly – that these particular forms of rule do not differ but are entirely the same.

14. He sets forth their rationale for this, which is as follows. The things that differ only by reason of large and small numbers do not differ specifically, because a difference according to more or less does not distinguish a species. But the rules just mentioned differ only by reason of large or small numbers, a claim which they defend as follows.

For if the community that is ruled contains a small number of people, as in the case of some small household, he who presides over them is called the head of household, to whom pertains despotic rule.

However, if the community is made up of a large number of people, so that it contains not only slaves but also a large number of free persons, the one who commands them is called the domestic head.

But if the community is made up of an even greater number of people, for example, not only those who are one household, but those who are of one city, then the rule is said to be political or royal.

15. The falsity of what certain people have said, insofar as they hold that the household and the city differ only by reason of their smallness and greatness, so that a large household is a small city and vice versa, will become clear from the following. Likewise, they have also maintained that political and royal rule differ only by reason of larger and smaller numbers. For when a person commands pure and simple and in all matters, the rule is said to be

royal. Yet when one rules in part, according to the precepts of a certain body of knowledge, that is, according to the laws set down by political education, and when one is in part a subject, namely, subjected to certain commands of law, the form of rule is said to be political. From all this, they have concluded that all the rules previously mentioned, some of which pertain to the city and others to the household, do not specifically differ.

16. He shows the way in which the falsity of this opinion may be revealed; and he says that what has been stated is not true. This will become apparent to those who consider the matter according to his teachings, that is, according to the art of examining the matters which are set forth below. Now the method of this art is the following. Just as in other things, in order to have knowledge of the whole, it is necessary to divide the compound all the way into its elements, that is, into its indivisibles, which are the smallest parts of the whole (for example, to understand a sentence, it is necessary to divide it into its letters, and to understand a mixed body, it is necessary to divide it all the way into its elements), so if we examine those things from which the city is constructed, we will be better able to see what each one of the previously stated rules is according to itself, and how they differ from one another according to whether in each case something is able to be considered in an artful manner. For in all matters we see that, if someone inspects things according to how they arise from their principles, one will be best able to contemplate the truth in them.

And just as this is true in other matters, so it is also true of those matters upon which we focus our attention now. In regard to these words of the Philosopher, it should be noted that, in order to arrive at a knowledge of compounds, it is first necessary to work according to the resolutive method, so that we may divide the compound all the way into its elements. Afterwards, however, the compositive method is necessary, so that from these indivisible principles already known we may determine the things that are caused by these principles.

17. According to the previously mentioned method, he lays out the relationship of the other communities to the city; and in this regard he makes two points. First, he discusses the other communities which are ordered to the city. Second, he addresses the community of the city....

BOOK 3, LESSON 1

348. After the Philosopher inquires into the forms of government according to the teachings of others in Book 2, he begins to develop them according to his own opinion.

And this is divided into two parts. In the first, he makes clear the diversity of governments. In the second, he teaches how to establish the best government, in the beginning of Book 7.

Now, the first part is divided into two. In the first, he determines what pertains to the government in general. In the second, he divides the governments.

The first part [regarding government in general] is divided into two. In the first, he speaks about his intention. In the second, he pursues his proposal.

Concerning the first, he does two things. First, he shows that in order to treat governments, it is necessary first to consider the city. Second, he shows that in order to treat the city, it is necessary to consider what is a citizen.

349. Therefore, he says, first of all, that the person who wishes to consider the government and determine what each is according to its proper reason, and what kind of government it is, namely, whether it is good or bad, must first consider what is a city.

And this he demonstrates by two arguments. The first is that there can be doubt concerning this. For some people raise doubt concerning whether the city itself has engaged in certain actions when they were performed by a tyrant or by the rich of the city. In this case, some say that the city acted, while others say that the city did not act, but only the rich rulers or the tyrant; and thus there seems to be a question about whether the rich alone rule the city. And because there is a question, it is proper that it be resolved.

The second reason is that the whole aim of those who manage governments and legislation is to do business around the city, because the government is nothing other than the order of the inhabitants of the city.

350. He shows that it is necessary to define the citizen for two reasons. First, in everything that is composed from many parts, it is necessary first to consider the parts. Now, the city is a certain whole constituted of citizens, just like its parts, since the city is nothing other than a sort of multitude of citizens. Therefore, to know the city, it is necessary to consider what is a citizen.

The second reason is that concerning this point, there also happens to be doubt: for not everyone is in agreement as to what is a citizen. For sometimes a common member who is a citizen in a popular state, according to which the people govern, is not also considered a citizen in a state of the few, according to which the rich govern, because it is frequently the case that the people have no part in it. For this reason, it is evident that there is a controversy concerning the citizen, as to who is a citizen and what kind of person it is proper to call a citizen.

351. He pursues his plan. And it is divided into two parts. In the first, he shows what is a citizen. In the second, he shows what virtue makes a citizen good.

Concerning the first, he makes two points. First, he determines what is a citizen. Second, he raises certain doubts concerning this.

Concerning the first, he also makes two points. First, he shows what a citizen is according to virtue. Second, he excludes a certain false conclusion.

Concerning the first, once again he makes two points. First, he lays out certain ways according to which some people are citizens in compliance with what is not absolute. Second, he shows what a citizen is absolutely.

352. Therefore, he says, first of all, that we must, for the present, exclude those who are called citizens in certain ways, that is, according to metaphor or by comparison; these are not really citizens.

And the first way is according to residence. Now, people are not said to be truly citizens from the fact that they live in a city, because foreigners and slaves live in a city and nevertheless are not citizens absolutely.

The second way is that some people may be called citizens because they are subject to the jurisdiction of the city, namely, in that they participate in the justice of the city, through which they at some times receive a favourable judgement, and by which they are at other times judged, that is, condemned; yet this is also the case with those who have certain contracts among themselves but who are nevertheless not citizens of one city. And yet, in certain cities foreigners do not participate perfectly in this justice, as do citizens, but it is necessary that if they wish to establish justice they must assign a legal protector, that is, someone who vouches for their obedience to the law. For this reason, it is clear that outsiders participate imperfectly in the sharing of justice; and thus, according to this, they are not citizens absolutely, but are able to be called citizens in a qualified way.

In the same way, also, we call children citizens, although they have not yet been enlisted among the number of the citizens. And in the same manner, we call old men citizens, although they have already been released from the number of citizens, since they are no longer able to discharge the services of citizens. For in both cases we do not call them citizens absolutely, but with some qualification. In fact, we refer to the children as imperfect. But we call the old people advanced beyond the years which are required for the condition of citizenship, or if some other such qualification is also added, it makes no difference. For it is clear that what we intend to say: for we are asking about what a citizen is absolutely and without any qualification, which is necessary for assigning or explaining the name 'citizen'.

Now, there is a fourth way in which the same difficulty and the same solution occurs, namely, that which concerns fugitives and infamous people; for these are citizens in a qualified sense but not absolutely.

353. He shows what a citizen is absolutely. And concerning this he makes three points. First, he lays out a certain definition of the citizen. Second, he shows that this definition is not common in any government. Third, he shows how it may be corrected so that it will be common.

Therefore, he says, first of all, that there can be no better way of defining the citizen than by the fact that he participates in the conduct of justice in the city, so that he is able to judge certain matters, namely, he has the power of some authority in the affairs of the city.

But note that there are two kinds of ruling. For some forms of ruling have been fixed for a certain period of time, thus in certain cities the same person is not permitted to hold the same office twice, or he may hold it for a limited time, such as exercising a certain office for a year and afterwards not being eligible for appointment to the same office for another three or four years. Now, the other form of ruling is not fixed for a certain period of time, such as that of a praetor, who has the power to judge certain cases, and a speaker, who has the power to express his opinion in the public assembly. However, it can happen that some such judges or speakers are not called rulers, and it may be said that they do not have any authority on account of which they may judge or address the assembly. But this proposition is not relevant, because there is no doubt except for words: for we do not find any name common to the judge and the member of the assembly; and therefore, let a name be established for this office, so that it is called 'indeterminate'. Thus, we establish that those who participate in their kind of government are citizens; and this seems to be a better definition of the citizen absolutely.

354. He shows that such a definition is not common in all governments. And he says that it is proper that this be made clear in all matters where individual subjects differ according to species, and where one of them is first by nature, another second, another having followed it; and either nothing is common to them insofar as they are such, as in the case of equivocal names, or else there is something common, but it is difficult and obscure, that is, according to some measure. Now governments, as is said later, differ according to species, and some of them are superior and some of them inferior, because those which are ordered according to right reason ought to be preferred to others, while those which are corrupt and exceed the right order of government are by nature inferior to non-corrupt governments, just as in any genus the perfect by nature come before the corrupt. But just how some governments exceed the right order will become clear later on.

For this reason, it is clear that the notion of a citizen should vary with different governments. Therefore, the definition of citizen already mentioned applies above all to the popular state, in which anyone among the people has the power to judge in certain matters and to address the assembly. However, in other governments, it sometimes happens that any citizen has this power; nevertheless, this is not necessarily so, because some of the people do not have any power, nor is the assembly of the people taken into account, but only others who have been especially summoned; and these alone through their offices judge certain cases, just as in Sparta where the ephors judge cases amongst citizens and others give sentence on other matters, and different groups judge different cases. Hence, the elders judged regarding homicides, and other rulers ruled in other cases. And thus it is also among the Carthiginians, because all their sentences are judged by certain rulers and so the common citizens do not participate in the judgement. For this reason, in such governments the notion of the citizen mentioned already does not apply.

355. He corrects the definition of the citizen already mentioned; and he says that this definition can be discussed in regard to that which is in common, because in governments other than the popular state, the member of the assembly and the praetor do not hold office for an indeterminate time,

but these two pertain only to those who hold office for a determinate time, because it belongs to some of them or even all of them to judge what is proper and to deliberate either in some matters or in all.

And from this it is clear to see what is a citizen: for he is not the one who participates in justice or the assembly but the one who exercises the judicial or deliberative function. For those who are not able to be appointed to such offices seem to have no participation in government, and thus do not seem to be citizens.

Now finally, he concludes from this that a city is nothing other than a large multitude of people such as these, who are thus called citizens, so that by themselves they are able to live sufficiently in an absolute way. For a city is a self-sufficient community, as was said in the first book.

BOOK 3, LESSON 3

365. After the Philosopher shows what a citizen is and solves certain doubts, he now inquires about that virtue according to which the citizen is defined.

And this is divided into two parts. In the first, he shows that the virtue of the citizen is not the same absolutely as that of the good person. In the second part, he addresses certain difficulties concerning this.

Concerning the first point, he makes two points. First, he shows that the virtue of the diligent citizen is not the same absolutely as that of the good person. In the second, he shows that the virtue of a certain sort of citizen is, however, the same as that of the good person.

Concerning the first point, he makes two observations. First, he speaks of his aim: that whether, after what has been said and reasonably considered, we ought to assert that the citizen's virtue is the same as that of the good person or not; this is to ask whether someone is called a good person and a good citizen from the same cause, for virtue is that which makes the person possessing it good. Now, in order to investigate this question properly, it is necessary to show what is the virtue of the citizen by means of a figurative and metaphorical explanation.

366. He shows that the virtue of a citizen is not the same as that of the good person on three grounds.

In the first of these, he begins by offering an analogy to illustrate what is the virtue of a good citizen; and he says that just as 'sailor' signifies something common to many people, so it is with 'citizen'. For he reveals how 'sailor' is common to many people. Many people who differ in power, that is, by their art and their function, are called sailors, since one of them is a rower who moves the ship with oars, another is a pilot who guides the ship with rudders, yet another is on lookout, that is, the guardian of the prow, which is the front part of the ship, and others have other names and functions. Now it is clear that each one of these people had something that belongs to him according to his own virtue, as well as something in common.

144

For it pertains to the virtue of each one individually that he should have some diligent reason and care concerning his own function, for example, steering in the case of the pilot, and likewise for all the others. But the common virtue is one which belongs to all, for the work of all of them works towards the end of safe navigation: for it is this towards which the desire and intention of any sailor aims and the common virtue of sailors is ordered, which is the virtue of the sailor as sailor.

In the same way, also, since there are different citizens possessing dissimilar functions and dissimilar positions through which they exercise their proper operations in the city, the common work of all is the safety of the community. Indeed, this community consists in the order of the polity.

For this reason, it is clear that the virtue of a citizen as citizen is considered in an ordered relation to the polity, so that, namely, the good person is the person who works effectively for the preservation of the polity.

Now, there are several species of polity, as will be mentioned later as is to some extent clear from what has previously been said; but people are well ordered to different polities according to different virtues. For a popular state is preserved in some way, and the rule of a few or a tyranny in another. For this reason, it is evident that a perfect virtue does not exist according to which a citizen can be called absolutely good; but a certain person is called virtuous according to a single perfect virtue, namely, according to prudence, upon which all the moral virtues depend.

Therefore, it happens that someone is a good citizen, although he does not have the virtue according to which one is a good person; and this is the case in polities other than the best polity.

367. He lays out a second argument. And he says that by inquiring and objecting, we can arrive through another path at the same viewpoint, even concerning the best polity, namely, that the virtue of the good citizen is not the same as that of the good person, because it is impossible, however good the government may be, that all the citizens be virtuous; nevertheless it is the case that each one can perform properly his work for the city, and this happens as a result of the virtue of the citizen as citizen. And therefore, I say that all citizens cannot be the same, since then the same work would pertain to all. And from this it follows that the virtue of the good citizen is not identical with that of the good person.

This conclusion he reveals thus: in the best government, it is proper that every citizen must have the virtue of the good citizen. For in this way the city will be best; but it is impossible that all have the virtue of the good person, because all the people in a city are not virtuous, as has been said.

368. He lays out a third reason. And he says that every city is established from different elements, just like an animal. For an animal is composed immediately from unlike parts, namely, soul and body, and similarly, the human soul is composed of unlike elements, namely, a rational power and an appetitive power, and once again, the domestic community is composed

145

of different parts, namely, man and woman, and acquisition is also established from a master and a slave. Now, the city is established from all these different elements and from many others. But it has been said in Book 1 that the virtue of the ruler and the subject are not one and the same, neither in the soul nor in other things: for this reason, it follows that the virtue of all the citizens is not one and the same, just as we see that in a chorus, the virtue of the leader is not the same as that of the assistant, that is, the person next to the leader. But it is clear that the virtue of all good persons is one and the same: it follows, therefore, that the virtue of the good citizen and of the good person are not identical.

369. He then shows that the virtue of one citizen is the same as that of the good person.

And concerning this, he makes three points. First, he states the aim. Second, he infers the conclusion from what has already been said. Third, he addresses a certain difficulty concerning what has already been said and resolves it.

Therefore, he says, first of all, that one will perhaps be able to say that the same virtue of the good person is required of a certain good citizen in order that he be good. For a person is not said to be a good ruler unless he is good through the moral virtues and prudence. For it has been said in Book 6 of the *Ethics* that the polity has a certain part of prudence: for this reason, it is necessary that the political person, that is, the leader of the polity, must be prudent and, consequently, a good person.

370. From this he concludes that the virtue of the good citizen and the good person are not the same absolutely. And in order to prove this, he first inspects the statement made by some people that the instruction of the ruler, by which he is to be educated in virtue, is different from the instruction of the citizen, as is clear from the fact that sons of rulers are instructed in the knowledge of horsemanship and warfare. For this reason, Euripides also, speaking in the person of a ruler, said, 'It is not for me to know things which are beautiful', namely, those that are the concern of a philosopher, 'but things that function for ruling a city.' And this he said to signify that there is a certain training proper for the ruler.

And from this he concludes that if the training and virtue of the ruler and the good person are the same, but not every citizen is a ruler, for there are also citizens who are subjects, then it follows that the virtue of the citizen is not the same absolutely as the good person, unless perhaps it is a certain citizen, namely, the one who is able to be a ruler. And this is so because the virtue of the ruler and the citizen are not the same....

371. He addresses a difficulty concerning what has been said. And concerning this he makes two points. First, he objects against what has been said. Second, he resolves it.

Thus, he says, first of all, that the citizen is sometimes praised from the fact that he is able to rule and to be subject as well. If, therefore, the virtue of the good person is the same as that of the good ruler, but the virtue of the good citizen is something that attaches itself to both of these things, namely, to ruling and to being subject, then it follows that both things, namely, to be a good citizen and a good person, are not praised similarly, but that it is much better to be a good citizen.

375. He shows how the virtue of the ruler is the same as that of other people and how it differs. And he says that even in this form of rule the virtue of the ruler is different than the subject: but nevertheless, it is fitting that the person who is a good citizen absolutely should know both how to rule and to be subject to rule, namely, not to a despotic rule, which is that of slaves, but to a political rule, which is that of free people. And this is the virtue of a citizen, so that he should be well disposed towards one and the other; and absolutely good people know both, namely, how to rule well and to be a subject. And thus the virtue of the good citizen, insofar as he can rule, is the same virtue as that of the good person; but insofar as he is a subject, the virtue of the ruler and of the good person is different from the virtue of the good citizen; for example, the temperance and justice of rulers and the temperance and justice of subjects are a different species. For the subject who is free and good does not have only one virtue, for example, justice; but his justice has two species, according to one of which he is able to rule well, and according to the other of which he is able to be a good subject. And this is also the case concerning the other virtues.

BOOK 3, LESSON 4

378. After the Philosopher shows what the virtue of the diligent citizen is and whether it is the same as the virtue of the good person, he addresses a certain difficulty concerning what has already been determined.

In this regard, he makes three points. First, he addresses the difficulty. Second, he resolves it. Third, he clarifies the solution.

Therefore, he says, first of all, that there still remains a certain difficulty regarding the citizen: namely, whether he is a citizen who is able to share in the governance of a city; or if common craftsmen, who do not happen to share in the government, should also be placed among the citizens.

And he objects to both parts, because if labourers, to whom nothing pertains concerning cities, are called citizens, it will follow that the virtue which we ascribed to the good citizen, namely, that he is able to rule and to be ruled, does not pertain to every citizen, because this person is placed among citizens although he is not able to rule. For it is said that no one of such a kind is a citizen; there will thus remain a doubt about the category in which a labourer should be placed. For it cannot be said that they are strangers, as if they are coming from elsewhere to live in the city; and neither are they foreigners, like travellers, who on account of some business come to the city without the motive of staying. For these craftsmen have their home in the city and are born there, and do not come from elsewhere.

379. He solves this difficulty and says that on account of this latter reason there is doubt about the appropriate category for the placement of craftsmen, but if they are not citizens it does not follow that this is in some way inappropriate. For they are people who are not citizens, and nevertheless are neither strangers nor foreigners, just as is clear concerning slaves and free people who have been returned from servitude to freedom. For it is true that not all are citizens, who are necessary for the perfection of the city and without whom the city is not able to exist, because in the case of slaves as well as children, they are not perfect citizens, as are men. For men are citizens absolutely, since they have in effect the power of performing the duties of citizens; but children are citizens by supposition, that is, with some diminishing qualification. For they are imperfect citizens; and just as slaves and children are citizens in some sense, but not perfectly, so also are craftsmen. For this reason, in ancient times, common craftsmen and even foreigners were slaves in certain cities, in such a way as many are even now.

380. He clarifies the already mentioned solution: that even in the best disposed city, workers are not able to be citizens. And if it is said that a worker is a citizen in some way, then it has to be said that the virtue of the citizen which we have defined, namely, as being able to rule and be subject equally well, is not that of the citizen, although citizenship is cited in any case. But it is proper that this virtue should pertain to them because they are not only free but are discharged, that is, released from the duties necessary for life. For if those who are assigned to such necessities serve only one man, this is properly the work of slaves; for slaves have to perform such services for their masters. But if they perform these services for anyone in general, this pertains to the work of labourers and bad people who service anyone for money.

8

'ON CIVIL GOVERNMENT'
Giles of Rome

INTRODUCTION

Giles of Rome (1247–1316), sometimes referred to by a Latinized version of his name, Egidius Colonna, was born at Columna, Italy into a powerful noble family. He entered the Augustinian order in Rome, where he sufficiently impressed his superiors to be sent to Paris to complete his studies. The University of Paris was flourishing, and Giles was the first member of his order to study for the doctorate, where his most famous teacher was the Dominican, Thomas Aquinas. Soon after completing his studies, Giles was offered a chair at the University and asked by Philip III of France to become tutor to his son, Prince Philip the Fair.

It was thus at the king's own request, Giles reveals in his introduction, that he wrote *De Regimine principium*, his book on the education of the prince. It is divided into three books: 'On Self Government', 'On Household Government', and 'On Civil Government'. One of the most elaborate 'mirrors' for princes to be written in the Middle Ages, the work covers every aspect of their life and training. Its aim is to provide a ruler with everything he needs to know in order to govern effectively, whether in his personal life, in his household, or in his kingdom. In essence, Giles adapts the teachings of Aristotle's *Ethics* and *Politics* to the situation of his own time, infusing them with contemporary and Christian significance. As is typical of thirteenth-century political thought, when Giles wants to prove his own position, he is most likely to cite Aristotle as his authority.

Book III, from which our excerpt is taken, concerns civil government, and is also divided into three parts. In Part I, Giles discusses Greek political theories, especially those of Plato, showing that his suggestions may not be practical or in the best interest of the community. Part II is about the best government in time of peace. In it, he begins with Aristotle's discussion of forms of government, and moves to the proposition that hereditary monarchy is better than other forms. Following in the footsteps of other writers, he distinguishes the characteristics of the good king from those of the tyrant. Fundamentally that difference is simple: the king governs for the good of the community and by the rule of law. The tyrant rules in his own self-interest. A discussion of the nature of law follows and the analysis concludes with Giles' reflections on the good community. It is here especially that he shows his recognition of the changing society around him: he focuses on the need for a large middle class, and the responsibility that ruler and ruled have to each other. It is this latter discussion that is included here, translated for the first time into English.

Part III concludes the work with a discussion of government in time of war, with practical advice on military recruitment and training, weapons, fortifications, and naval warfare.

'ON CIVIL GOVERNMENT'

Chapter 33: The state, the kingdom and the people are best when there is a large middle class

In Book Four of [Aristotle's] *Politics*, three classes are distinguished; those who are rich, those who are poor, and those who are in the middle. Therefore, because there is this way of dividing the state into three parts, the people and the kingdom can also be divided. I intend in this chapter to describe the best condition for the state and the kingdom; that is, when the population has a large middle class. In Book Four of the *Politics*, the Philosopher [Aristotle] gives four reasons why kingdoms and states are well ordered when there is a large middle class: first, it is a more rational way to live; second, there is more esteem between the classes; third, there is more equality; fourth, there is less envy and distrust.

First, if there are many who are very rich, and many who are very poor, and few who are middle class, none are able to live according to reason. The very rich will not know how to conduct themselves towards the very poor, and thus will injure them and do them harm for no reason. Those who are poor will not know how to behave toward the rich and will think unceasingly about how to rob them and deprive the rich of their goods. But if the population is made up of many middle-class persons, they will achieve the rational mean, and can live together according to reason, as the fourth book of the *Politics* says.

Second, there is none of that mutual esteem which ought to exist in any kingdom, or between inhabitants in any state. As it says in Book Four of the *Politics*, obviously few poor people love princes, the powerful, or the rich; here as above, they are not good citizens. Thus, for mutual esteem among citizens, it is better to have a large middle class.

Third, in order to have equity and justice, which are necessary to the state, there must be a large middle class. For, as the Philosopher tells us, those who have excessive fortune, power, riches, friendship, and other good things do not know how to be subjects. If there are too many who are indigent and poor, they do not know how to rule. When the population is constituted by only two classes, the very rich and the very poor, and there are too few middle-class persons, it is difficult to have equity and justice because the rich want to rule and subject the others. However, if the poor have power over the rich, they will treat the rich and mighty badly, because they do not know how to rule.

Fourth, it is spoiled by envy and contempt. As the fourth book of the *Politics* says, the very poor will envy the rich and the very rich will have contempt for them. No society survives long where there is a lot of envy and contempt.

It is best to have a population with a large middle class which then has the ability to live rationally, with mutual esteem, sustained by justice and equity, avoiding contempt and envy amongst them. Truly, without this, there will be envy towards one class and contempt towards the other and equality cannot exist. This is attested to by authorities such as Solon, Charondas, and Lycurgus, says the *Politics*. They say that it is better if [society] is constituted by middle-class persons. Therefore kings and princes are counselled to have a large middle class in their kingdoms and not too many people who are rich or poor. And a king can do this by establishing that no one can buy or sell an inheritance from father or mother, except for good and trustworthy reasons. If he diligently regulates the sale and acquisition of farms and land, he will be able to have equality between citizens.

Chapter 36: How kings and princes ought to make themselves loved by their people, and that they ought to desire to be loved more than feared

Since in the first book we set forth how the people ought to behave towards kings and princes, now we will discuss how kings and princes should treat their people, so that they will be loved and feared. Know that they ought to be three things: first, they ought to be generous and liberal; second, to be strong and courageous; third, to be equitable and just.

First, they ought to be generous and liberal, because the common people, who know nothing about them except that they have a great deal of money, love and revere those who are generous and spend a lot, and who willingly give what is theirs. Chapter Two of [Aristotle's] *Rhetoric* says that the people love and honour those who generously benefit them with money.

Second, kings who want to be loved by the people ought to be strong and courageous, putting themselves in peril of death for the good of the community and the defence of the kingdom. This idea is found in Book Two of *Rhetoric*: We love our benefactors, and those who benefit us generously, we love wholeheartedly.

The third thing which makes a king loved by his people is if he is just and equitable. Nothing makes a people hate him more than if he does not observe justice. Thus the *Rhetoric* says that we love most those who are just. This is how the king and prince who want to be loved by their people ought to conduct themselves.

And we ought to note that the people fear the king for three reasons. First, because of the harsh penalties which he can inflict upon his subjects (as Book Two of the *Rhetoric* says). Second, kings and those in authority are feared, not only because of the punishments they can inflict, but because those punishments are rational. Punishments are just because they are on behalf of justice; no one ought to be spared. Thus Book Seven of the *Politics* says that it is good to do no less than justice, whether for a father or a son or a friend or for any other, excusing no one from what is just and right. Then everyone will fear to do wrong, for he will know that if he does he will be punished. In Book Seven of the *Politics*, the Philosopher says that the king is feared by the powerful when he has the strength to observe justice and to punish the powerful, even to punish his friends with severity if they deserve it.

Third, kings and princes are feared when punishment is rational, and it is the same for those around them, so that judges and officials of the king handle themselves so wisely in the exercise of punishment and giving justice that the evil cannot escape being punished. So Book Two of the *Rhetoric* says that it is evident that those at the side of the great are feared.

We said above that the principal intention of kings and any princes ought to be to encourage others to act virtuously. The intention of the legislator ought to be to have citizens who are very good and virtuous. With citizens and inhabitants in the kingdom acting rightly and observing the law, and the commands of the king honoured out of love and affection, both for the common good and for the sake of the king, the citizens act out of goodness and virtue rather than acting out of fear of punishment. When kings and princes are loved by the people, the people act rightly; and when feared by them avoid doing wrong out of fear of punishment; which is why both fear and love are necessary. Now, not all are good and perfect, desiring only honesty and the common good, acting out of affection for the legislator, intending the common good, and doing nothing evil. It is necessary therefore to encourage them to do good and to deter them out of fear of punishment from doing evil. Nevertheless, it is better to choose to be loved than feared as we have shown.

FURTHER READING: THE THIRTEENTH CENTURY

Primary sources

Thomas Aquinas, *On Kingship*, trans. G.B. Phelan, Toronto, Pontifical Institute of Medieval Studies, 1949.

Thomas Aquinas, *Summary of Theology*, 61 vols, ed. T. Gilby *et al.*, New York, McGraw-Hill, 1964–80.

Thomas Aquinas, *St. Thomas Aquinas on Politics and Ethics*, ed. P. Sigmond, New York, Norton, 1987.

Henry de Bracton, *On the Laws and Customs of England*, 4 vols, trans. S.E. Thorne, Cambridge, Mass., Harvard University Press, 1968–77.

[Anonymous], *Disputation between a Cleric and a Knight*, ed. and trans. N.N. Erikson in *Proceedings of the American Philosophical Society*, 111, 1967, 288–309.

Pierre Du Bois, *The Recovery of the Holy Land*, New York, Columbia University Press, 1956.

[Anonymous], *Fleta*, 3 vols, ed. and trans. H.G. Richardson and G.O. Sayles, London, Selden Society, 1955–72.

Secondary sources

Beer, S., 'The Rule of the Wise and the Holy: Hierarchy in the Thomistic System', *Political Theory*, 14, 1986, 391–422.

Blythe, J.M., 'The Mixed Constitution and the Distinction between Regal and Political Power in the Work of Thomas Aquinas', *Journal of the History of Ideas*, 47, 1986, 547–65.

Blythe, J.M., 'Family, Government and the Medieval Aristotelians', *History of Political Thought*, 10, 1989, 1–16.

Canning, J.P., 'Ideas of the State of Thirteenth- and Fourteenth-Century Commentators on Roman Law', *Transactions of the Royal Historical Society*, 5th ser., 33, 1983, 1–27.

Catto, J., 'Ideas and Experience in the Political Thought of Aquinas', *Past and Present*, 71, 1976, 3–21.

Gilby, T., *Principality and Polity: Aquinas and the Rise of State Theory in the West*, London, Longman, 1958.

Kayser, J.R. and R.J. Lettieri, 'Aquinas's *Regimine benecommixtum* and the Medieval Critique of Classical Republicanism', *The Thomist*, 46, 1982, 195–220.

Kuiters, R., 'Aegidius Romanus and the authorship of *In utramquepartem* and *De ecclesiastica potestate*', *Augustiniana*, 8, 1958, 267–80.

Malloy, M.P., *Civil Authority in Medieval Philosophy: Lombard, Aquinas and Bonaventure*, Lanham, University Press of America, 1985.

Martin, C.J., 'Some Medieval Commentaries on Aristotle's *Politics*', *History*, 36, 1951, 29–44.

Nederman, C.J., 'Bracton on Kingship Revisited', *History of Political Thought*, 5, 1984, 61–77.

Nederman, C.J., 'The Royal Will and the Baronial Bridle: The Place of the *Addicio de Cartis* in Bractonian Political Thought', *History of Political Thought*, 9, 1988, 415–29.

Parel, A., 'Aquinas' Theory of Property', in A. Parel and T. Flanagan, eds, *Theories of Property, Aristotle to the Present*, Waterloo, Ont., Wilfred Laurier University Press, 1979.

Renna, T.J., 'Kingship in the *Disputatio inter clericum et militum*', *Speculum*, 48, 1973, 675–93.

Renna, T.J., 'Aristotle and the French Monarchy, 1260-1303', *Viator*, 9, 1978, 309–24.

Tierney, B., *The Foundations of the Conciliar Theory*, Cambridge, Cambridge University Press, 1955.

Part III

THE FOURTEENTH CENTURY

9

ON ROYAL AND PAPAL POWER
John of Paris

INTRODUCTION

With the rise of universities and of scholastic philosophy during the thirteenth century, the most common source of political theory soon became the Masters of the schools. John of Paris (*c.* 1250–1306), for example, had excellent academic credentials. A member of the Dominican order, John followed the prescribed course of study towards the position of Master of Arts at the University of Paris. He probably studied with Thomas Aquinas, and he certainly wrote a defence of Thomistic thought in about 1285, in response to Franciscan critics. In addition, John's name has been assigned to a wide range of other writings (approaching two dozen in number) on philosophical and theological topics. By the end of the thirteenth century, he was counted among the most prominent scholars at Paris. John's interest in political affairs seems to have developed late: his best known work on politics, *On Royal and Papal Power*, has been dated to 1302 (or possibly 1303), while his (just recently established) contribution to the composition of the treatise *Questions Regarding Papal Power* (commonly known by its opening words, *Rex pacificus* ['Peaceful king']) dates to the middle of 1303. These writings did not stimulate any direct ecclesiastical censure of John. Although he was deprived of his papal licence to teach in 1304 (a judgment which was under appeal at the time of his death), it was his theological views on the Eucharist which formed the source of his conflict with Church authorities.

John's sudden concern for political theory was mainly conditioned by contemporary events. Since 1296, the French King Philip IV (the Fair) had been engaged in a conflict with the papacy regarding his right to tax and exercise control over the French Church and its minions. The controversy had been conducted both through legal means (such as royal decrees and ecclesiastical censure) and through polemical disputes, in which increasingly extravagant claims were made by both parties and their advocates. The reigning pope, Boniface VIII, asserted for himself universal lordship over the entirety of the possessions and offices of the temporal realm, accruing to him because of his unique status as successor to Christ through his occupation of the See of St Peter. The proponents of the cause of the French Crown argued in response that the king was subject to no superior in earthly affairs within his jurisdiction, and could thus collect revenues from, appoint officials to, and impose judgement upon the Church. The French clergy (and especially the Dominicans) teaching at the University of Paris had sided over-whelmingly with the royal position; John of Paris' name is to be found among very many others on a petition urging Philip to bring Boniface to trial before a general council of the Church.

In developing the arguments of *On Royal and Papal Power*, John charts a relatively independent course. Despite his Dominican and Thomist asso-ciations, he does not merely restate the doctrines of Thomas Aquinas. In his conception of the nature and extent of papal power, especially, John develops a line of thought which lacks any foundation in the writings of Thomas, and which indeed reveals a thorough knowledge of canon law texts and of varying theories of church government. Likewise, he does not prove to be an unalloyed royalist: he maintains, for instance, that the property of lay persons belongs in the first instance neither to the pope nor to the king, but instead to private individuals themselves; although the secular ruler can claim what he requires for the sake of defending the common welfare, he is no more lord over the temporal goods of his subjects than the pope. As John intimates in his Prologue, his intellectual sensibilities lead him to seek a moderate path, a golden mean between contrasting excesses.

ON ROYAL AND PAPAL POWER

Prologue

It occasionally happens that in attempting to avoid a certain error one is impaired by a contrary error. Thus, we read of numerous people asserting on the basis of the *Decretum* [16.1.8] that monks, because they are dead to the world, cannot dispense the sacrament of baptism or bestow penance, since these are inconsistent with the calling which the monk answers. Others, attempting to avoid or perhaps forestall any such error, have said that the calling of monks, by which they are elevated to the perfect state, obliges them to hear confessions, to absolve, and to impose salutary penances. Sound doctrine is the mean between these two errors, considering that it is neither repugnant to the calling of the monk nor an obligation thereof, but it can be appropriate for him if it is entrusted to him by his bishop, who ought rightfully to do so. In the same way, it is shown in the book *On the Two Natures and One Person of Christ* [attributed to Boethius] that faith occupies a middle ground between two contrary errors, namely, that of Nestorius and that of Eutyches.

In a similar way, the truth regarding the ecclesiastical power of pontiffs lies in the middle between two errors. On the one hand, the Waldensians were mistaken that the successors of the apostles, namely, the popes and ecclesiastical prelates, are to resist lordship in temporal goods and are not permitted to possess temporal wealth. For this reason, they say that the Church of God, along with the successors of the apostles and true prelates of the Church of God, had lasted only down until Pope Sylvester I, in whose time (they say) the act of donation by the Emperor Constantine instigated the Roman Church, which is not the same thing as the Church of God, according to them. But they say that the Church of God has been extinguished except inasmuch as it is perpetuated by them and renewed by them. In support of such claims, they present these texts among others: 'Do not store up riches for yourself here on earth' (Matthew 6:19); 'Having food and that which clothes us, we are to be content with these.... Those who wish to become rich' etc. (1 Timothy 6:8–9); 'No one can serve God and mammon' (Matthew 6:24); 'Do not worry about what you eat in order to continue your life nor about clothes for your body' (Matthew 6:25); 'Look at the birds of the sky which neither sow nor reap' (Matthew 6:26); and Christ said to his disciples: 'Do not possess any gold or silver or money' (Matthew 10:9); 'Unless one has renounced everything which he possesses' etc. (Luke 14:33); 'Silver and gold is not mine' etc. (Acts 3:6). On the basis of these passages, they say that the prelates of the Church of God, the successors of the apostles, ought not to have lordship over temporal wealth.

On the other hand, there is the error of Herod, who, upon hearing of the birth of Christ the King, believed him to be an earthly king. An opinion seems to have been derived from this by certain modern men, who have turned away from the errors of the Waldensians to such a degree that they incline to the totally opposite view, so that they assert that the pope, inasmuch as he occupies the position of Christ on earth, has lordship over the temporal goods of rulers and barons, and rights of trial and jurisdiction over them. Moreover, they say that the pope has this power over temporalities in a more overarching manner than the ruler, since the pope has it on account of a primary authority and from God immediately, while the ruler has it from God mediated by the pope. And further they say that the pope does not have immediate power of execution except in certain cases as specified by the decretal *Per venerabilem* [*Decretals* 4.17.13]; it is the ruler who normally has the immediate power of execution, and those whom they single out as differing in viewpoint are said to be supporters of rulers. And if the pope sometimes says that he does not have temporal jurisdiction, this is to be said in respect of regular and immediate power of execution, or because he wishes to preserve the peace between rulers and the Church, or lest prelates become excessively prone to involve themselves with regard to temporal goods and secular affairs. In addition, they say that the pope possesses temporal goods differently than rulers and prelates, because only the pope is the true lord, so that he can absolve usurers at will from the penalties for usury and can at his own will remove property from someone else; and the pope's acts stand unchallenged even when he commits a sin, although he ought not to do these things except for a reasonable cause such as defence of the Church and the like; but other prelates and rulers are not lords but protectors, administrators, and stewards.

This opinion in regard to lordship over property was born not only out of the error of Herod, but it also seems to carry forward the error of Vigilantius. For everyone holds and ought to hold this: that the lord pope does nothing inconsistent with his proper condition, which is one of evangelical perfection. It is thus evident that, if the pope in his proper condition (inasmuch as he is pope and vicar of Christ) as lord of everything has abdicated property rights and rejected lordship over temporal goods, this is inconsistent with his proper condition, since it is suited to the opposite condition. Therefore, poverty and the deprivation of private lordship over external property is not evangelical perfection, as had been said by Vigilantius, about whom Augustine remarks in the book *On Christian Combat* that there are some people who, although seeming to be catholic, are in fact self-interested or who, seeking their own glory in the name of Christ, commit heresy. Among their number, Vigilantius had long ago emerged in Gaul (which had previously been free of such monstrous errors), supposing the condition of true wealth to equal that of poverty, just as earlier on Jovinian in Italy supposed true chastity to be equivalent to marriage.

Furthermore, this opinion seems to capture something of the arrogance of the Pharisees, who proclaimed that people offering tithes and sacrifices to God were not bound to render anything to Caesar, in order that they would receive an enlarged portion from those who had been made richer, as Jerome observes. In addition, this opinion seems hazardous, since by converting to the faith, the lordship over property which one had previously enjoyed is transferred to the supreme pontiff, as a result of which the faith is rendered less appealing and people refrain from belief, as the *Gloss on 1 Peter* 2:13 says. Indeed, there is to be apprehension regarding this opinion lest, while business affairs are conducted in the house of the Lord, an angry and stern Jesus might enter and cleanse his temple with nothing short of a whip and refashion it from a den of thieves into a house of prayer, just as Chrysostom says in the *Commentary on Matthew*.

Therefore, between these contrary opinions, the first of which everyone admits to be erroneous, I think that the truth lies in the middle, namely, that it is not inconsistent for prelates of the Church to have jurisdiction and lordship over temporal goods, contrary to the first erroneous opinion, and yet that this authority is not owed to them on the basis of their own proper condition and the fact that they are vicars of Christ and successors of the apostles. Rather, it can be appropriate for them to have such property as a result of the concession or permission of rulers, if it has been conceded to them by the devotion of some such persons or if they have acquired it elsewhere.

I proclaim that nothing I plan to say in any of my statements contradicts faith, good morals, sound doctrine, or reverence for the person or status of the supreme pontiff. And if any such thing might be presented, either directly or incidentally, among my words and remarks, I wish it to be taken as not said at all, wanting this declaration to apply and be in force as if specifically repeated before each and every statement made here....

Chapter 1: What royal government is and whence it had its origins

In the first place, it is to be understood that a kingdom can be defined thus: a kingdom is the perfected government of a multitude by one person for the sake of the common good.

In connection with this definition, 'government' is taken to be the genus, while 'multitude' is added in order to differentiate it from government in which each person governs himself, whether by natural instinct (in the manner of brute animals) or by one's own reason (in the case of those who lead a solitary life). It is called 'perfected' in order to differentiate the multitude from the family, which is not perfected because it is not self-sufficient, except for a short time, and is not adequate for a full life in the manner of the civil community, according to the Philosopher in Book 1 of the *Politics*. 'Arranged for the good of the multitude' is mentioned in order to differentiate it from tyranny, oligarchy and democracy, in which the governing party attends only to its own good, especially in the case of tyranny. 'By one person' differentiates a kingdom from an aristocracy, that is, the rule of the better or the best, wherein a few hold sway on account of their virtue, which certain people call government according to the advice of the prudent or the expertise of the senate, and differentiates it from *polycratia*, in which the people hold sway by means of popular decrees. For the king is no one but he who holds sway alone, as is said by the Lord through Ezekiel [34:23]: 'My servant David will be king over everyone and he will be the sole pastor over them all.'

Such government is derived from natural law and from the law of nations. For since a human is naturally a political or civil animal, as is stated in *Politics* Book 1 (which is demonstrated, according to the Philosopher, by the cases of food, clothing and defence, in which one person alone is inadequate, as well as by speech, which is directed towards others – all factors which are uniquely intrinsic to human beings), it is necessary that human beings live in a multitude and in such a multitude as suffices for life itself, which is not the household or the village community, but the city or kingdom, for in a single house or village, one does not find everything in respect of food and clothing and defence necessary for a full life, as one does find in a city or kingdom. A multitude in which everyone strives only for what is one's own will disperse and divide into diverse parts unless it is ordered towards the common good by some one person, just as the human body would pass away unless there were some common force within the body which directed it towards the common good of all the members. On account of this, Solomon says in Proverbs 11:14: 'Where there is no governor, the people will disperse.' For this is necessarily the case, insofar as what is individual and what is common are not the same. Everyone differs in regard to individual matters, yet they are united in regard to common matters. Moreover, diverse things have diverse causes, for which reason it is necessary that everyone should incline towards what is for the common good of the many as well as inclining towards what is for one's individual good.

Furthermore, the governance of a multitude by one person who is pre-eminent on account of virtue is more expedient than by many or a few virtuous people, as is evident not only in regard to potency, since virtue is more united and therefore stronger in one ruler than in many different ones, but also in regard to the unity and peace which ought to be the aim of the government of a multitude. For many rulers do not preserve the peace of a multitude unless they are united and harmonious. Therefore, if on account of these factors a single ruler in accordance with virtue can better serve the peace, and the peace of the citizens cannot be as easily disturbed, then also the single ruler aiming at the common good has more of an eye on common affairs than if many people were to hold sway in accordance with virtue, because when more people are removed from the community, there is less that remains in common, and when fewer people are removed, there is more remaining in common. On account of this, the Philosopher says that among all of the forms of government aiming at their own advantage, the tyrant is the worst because he aims more greatly at his own advantage and more greatly despises common affairs. Besides, in the natural order, we observe that everything is reduced to a single order, so that in a body composed of mixed elements a single part holds sway: in the heterogeneous human body there is one principal member, namely, the soul, which restrains all the elements throughout the whole body; likewise, gregarious animals such as bees and cranes, for whom it is natural to live in society, naturally submit to one ruler.

From what has been said above, it is evident that it is necessary and expedient for human beings to live in a multitude and particularly a multitude which can meet the needs of a full life, such as a city or territory, and most especially under one person ruling by reference to the common good, who is called a king. And it is also evident that this government is derived from natural law, namely, by reason that a human is in large measure naturally a civil or political and social animal, since before Belus and Ninus, who for the first time exercised rulership, human beings lived neither naturally nor even in human fashion, but instead they lived in the manner of beasts without rulership, as is reported by certain people mentioned by

Orosius in his *Against the Pagans*. And Tully [Cicero] says quite the same thing at the beginning of the *Old Rhetoric* [*De inventione*] and the Philosopher says of such creatures in the *Politics* that they do not live as human beings but as gods or beasts.

And since such human beings could not be recalled from the life of beasts to the communal life to which they are naturally suited solely through of their common speech, those human beings who were more experienced in reason struggled by means of persuasive reasoning to recall their erring companions to a common life ordered under some one person, as Tully says; and so recalled, they were bound by fixed laws to the communal way of life; these laws can indeed be called the laws of nations. And thus it is evident that such rulership is derived from both natural law and the law of nations.

Chapter 4: Which is prior in time, kingship or priesthood?

It ought now to be considered whether kingship or priesthood is prior in time. In regard to this, it is to be understood that 'kingship' is meant in its proper sense, inasmuch as it denotes not the rule of merely a household or village or city but of a province in which is found the greatest sufficiency of those things which pertain to a full life, and if we speak of priesthood in its proper sense, kingship was prior to priesthood. For as Augustine says in the *City of God*, Book 16, Chapter 17, the earliest of kingdoms was the kingdom of Assyria, which was founded long before the giving of the Law, since Belus first reigned in Assyria for 65 years, and upon his death his son, Ninus, reigned for 52 years, enlarging the kingdom over the whole of Asia Minor except India.

Having been king for 43 years when Abraham was born, Ninus existed about 1,200 years before the City of Rome was founded. Together with this kingdom, the kingdom of Sicyonii – the first king of which was Egyachus, whose son was Europs – was founded in Africa, although it was not so great in the beginning.

At the same time, among the worshippers of the true God may be found the King of Salem, whom the Hebrews called Sem, the son of Noah, and who is said to have lived up until the time of Isaac.

During these times, with the existence of true kings already long established, there was not yet a true priesthood for the sake of mediation between God and human beings until Jesus Christ. From this it is evident that, if it were said that there were priests among the Gentiles, these were not true priests, because they neither offered valid sacrifices nor knew the true God but only an approximation of Him; as Deuteronomy 32:17 says, 'They made sacrifices to demons and not to God.'

Therefore, if, according to the Old Law, certain persons of the tribe of Levi have been called priests of the people of God, still they were not true priests but they were a foreshadowing of the true priesthood, and their sacrifices were merely intimations and their sacraments were not real but intimations because they neither absolved from sin nor opened up heaven, but they foreshadowed the absolution of certain irregularities and they opened up the temple made by human hands, through which they foreshadowed the opening up of the temple made not by human hands but by Jesus Christ; and they did not promise spiritual goods except in a temporal form, as the Apostle says in Hebrews 10:1: 'The Law contains a hint of future goodness.' Prior to the Law, one encounters Melchisedech, the priest of the most high God, whose priesthood, although it may have been more perfect and more eminent than the priesthood of the Levites, was still solely an intimation and not true. For it was more perfect because it manifested precisely that feature of priesthood in which the priesthood of Christ had excelled the priesthood of Aaron. And the priesthood of Aaron was defective in its foreshadowing of the priesthood of Christ, namely, in regard to its perpetuity, since nothing is said in Scripture about Melchisedech having a beginning or end just as Christ does not have one, and in regard to many other points which the Apostle lays out in Hebrews [7]; yet such a priesthood was still an intimation and was not true in just the same way as the priesthood of the Levites.

It is to be understood, therefore, that there was no true priesthood until the priesthood of Jesus Christ for the sake of mediating between human beings and God; He makes us participants in and vicars of His priesthood.

Therefore, since before the birth of Abraham there were kings of the Assyrians, Sicyonii, Egyptians and some other peoples, and since there were, according to Methodius, two millenia from Abraham until the birth of Christ (or approximately so, according to others), it is evident that for a long period of time before there had been true priests, there had been true kings whose duties existed for the sake of the necessities of the civil life of human beings. For they were true kings, although in addition to this those kings who were anointed amongst the people of God also foreshadowed Christ....

Chapter 5: Which is prior in dignity, kingship or priesthood?

From the preceding, it should be evident whether kingship or priesthood is prior in dignity, for what is later in time is routinely held to be prior in dignity, as in the case of what is imperfect in relation to what is perfect or a means in relation to an end. And therefore we say that priestly power is greater than royal power and surpasses it in dignity, because we always perceive that whatever pertains to the ultimate end is more perfect and better, and it directs whatever pertains to an inferior end. Now kingship is ordained in order that the assembled multitude may live in accordance with virtue, as has been stated, and it is furthermore ordained for the sake of a higher end, which is the enjoyment of God, whose guiding trusteeship is entrusted to Christ whose ministers and vicars are priests. And therefore priestly power is of greater dignity than secular power, and this is commonly conceded: 'As lead

is not as precious as gold, so the priestly order is higher than royal power'
[*Decretum* 96.10]; and the decretal *Solitae* says that spiritual ends are to be
preferred to temporal goods just as the sun is preferred to the moon
[*Decretals* 1.33.6]; and Hugh of St Victor says: 'To the extent that the spiritual
life is of greater dignity than the earthly, and the soul than the body, so
spiritual power surpasses the honour and dignity of secular or earthly power'
[*On the Sacraments* 2.2.4]; and Bernard writes to Pope Eugenius: 'Does it
seem to you that dignity or power rests with the forgiveness of sins or rather
with the allotment of property? But there is no comparison', as if to say,
'Spiritual power is greater, therefore it is surpassing in dignity' [*On
Deliberation* 1.6].

And yet, if the dignity of the priest is ultimately greater than that of the
ruler, it is not necessary that it is greater in all ways. For the lesser, secular
realm does not hold its power from the greater, spiritual realm in such a
manner that the former originates in or was derived from the latter, as in the
case of the power which a proconsul holds from the emperor who is greater
in all matters, since the proconsul's power is derived from him; but secular
power is held in the manner of the head of the household in relation to that
of the commander of an army, since one is not derived from the other, but
both are given from some superior power. And therefore secular power is in
certain matters superior to spiritual power, namely, in respect of temporal
affairs, regarding which it is not subject to the spiritual realm since it does not
originate in that source, but instead both have immediate origins in a single
supreme power, namely, the divine one, on account of which the inferior is
not subject to the superior in all matters but only in regard to those in which
the supreme power has placed it beneath the greater realm. For who would
claim that, because a learned teacher of letters or a moral educator arranges
all the affairs of a household towards a more noble end, namely, knowledge
of the truth, he should therefore also subject the physician, who is concerned
with an inferior end, namely, knowledge of the body, in regard to the
administration of his medications? Surely this is not reasonable, since the
head of the household, who brought them both into the house, would not
have placed a greater authority over the physician in this way. Therefore, the
priest is greater than the ruler in spiritual matters and conversely the ruler is
greater in temporalities, although ultimately the priest is greater inasmuch as
the spiritual is greater than the temporal.

This is also demonstrated by examples from the authorities cited previously, for although gold may be more precious than lead, still lead is not
formed out of gold. This is expressly stated in *Decretum* 2.7.41. Yet it ought
to be observed that what is said here we must understand in regard to the true
priesthood of Christ. For the priesthood of the Gentiles and all veneration of
deities existed by means of temporalities arranged for the common good of
the multitude whose care fell under the king. Thus, the priests of the Gentiles
were set under the kings, and kingship was greater than priesthood in just

the same way as that power which concentrates upon the common good is greater than that which concentrates solely upon some particular good. Similarly, in the Old Law the only goods which the priesthood promised explicitly were temporal ones, although these were conferred upon the people not by demons but by the true God. Thus, in the Old Law the power of the priesthood was of less dignity than royal power, and the former was subjected to the latter, because the king was not directed by the priesthood towards anything other than the good of the multitude whose care fell upon him. And the converse is true of the New Law.

Also, it ought to be observed how, through the miraculous exercise of divine providence, there gradually grew up in the City of Rome, which God had prepared as the future principal seat of His priesthood, the practice among the leaders of the city of voluntarily subjecting themselves to priests more readily than in other places, although this was done not out of an obligation of justice, since they were greater in absolute terms than priests, but as a sign of the excellence of the future priesthood, to whom fuller reverence would be owed. In the words of Valerius:

> Our city always regards everything to be less important than religion, even in regard to matters in which those of the greatest distinction wish to display their own prestige, on account of which leaders do not hesitate to serve sacred causes, thus discerning that one will control human beings if the divine powers are properly and steadily served.
> [Valerius Maximus, *Memorable Words and Deeds* 1.1.9]

Moreover, since it would later be the case that the priesthood of the Christian religion would thrive best in France, it was divinely provided among the Gauls that Gentile priests (who have been named druids) were especially central throughout the whole of Gaul, as Julius Caesar writes in his book, *On the Gallic War*. Therefore, the power of the priesthood of Christ is of greater dignity than royal power.

Chapter 7: In what way the supreme pontiff is related to the goods of the laity

The preceding makes evident the way in which the pope relates to the goods of the laity, because as little as he has lordship over the external goods of the laity, even less is he steward over them, except perhaps in instances of extreme necessity, in which case he is not really a steward, but a proclaimer of right. In regard to what has been stated, it ought to be observed that the external goods of the laity are not bestowed upon the community as are ecclesiastical goods, but they are acquired by the personal art, labour or industry of individual people, and individuals, inasmuch as they are individuals, have right and power and true lordship over their goods, and each can ordain, dispose, administer, preserve and alienate his own goods according to his will without injury to anyone else, since he is lord. And thus such goods do not have an order or connection either between them or in relation to a single common head that may have them to dispose or administer, since each person is to be arranger of his own property according to his own will. Thus, neither the ruler nor the pope has lordship or stewardship over such things.

Yet because it sometimes occurs that the communal peace is disturbed on account of such external goods, insofar as a certain person usurps what belongs to another, and also because sometimes human beings who are too fond of their own goods do not share them in cases of necessity nor release them for the utility of the country, so a ruler, who takes charge of such matters, is appointed by the people with the result that there is a judge discerning between justice and injustice and an avenger of injuries and a fair measure in the acquisition of goods from individuals in accordance with just proportion for the necessity or utility of the community. Because the pope is a type of supreme head not only over the clergy but generally over all the faithful inasmuch as they are believers, in the manner of a general instructor of faith and morals, he has the power, in the case of a great threat to faith and morals (in which instance all the goods of the faithful, even the chalices of the churches, are communal, that is, are to be shared), to administer the external goods of the faithful and to discern how these are to be put to use in proportion to what the community contributes towards the needs of the faith, which might otherwise be subverted by the invasion of pagans or something of the sort; and such danger can be so dire and so clear-cut that the pope can extract tenths or fixed payments from individual believers for the sake of alleviating the threat to the common faith, although in accordance with due proportion lest someone is unjustifiably burdened more greatly than the others. And such a decree by the pope is nothing other than the proclamation of right. Moreover, he can compel resisters and opponents by means of ecclesiastical censure. In the same way also, the pope can ordain that the faithful contribute additional amounts from their goods up to what is adequate to meet the debts of their parish, if in some parish there were a multiplication of new believers to such an extent that traditional revenues could not suffice for the care of parishioners because it would be necessary to retain new priests to perform services; in this case, such a papal decree would be the proclamation of right. Yet except for such cases of necessity on behalf of the spiritual community, the pope does not have stewardship over the goods of the laity, but each disposes of his own goods just as he wills, and the ruler administers them in special cases for the good of the temporal community. In instances where there is no necessity, but where there is some spiritual utility, or where it is not agreed that the external goods of the laity are to be granted on account of such utility or necessity, the pope may not compel anyone, but the pope can give indulgences to the faithful for the performance of services and, I think, nothing else is granted to him.

10

THE BANQUET
Dante Alighieri

INTRODUCTION

Dante Alighieri (1265–1321) is best known to modern readers for his *The Divine Comedy*, the great three-volume tour through hell, purgatory, and heaven, which not only established Dante as a poet, but affected our culture deeply, providing for generations of readers imagery that has entered deep into our language. But Dante was very much involved in the political life of thirteenth-century Florence as well. Among other positions, he served on the city council several times, was city prior, and attempted to negotiate a peace treaty between the city's warring factions as its ambassador to Rome. Political turmoil, intrigue, and betrayal led to his exile, along with other political leaders of the outlawed White Guelf party.

In the time-honoured tradition of the philosopher-statesman, his exile led him to write his own 'Consolation', inspired, he tells us, by Cicero and Boethius, both philosophers and statesmen who became victims of political injustice. That work is *Convivio*, or *The Banquet*, in which the author describes himself as gathering the crumbs that fall from the philosophers' table (*Con.* 1 i). In this work, Philosophy, 'the daughter of God, queen of all, fairest and most noble', (*Con.* 2 xii) is the love of wisdom. Written from experience of political turmoil and injustice, out of dissatisfaction with the greed and envy of 'the social animal', Dante believed the only solution to be an imperial monarchy, a world united in an empire founded on Roman law and directed to the common good. This he describes in *Convivio*, from which our selection is taken. His more well known political work, *De Monarchia*, was written about 1309 when there was a newly elected emperor, Henry VII, who appeared to have the characteristics for which Dante hoped. After Henry's premature and suspicious death in 1313, a disillusioned Dante began what was to be his most famous work, *The Divine Comedy*, which was finally finished just before his death in 1321.

THE BANQUET

BOOK FOUR

Chapter 4 [The origins of imperial majesty]

The fundamental root of imperial majesty is the necessity of human society, which has only one purpose: a life of happiness. No one is sufficient in himself for its attainment without the aid of others, since a person needs many things which he cannot satisfy by himself. Thus, the Philosopher says, 'The human being is by nature a social animal.' And just as a person needs the domestic society of the family, so a household needs a neighbourhood, otherwise its deficiencies are an impediment to happiness. And a neighbourhood by itself cannot satisfy every need, so that a city is necessary. Yet the city also needs to cooperate and have friendly relations with surrounding cities for the sake of defence and trade. And so the kingdom was born.

Since the consciousness of the human spirit is not content with the possession of a limited amount of land, but always desires to acquire more land, experience has shown us that conflict and war spring up between kingdom and kingdom. Wars are an affliction to cities, and through cities, to neighbourhoods, and through neighbourhoods, to households, and from households to the individual; and these things are impediments to happiness.

And in order to end these wars and all their causes, it is necessary that the whole earth and all that humans can possess be a monarchy, that is, one government under one ruler. Because he possesses everything, the ruler would not desire to possess anything further, and thus, he would hold kings contentedly within the borders of their kingdoms, and keep peace among them. Thus cities would have peace, and in peace, neighbourhoods would have friendship, and because of this friendship, households would take care of all their needs, and finally, the person would live in happiness, which is the condition for which he was born.

And this is proven by the words of the Philosopher, who in his *Politics* says 'when the polity is directed to a single end, it is suitable that one person rules and directs, and that all the others are ruled and directed'. Just as on a ship there are many duties and many purposes directed towards one goal – to reach the desired port after a profitable voyage – in order that each officer plans his own activities to their proper goal, there is one whose responsibility is all the individual goals and who directs them to their final goal. He is the captain and all ought to obey him. The same principle is true in religious communities, in armies, and in anything where there is one end.

It is obvious that for the perfection of the universal religion of the human species, there must be someone like a captain. It is necessary to have one office with a universal and irrefutable right to command all the other officers needed according to the various situations in the world. And this supreme office is called 'rule' [*imperio*] without qualification, because its function is to govern all other offices. And the person who is appointed to this office is called 'emperor' [*imperadore*] because he rules all other rulers; what he says is law for everyone, and must be obeyed by all. The strength and authority of all other rule must come from his. And this is unmistakable; imperial majesty and authority are the highest in human society.

Of course, someone could argue, saying

> Although the office of emperor is necessary for the good of the world, it does not follow that the authority of the Roman prince as highest is rationally established, as you have intended to show. Roman power was not founded on reason, nor by a decree from a universal convention, but by force, which seems to be the opposite of reason.

To this the response is obvious: the choice of the highest official originates in the decision of God, otherwise the choice would not be equitable for all, since there was no other official whose intent is the good of all, who predates Him. Furthermore, there never has been, nor will there ever be, any sweeter nature in ruling, greater strength in maintaining, more subtlety in acquisition than the Italians have, especially that holy people [of Rome] whose blood is mixed with the noble blood of the Trojans. God has chosen them for that office.

This was the people most suitable for that office since it could not be obtained without the greatest strength of character or used without the greatest and most humane benevolence.

Thus it was not force that was the principal means to office of the Roman people, but divine providence which is the ultimate source of reason. With this Virgil agrees when in the first book of the *Aeneid* he has God say: 'To them [the Romans] I set no boundary in space or time. I have granted them empire, and it has no end.' Force, then, was not the moving cause (as believed the one who argued above) but the instrumental cause. Just as the blows of the hammer are a 'cause' of the knife, but the mind of its maker is the efficient or moving cause, so it is not force, but reason, indeed divine reason, that is the first cause of Roman empire and rule.

Chapter 9 [The limits of imperial authority]

To show truly that in the case of refuting or confirming the opinion of the Emperor on this subject, I do not owe him submission, I must call to mind what was said about the office of emperor. Imperial authority was established for the perfection of human life; it justly regulates and oversees all our activities and in so far as our activities extend, imperial majesty has jurisdiction, and is limited to its boundaries. Just as human arts and functions have boundaries limited by imperial rule, so that rule has boundaries and limits set by God. This is not so surprising since the functions and the arts of nature are limited in all its activities. So if we take the case of universal nature, its jurisdiction is limited to the universe, that is, the heaven and the earth, as is proven in the *Physics* and *On the Heavens and the Earth*. Thus the jurisdiction of universal Nature has certain finite limits and as a consequence particular limits, and so He has set limits who has no limits Himself. He is the first Good, that is, God, who has infinite capacity to enclose infinity.

Let us see the limits of our activities, that is, only those activities that are dependent on reason and the will, like digestive activity which is not human but natural. Properly speaking, our reason has four kinds of activity diversely considered and ordered. Some activities are only considered; it does not and cannot create any of them. This is the case of subjects like physics, metaphysics and mathematics. There are activities that reason examines and can create in itself, intellectual studies, like rhetoric. There are activities that reason examines and can create material things outside itself, as in the mechanical arts. All these activities, although equally the consequence of our will, do not depend on our will; just as perhaps we might wish that heavy things would move up by their own nature, or that a syllogism based on false premises would lead to a true conclusion, or that a house would be equally solid when set on an angle as lying square, it is not possible. For each of these activities is not, properly speaking, created by us; we discover them. They were created and made by a greater Maker.

Some other activities of our reason are a consequence of the will, such as hurting or helping someone, standing firm or running away in battle, chastity or lechery; each of them is dependent on our will. We are judged good or bad by them, for they are all properly ours, for what the will can accomplish is truly 'our' activity. And in all these activities there is equity to be conserved and inequity to be avoided, which equity can be lost for two reasons – either because we lack knowledge, or because we do not have the will to carry it out. Therefore, we have written law which shows it and commands it. As Augustine said, 'If this (equity) were known by humans, and carried out what they knew, written law would not be needed.' And the same principle begins the *Old Digest*, 'Written law is the art of goodness and equity.'

To write, to demonstrate, and to command this is the role of the official of whom we spoke, the emperor; we are subject to him in those areas that are included in our activities strictly speaking, and in no others. This principle is found in every art and craft: artisans and apprentices are subject to whomever is leader or master in the craft or in the art. Outside that area they are no longer subject, because there is no longer a leader. So one can speak of the emperor metaphorically as the 'rider' of the human will. How the horse behaves in the pasture when it is without the rider is clear enough, especially in miserable Italy which is left without government to care for it.

It ought to be realized that the more a thing belongs to an art or its master, the greater is it subjugation, for the greater the cause, the greater the effect. This means that certain matters are arts so purely that nature becomes an instrument of the art, for example, to row with an oar. There the art makes propulsion – a natural movement – its instrument. In forging iron, the art uses heat as its instrument, which is a natural quality. In such cases the obligation to be subject to the ruler or master is greater.

Then there is the case where the art is merely the instrument of nature; these are lesser arts. In these, the artisan is less subject to the ruler; for example, sowing seeds in the earth where the whole waits on the will of nature, or sailing out of port, where the principle is the natural disposition of the weather. Here we see more arguments among the artisans, and the superior taking counsel with the inferior.

There are other things, which are not an art, but appear to be, and then many people fall into error. In this case, the apprentices in the art are not subject to the master and are not obligated to follow him, as they are in what concerns the art. For example, fishing appears at first to belong to navigation, and knowledge of the qualities of herbs appears to be a part of agriculture. But they are not subject to the same rules; for fishing is part of the art of hunting, and the knowledge of herbs is a part of medicine, or some other, even more noble, discipline.

Similarly, the argument given for the other arts pertains in the art of ruling also. In this case, the laws which are about things that are pure arts, such as the laws regulating marriage, slavery, the military, and inheritance – in all these, without any doubt, we are subject to the emperor. Other laws, almost dictated by nature, such as that age which constitutes the status sufficient to hold office, we are not entirely subject. Now defining what constitutes youth or nobility, for example, might appear to belong to the art of ruling, but it is and will be an error to believe that the statement of the emperor is authoritative on this. Outside governing, no opinion of the emperor's is given consent merely because it is the emperor's. 'That which is God's, render to God.' So [for example], we ought not to believe or consent to the opinion of Nero who said that maturity consists in beauty and strength of body, but rather with him who says that maturity is the culmination of natural life, as a philosopher would say. It is thus clear that to define nobility [for example] is not part of the art of ruling, and if it is not part of the art, we are not subject to him in this, and if not subject we are not obligated to show him respect in it. This point has been the purpose of my discussion. Now with all liberty and freedom of spirit, we may run a sword through the common opinions, throw them on the ground, so that by my victory over them, true opinion may hold in the minds of those for whom the truth shines vigorously!

11

THE DEFENDER OF THE PEACE
Marsiglio of Padua

INTRODUCTION

No political thinker of the late Middle Ages has been more controversial than Marsiglio of Padua (*c.* 1275–1342/43). Born into a prominent professional family, Marsiglio received his advanced training in medicine. During the 1310s and early 1320s, he was a Master of Arts at the University of Paris, of which he was the Rector in 1313. Simultaneously, he served as an advisor to and delegate on behalf of several important figures in Northern Italian politics. Marsiglio completed his most famous work, *The Defender of the Peace*, in June 1324. Initially, the work circulated anonymously, and when his authorship of it was made public in 1326, he immediately fled Paris, seeking protection at the court of the embattled German Emperor, Ludwig of Bavaria. Ludwig was in the midst of a lengthy (and ultimately unresolved) conflict with the papacy (which since 1305 had been domiciled at Avignon in France) over its refusal to recognize his claim to the imperial title and thus to the prerogatives to which office entitled him in Germany and Italy. Marsiglio seems to have had a hand in planning and promoting Ludwig's 1327 expedition across the Alps and down the Italian peninsula, which culminated in the Emperor's entry into Rome and coronation by representatives of the Roman people. Marsiglio acted as Ludwig's aid and ambassador throughout the journey, for which he was rewarded with imperial appointment as 'Spiritual Vicar' of Rome. The Roman citizenry soon became disenchanted with their new master and his entourage, however, and an embarrassed Ludwig was forced to return to Germany in 1329. Marsiglio remained at Ludwig's court during the 1330s, but produced no new writing of which we are aware until the end of the decade, when he composed a summary and restatement of the main principles of *The Defender of the Peace*, entitled *The Defender Minor*, as well as several shorter pieces.

The Defender of the Peace is organized into three major sections (or discourses). Discourse I discusses the origins and nature of earthly political authority; the second discourse, nearly quadruple the length of the first, critically surveys a variety of claims made on behalf of the power of the priesthood and, particularly, the papacy; a brief third discourse summarizes those conclusions derived from the preceding discussions that Marsiglio regards as especially useful or worthy of emphasis. The structural division between the substance of Discourses I and II is unusual for its time, inasmuch as it implies a distinction between the treatment of temporal government and of ecclesiastical affairs. Yet *The Defender* is by no means two separate, self-subsistent and internally coherent treatises. Rather, a single central theme binds it together as a whole: the danger posed to human happiness (as experienced in the peaceful and self-sufficient community) by the interference of papal government in secular life. Marsiglio expressly proclaims the purpose of *The Defender* to be the demonstration of the 'singular cause' of dissension that infects parts of Europe (specifically, Northern Italy, sometimes called the 'Italian kingdom'). The force of *The Defender*'s argument is directed towards revealing the disruptive effects of the papacy's attempts to regulate temporal affairs. The first discourse stipulates the arrangements necessary to bolster the stability and unity of secular communities so as to repulse papal interference, while Discourse II substitutes the principles of papal monarchy with those of a Church governed by a General Council of faithful Christians.

The secular political theory of *The Defender* has sometimes been characterized in terms of 'popular sovereignty' or has been singled out for its 'democratic' overtones. It is true that Marsiglio seems to regard consent as the touchstone of good government. But his notion of consent is very different from our own; agreement to laws and rulers is for Marsiglio a product of rational reflection on the dictates of justice and the common welfare, rather than the result of the calculation of self-interest narrowly construed. Moreover, consent is the outcome of a discursive, rhetorical process through which all, or virtually all, citizens agree to accept the proposed statute or ruler; Marsiglio's argument supports communal decision-making which arises from active civic participation and consensus rather than the more passive notion of consent associated with the representative and majoritarian conception of government.

THE DEFENDER OF THE PEACE

DISCOURSE I

Chapter 1: Regarding the overall plan of the matters to be considered, and the rationale for the plan, and the division of the books

1.

Every kingdom ought surely to be desirous of tranquility, through which peoples profit and the utility of nations is maintained. For this is the proper mother of worthwhile acts. Increasing each new generation of human progeny, this extends the faculties and refines the characters of mortal creatures. And he who is seen to have no desire for it is understood to be ignorant of such matters.

[Cassiodorus, Variae I.1]

Cassiodorus, in the first of his letters which we have just quoted, extols the advantages or fruits of the tranquility or peace of civil governments, so that by setting forth the importance of these things as the greatest of human goods, namely, the sufficient life, he stimulates the wills of human beings towards the maintenance of peace amongst one another and hence tranquility. In this regard, he has expressed himself in conformity with the judgement of the blessed Job, who said in his twenty-second chapter [22:21]: 'Maintain peace, and through this you shall have the greatest fruits.' Consequently, also, Christ, the son of God, decreed that this was to be the sign and declaration of his new birth, insofar as he wished the choir of the heavens to sing in these words: 'Glory to God in the highest, and on earth peace to men of good will' [Luke 2:14]. On account of this also, Christ had very often desired the peace of his disciples, for which reason it says in John [20:19]: 'Jesus came and stood among the disciples and said: "Peace to you."' Instructing them in regard to the observance of peace amongst one another, he said in Mark [9:50]: 'Maintain peace between you.' He had taught them not only to maintain this amongst themselves, but to desire it for others, for which reason he says in Matthew [10:12]: 'Upon entering a house, pay respects to it, saying, "Peace to this house."' Once again, this was the inheritance which he left in his testament to his disciples at the time of his passion and death, insofar as he says in John 14[:27]: 'I leave you peace; my peace I give you.' And in his likeness, the Apostles, as the true heirs and imitators of him, desired this for those to whom they directed letters of evangelical teaching and advice, knowing peace to be the greatest fruit, just as is revealed by Job and explained more fully by Cassiodorus.

2. Yet since 'contraries are created by their contraries' [Aristotle, *Physics*, 5.8], there emerge from the opposite of tranquility, discord, the worst fruits or disadvantages of any city or kingdom, as one may adequately see, and as is revealed to virtually everyone, in the case of the Italian kingdom. For so long as the inhabitants of Italy had lived together peacefully, they had harvested the sweet fruits of peace already enumerated, from which and in which they had gained such advantages that they subjected the inhabitants of the whole world to their rule. Yet discord and conflict arose between them, their kingdom was plagued by many sorts of burdens and inconveniences, and their authority was assailed by foreign and unknown nations. And in this way it is once again buffeted from all sides on account of virtually unrestrained conflict, so that it is presently open to easy invasion by whomever wishes to occupy it and is capable of doing so; nor do I deem such

an event worthy of surprise, since (in regard to the matter of Jugurtha) Sallust testified: 'Small matters increase by concord, but great affairs are ruined by discord' [*Jugurtha* 10.6]. On account of being led astray into error, the natives are deprived of a sufficient life, suffering heavy burdens instead of sought-after calm and the harsh yoke of perpetual tyranny instead of liberty; and consequently, they are made so much more unhappy with civil lives than others that eventually their inherited name, customarily occasioning invocations of glory and freedom, is reproached for its dishonourable passions by all other nations.

3. Into this headlong fall into darkness, therefore, these miserable creatures are carried on account of the discord and quarrels among them which, like the sickness of an animal, is thus diagnosed to be the deformed disposition of civil government. Although there are many primary causes of discord, and there are not a few interconnections among them, which are capable of occurring in the normal manner, almost all were described by the distinguished Philosopher in the *Civil Science*; yet there is a certain additional unique and extremely obscure cause, which has long burdened the Roman Empire, and burdens it still, one which is never less than highly contagious and is inclined to spread slowly into all cities and kingdoms, and has already attempted in its covetousness to invade most of them. And the origins and character of this could have been perceived neither by Aristotle nor by any other philosopher of his time or earlier. For this cause is and was a certain perverted opinion, to be explicated subsequently by us, occasioned as the result of a miraculous effect (produced by the Supreme Cause beyond the possibilities of inferior nature and the normal actions of causes in physical objects) which occurred long after the time of Aristotle. This sophism, wearing an honourable and useful face, is wholly pernicious to the human species and to all civil bodies and countries; if it is not restrained, it will ultimately beget unbearable injuries.

4. Therefore, as we have said, peace and tranquility are the greatest goods; the opposite, quarrels, are unbearable injuries; on account of this, we ought to desire peace, to seek it when it is not maintained, to preserve it when it is obtained, and to repel with every effort the quarrels which oppose it. Towards this end, also, individual brethren, and even more associations and communities, are bound to aid one another, as much out of the affection of heavenly love as out of a bond or right of human society. In regard to this, Plato admonishes us (as witnessed by Tully in *On Duties*, Book I[.7.22]), when he says: 'We are not born for ourselves alone, but our country claims for itself one part of our birth, and our friends another part.' To this statement Tully added the conclusion:

> Moreover, as the Stoics believe, everything on the earth is created for the use of human beings, so that they may be able to assist one another. We ought in this to follow nature as our leader, to contribute to the common stock that which benefits everyone together.

It would be of no little common utility, indeed a necessity, to reveal the sophism of the unique cause of those quarrels already mentioned, which are threatening no little injury to kingdoms and also communities; each person who is willing and able to discern the communal utility is bound to supply his vigilant attention and diligent effort to this goal. For if this is concealed, then the disease can in no way be avoided, nor can its pernicious effects upon kingdoms and cities be completely curtailed.

5. Moreover, no one ought to neglect attention to this out of fear or sloth or any other form of mean spiritedness. For as 2 Timothy 1[:7–8] says, 'God gives us not the spirit of fear but of strength and affection': the strength and affection, I say, to set forth the truth, for which reason the same Apostle adds: 'And so do not be embarrassed at the testimony of our Lord'; moreover, this was the testimony of truth, for the sake of the demonstration of which Christ said that he had come to the world, insofar as John 18[:37] says: 'I was born for this, and I came into the world for the sake of this: that the truth be demonstrated by testimony', namely, in order to lead the human species to eternal salvation. Therefore, his example of teaching truth, by which the already mentioned disease of civil governments is able to be halted within the human species, especially the worshippers of Christ, is to lead to the life of civil well-being, while also progressing in no little way towards eternal salvation. This is meant to be more binding on him upon whom the Giver of grace has bestowed greater understanding of such matters, and all the more heavily upon him who, in an ungrateful manner, sins by disregarding what he knows and can do, as James testifies in Chapter 4[:17] of his canon when he says: 'It is a sin that one knows to do the good and does not do it.' For otherwise this injury, the common enemy of the human species, would not be completely cut down, nor would the pernicious fruits which have thus far been yielded wither away, unless the iniquity of its cause or root is first exposed and censured. For in this way and in no other can the coercive power of rulers safely be devoted to the final assault upon the unscrupulous patrons and obstinate defenders of this malice.

6. And so, heeding and obeying the above mentioned advice of Christ, the saints and the philosophers, I, son of Antenor, out of an understanding of these matters (if such grace may be credited to me), and in a spirit which was furnished from above (about which James testifies in the first chapter of his canon [1:17]: 'Every great good and every perfect gift given descends from the father of lights above'); on account of reverence for the Giver, love of setting forth the truth, fervent charity towards country and brethren, compassion for the oppressed, and for the sake of preserving the oppressed, recalling the oppressors from their straying errors, and inciting those who surrender to these conditions to oppose them instead insofar as they should and can do so; in connection with perceiving that you uniquely, the most glorious Ludwig, Emperor of the Romans, who as God's minister will confer upon the goal of these actions that fulfilment the occurrence of which is

desired, and who as though by some special ancient right of birth, no less than by your heroic nature and splendid virtue, is innately and firmly devoted to eradicating heresies, to exalting and preserving the universal truth and every other discipline of study, to destroying vice, to extinguishing quarrels, and to spreading and nourishing peace and tranquility everywhere; I have thus committed the following thoughts to the written page, after a period of diligent and intense reflection, thinking that your vigilant majesty could derive something beneficial from them, since you are attentive to the already noted faults and other occurrences and to caring for other matters of public utility.

7. It is my intention, therefore, with the aid of God, to reveal only this unique cause of quarrels. For it would be superfluous to rehearse the number and nature of the causes which were ascribed by Aristotle; but we wish to uncover the veil from that one cause which Aristotle could not have perceived and which no other person who could have done so has undertaken to delineate, so that it can be readily excluded from succeeding kingdoms and cities, and by this exclusion devoted rulers and subjects can live in more secure tranquility. This was the desirable aim that was proposed at the beginning of the present work, necessary for civil happiness to be enjoyed, which seems to be the greatest possible good to be desired by human beings in this world and the end of human action.

8. And so I shall arrange my already mentioned proposed endeavours by means of three discourses. In the first of these, I shall demonstrate my intent by a certain method ascertained by unaided human nature, consisting of propositions self-evident to the mind of whomever is not perverted by a corrupted nature, habit or affection. In the second, that which I believe to have been demonstrated, I shall confirm by securing the testimony of truth in eternal form, and its interpretation by saintly authors and other approved learned teachers of the Christian faith, so that this book may stand on its own, not lacking in external evidence. Hence, I shall impugn the falsehoods opposed to my conclusions, and I shall expose the complicated sophisms through which their opponents obstruct such conclusions. And in the third, I will infer certain conclusions or useful precepts, to be observed by civic rulers as well as subjects, on the basis of the clear certainty contained in the earlier conclusions....

Chapter 2: On the first questions in this book, and the definition and meanings assigned to the word 'kingdom'

1. And undertaking our plan, we first aim to reveal what constitutes the tranquility and intranquility of the kingdom or city, yet starting with tranquility, for without revealing this, one is necessarily ignorant of what constitutes intranquility. And since both of these seem to be dispositions of the city or kingdom, as was supposed by Cassiodorus, we shall consequently reveal what is initially to be disclosed: what constitutes a kingdom or city and

for what reason; thereafter, the definitions of tranquility and its opposite will become more fully apparent.

2. Resolving to define the tranquility of the city or kingdom in accordance with the aforementioned design, lest on account of the multiplication of terminology ambiguity might emerge in our plan, it is necessary not to keep obscured that the word 'kingdom' in one of its meanings denotes a plurality of cities or provinces held together under one government; according to this understanding, a kingdom does not differ from a city in regard to the species of polity, but more on account of quantity. In another of its meanings, the word 'kingdom' signifies a certain species of temperate polity or government which Aristotle calls 'temperate monarchy'; in this manner, a kingdom can exist in a single city just as in many, as was the case at the time of the origin of civil communities, for in virtually all of them there was one king in a single city. The third and most renowned meaning of this term is composed out of the first and second ones. Its fourth sense expresses something common to every species of temperate government, whether in a city or in a plurality of cities, which was the meaning of the term adopted by Cassiodorus in the statement which we quoted at the beginning of this book, and according to which we will use the word in the resolution of the questions at hand.

3. Thus, turning to the definition of tranquility and its opposite, we maintain in accordance with Aristotle in his *Politics*, Book I, Chapter 5 and Book 5, Chapter 3, that the city is somewhat like an animate nature or animal. For just as an animal well disposed in accordance with nature is composed out of certain parts arranged in proportion to one another, and with their functions arranged according to mutual intercommunication and for the sake of the whole, so the city is constituted out of certain such components when it has been well disposed and instituted in accordance with reason. Therefore, the sort of relation between an animal and its parts that exists for the sake of health would seem to be on par with the relation between a city or kingdom and its parts that exists for the sake of tranquility. The credibility of such an inference we can accept on the basis of what everyone understands about each of these relations. For as health appears to be the best disposition of animals in accordance with nature, so likewise tranquility appears to be the best disposition of the city in accordance with its institution by reason. Moreover, health, as the more skilled physicians say in describing it, is the good disposition of the animal, in which each of its parts can perform completely the tasks appropriate to its nature; in accordance with this analogy, tranquility would be the good disposition of the city or kingdom, in which each of its parts can perform completely the tasks appropriate to it in accordance with reason and its institution. And because a proper definition equally indicates its contrary, intranquility will be the diseased disposition of a city or kingdom, in the manner of an illness of an animal, in which all or some or its parts are impeded from performing their appropriate functions, either entirely or satisfactorily.

In this figurative way, therefore, tranquility and its opposite, intranquility, may be defined by us.

Chapter 3: On the origin of the civil community

1. Moreover, since we have called 'tranquility' the good disposition of the city for the sake of the functions of the parts, it is consequently necessary to attend to what and why the city on its own account exists; which and how many are its primary parts; and, furthermore, what function is appropriate to each one of them, and what the cause is, and how they are arranged in relation to one another; for these are the foremost tasks for the sake of a complete definition of tranquility and its opposite.

2. Yet before we deliberate about the city, which is the perfected community, and its species or modes, we ought first to present the origins of civil communities and their governments and modes of life. From imperfect sorts [of associations], human beings have proceeded to perfected communities, governments and modes of life in them. For the progress of nature, and also of its imitator, art, is always from the less perfect to the more perfect. Human beings do not suppose that anything is otherwise known except 'when they know its first causes and primary principles right down to its elements' [Aristotle, *Physics* 1.1].

3. Consequently, advancing in accordance with this method, it is necessary not to conceal that civil communities began with very small units spread throughout different regions and times, and gradually taking hold, they were led by a series of steps to final completion, just as we already observed occurring in every process of nature or art. For the first and smallest combination of human beings, from which all others originate, was that of male and female, as the most distinguished of the philosophers says in *Politics*, Book I, Chapter 1 and as is furthermore apparent from his *Economics*. As a result of this, of course, human beings are propagated, all of whom at first fill one household; from this, more such combinations are created, and the propagation of human beings is achieved to so great an extent that a single household is not adequate for them, but it is necessary to create many households, a number of which taken together are called a village or neighbourhood, and this was the first community, as is also written in the above mentioned work.

4. Yet so long as human beings lived in a single household, all their actions, especially those which we will later call 'civil', were regulated by their elders as persons of greater discernment, although without any laws or customs, because these could not yet have been invented. And not only were the human beings of a single household ruled in this way, but also the first community, called the village, was ruled in virtually the same fashion, although some of them were ruled differently. Even though the head of a single household was permitted to forgive or punish domestic injuries

entirely on the basis of his will and pleasure, still this would not have been permitted to the chief of the first community, called the village. For in the latter case, the elder ought to determine matters of right and advantage on the basis of some reasonable regulation or quasi-natural law, since this would have seemed appropriate to everyone as the result of a certain equity, without great investigation but only out of the common direction of reason and a certain duty of human society.

The reason for such a difference between the governance of a single household and a neighbourhood is and was: if one brother from the single and first household or domestic family had killed or otherwise committed an offence against his brother, then the head of the household was permitted, if he willed, not to punish the transgressor by the most extreme penalty without risk of untoward consequences thereafter, because the injury would seem to be done solely to the forgiving father, and on account of the scarcity of human beings, as well because the head of the household would be less injured and sorrowful to be deprived of one son than two; this is what our earliest ancestor, Adam, would seem to have done when his first-born son, Cain, murdered his brother, Abel. For the relation of father to son does not properly pertain to civil justice, as is written in the *Ethics*, Book 4 [Chapter 10], in which the 'treatise on justice' is contained. In the first community of the village or neighbourhood, however, such a situation neither was permitted nor would be permitted, on account of the aforementioned differences; indeed, unless injuries had been avenged or were rendered subject to equity by the elder, there would have occurred or will occur the fighting and consequent separation of the neighbours.

In spite of the multiplying of villages and the enlargement of the community, the progress of which was necessitated by propagation, these would still have been ruled by one person (whether on account of the lack of a large number of prudent persons, or some other such cause, as is written in *Politics*, Book 3, Chapter 14), yet one who would have been older and better, so that the regulations according to which they were arranged were less imperfect that in the individual village or household. The first communities did not, however, have so great a differentiation and ordering of parts, or the most necessary arts and rules of living, as were later to be contrived in the ensuing perfected community. For sometimes the same person was a ruler and a farmer or shepherd, as in the case of Abraham and a large number of his offspring; yet in perfected communities this is neither expedient nor permitted.

5. With the ensuing development of this community, the experience of human beings was augmented, arts and rules and more perfected modes of living were invented, by means of which a more complete differentiation of the parts of the community was achieved. At last, these things which were necessary to live and to live well were led to completion by means of human reason and experience, and the perfected community (called the city) was

instituted along with its different parts, to the demarcation of which we shall immediately advance.

Such comments, therefore, suffice in regard to the origin of the civil community.

Chapter 4: On the final cause of the city, and the aims of the civil body, and the differentiation in general of its parts

1. According to Aristotle in the *Politics*, Book I, Chapter 2, the city is 'the perfect community having all the marks of self-sufficiency, as a result of which it is said to be created for the sake of living, but to exist for the sake of living well.' When Aristotle says, 'to be created for the sake of living, but to exist for the sake of living well', he means its perfect final cause, since those living civilly not only live, as do beasts or slaves, but they live well, namely, free for liberal activities such as are constituted by the practical as well as the theoretical virtues of the soul.

2. Consequently, settling upon the end of the city as living and living well, it is necessary first to consider living and its modes. For, as we have said, it is for the sake of this end that the city is instituted, and it is necessary for everything which exists and is done for means of human association within it. Therefore, we establish as the starting point of everything to be demonstrated a view which is naturally accepted, believed and freely conceded by everyone: namely, that all human beings who are not deranged or otherwise impeded naturally desire a sufficient life, and also evade and shun injuries to it. This is granted not only about human beings, but also about all species of animals by Tully in *On Duties*, Book I, Chapter 4, insofar as he says:

> From the beginning nature has assigned to every type of creature the tendency to preserve itself, its life and body, and to reject that which seems to be of harm, and it seeks and procures all of those things which are necessary for the sake of living.

Moreover, this can be understood on the basis of sense experience evident to everyone.

3. The form of living and living well appropriate to human beings exists in two ways: the one sort is temporal or earthly, the other is normally called eternal or heavenly. This second way of living, namely, eternally, could not be demonstrated by the proofs of all the philosophers, nor was it a self-evident truth, therefore they were not concerned about instruction in those matters which were related to it. But in regard to living and living well or the good life in accordance with its first mode, namely, the earthly one, and also those things which were necessary on account of it, such matters were comprehended almost completely by the proofs of the glorious philosophers. For the sake of the attainment of the good temporal life, they deduced the necessity of the good civil community, without which this

sufficiency of life could not be obtained. The most eminent of them, Aristotle, says in his *Politics*, Book I, Chapter 2: 'All human beings are led toward it, and are drawn close to it in accordance with nature.' Although sense experience teaches this, still we wish to present more distinctly that cause of which we have spoken, by pointing out that because humans are born composed out of contrary elements, on account of which something of their substance is almost constantly being destroyed by contrary actions and passions; and because they are born naked and weak in relation to the excesses of enveloping air and the other elements, and are exposed and corruptible, as is said in the science of nature; so they require arts of diverse kinds and types for the sake of avoiding the already mentioned injuries. Since these cannot be exercised except by a large plurality of human beings, and cannot be enjoyed except by means of their association with one another, it was necessary for human beings to be congregated together for the sake of obtaining advantage from these arts and shunning disadvantage.

4. Yet because between human beings thus congregated contentions and disputes occur, which would cause fighting and the separation of human beings and eventually the decay of the city were they not regulated by means of a norm of justice, it is necessary to establish in this association both just rules and a custodian or administrator of them. And because this custodian has to prevent the transgressions of criminals and other individuals inside as well as outside the community from disturbing or attempting to oppress it, it is necessary for the city to have within it something which may stand up to these persons. Again, because the community requires certain sorts of advantages, repairs, and guardianship over common affairs, and one sort in time of peace and another sort in time of war, it was necessary for these to be providers of such things, in order that common needs could be met when it was expedient or necessary. In addition to those things already specified, which only meet the needs of the present life, there is something else which members of the civil association require for the sake of the condition of the future world, promised to the human species by the supernatural revelation of God, and also useful for the sake of the condition of the present life, namely, the worship or honour of God, and the act of offering thanks for benefits received in the present world as well as those to be received in the future; towards this end, the city ought to assign certain learned teachers to give instruction to human beings and to direct them in connection with supernatural affairs....

5. Therefore, human beings were drawn together on account of a sufficient life, through which they were able to procure for themselves the requisites enumerated before and to exchange them amongst one another. This assemblage, thus possessing perfection and ultimate self-sufficiency, is called the city, the final cause of which and of many of its parts was already stated by us to some extent and will be further delineated in what follows. For because different things are required by those who wish to live

sufficiently, which cannot be procured by human beings of a single order or office, it is necessary for there to be different human orders or offices within this association, occupying themselves with or procuring such different sorts of things as human beings require for a sufficient life. Moreover, these different human orders or offices are nothing other than the many and separate parts of the city.

It may suffice, therefore, to have thus summarized briefly in outline form what constitutes the city, and for what reason such an association may be created, as well as the number and apportionment of its parts.

Chapter 12: Regarding the demonstrable efficient cause of human laws, and also that one which cannot be proved by means of demonstration; to inquire what is the legislator. For this reason it also appears that what is established by election is granted authority from election alone apart from other confirmation of it

1. This is to be the occasion for speaking about that efficient cause of law which can be identified by means of demonstration; for I do not intend to make comment here about those ordinances which the deed or word of God without human decision is capable of creating or which already exist, in the manner of the institution of the Mosaic Law about which we have spoken, even though some of them are precepts in regard to civil acts for the sake of the condition of the present world; but I intend only to comment upon the institution of those laws and governments which arise from the decision of the human mind.

2. In advancing towards this goal, we may say that the ascertaining of the law, taken in an almost material fashion and in accordance with its third meaning [in Chapter 11], namely, the science of civil justice and advantage, can pertain to any citizen whomsoever, although this examination can be conducted more conveniently and completed better by those able to have the time for such observation – those persons of greater age and more proven in matters of action who are called 'prudent' – rather than by the consideration of mechanics, who direct their tasks towards the acquisition of the requisites of life. Yet since the knowledge or discovery of the true, the just and the advantageous, and also of their opposites, is not law in accordance with its final and proper sense, according to which it is the standard of the civil acts of human beings, except insofar as a coercive precept is declared in regard to its observance or something had been propounded on the basis of such precepts by the authority of one who can and should restrain transgressors, therefore it is appropriate to identify the persons who have the authority of making such precepts and of restraining transgressors against them; this is, in fact, to inquire after the legislator or law maker.

3. We may affirm in accordance with the truth and counsel of Aristotle's *Politics*, Book 3, Chapter 11, that the 'legislator' or primary and proper

efficient cause of the law is the people or corporate body of citizens, or the more dominant part of them, by means of their election or volition expressed through words in a general assembly of citizens regarding the commanding or prescribing of things to be done or omitted in regard to the civil acts of human beings under threat of temporal penalty or punishment: I say 'more dominant part' in order to take into account the quantity and quality of the persons within that community over which the law is decreed; either the above mentioned corporate body of citizens or its more dominant part has made law by itself immediately or it has some person or persons to do so, in which case they neither are nor can be the legislator in an absolute sense, but they only legislate in regard to a given matter and for a limited time and in accordance with the authority of the primary legislator. And I consequently assert that this same primary authority and no other ought to undertake the necessary approval of laws and anything else to be instituted by means of election, regardless of what may be conceded with regard to certain ceremonies or rites which are conducted not for the sake of the actual performance of the election but for the sake of its thorough performance, even though such an election would be no less valid without their performance; moreover, the laws and other matters which are established by means of election should by the same authority undergo additions or deletions or total alterations, interpretations and suspensions, according to the demands of time or place and other circumstances in view of which some such changes were appropriate on account of the common advantage. In addition, the laws ought to be promulgated or proclaimed by the same authority after their institution, lest any citizen or foreigner be excused from them on account of his ignorance.

4. I also say that the citizen, according to Aristotle in the *Politics*, Book 3, Chapters 1, 3 and 13, is he who participates in the ruling or counselling or adjudicating functions of the civil community according to his rank. By means of this definition, citizens are distinguished from children, slaves, foreigners and women, although according to different factors. For the children of citizens are citizens in proximity of capacity merely on account of the defect of age. One ought to treat the more dominant part of the citizens in accordance with the honourable customs of polities, or one ought to prescribe it in accordance with the judgment of Aristotle in the *Politics*, Book 6, Chapters 3 and 4.

5. In view of such a delineation of the citizen and of the more dominant multitude of citizens, we may return to the proposed intention, namely, demonstrating that the authority of the human legislator pertains solely to the corporate body of the citizens or its more dominant part. That this is the case we may first attempt to conclude as follows. The primary absolute human authority of making or instituting the laws of human beings pertains solely to those from whom the best laws can originate. This is the corporate body of citizens or its more dominant part, which represents the whole corporate

body, since it is not easy or not possible for all persons to agree upon a single judgement, on account of the fact that some people are naturally deprived, dissenting from the common judgement as a result of extraordinary malice or ignorance; the common advantage should not be impeded or neglected because of such irrational protest or opposition. Therefore, the authority of making or instituting law pertains entirely to the corporate body of citizens or its more dominant part.

The first proposition of this proof is very nearly self-evident.... I support the second proposition of the proof – namely, that the best law is decreed only with the hearing and command of the general multitude – with reference to Aristotle in the *Politics*, Book 3, Chapter 13, that the best law is that which is made for the sake of the common advantage. For this reason, he says: 'Perhaps also right', namely, law, 'exists for the sake of the advantage of the city and the community of citizens'. That this is best accomplished only by means of the corporate body of citizens or its more dominant part (which may be regarded as interchangeable) I demonstrate thus: on account of such a legislator, the truth towards which the minds and dispositions of the whole corporate body of citizens are directed is more certainly judged and its common utility is more diligently considered. For a defect in regard to a law proposed for establishment can be better noticed by a great plurality than by any of its parts, since every totality, at least of a corporeal nature, is greater in size and strength than any of its separate parts. In addition, the common utility of a law is better considered by the general multitude, because no one harms oneself knowingly. In that case, anyone can inspect whether a proposed law inclines more towards the benefit of one or a few people rather than others or the community, and can protest against it; this would not happen if the law itself was decreed by one or a few such people, who would consider their own benefit more than the common benefit....

6. The following point may also be made on behalf of the principal conclusions: the authority of making laws pertains only to those whose decrees will be observed either better or at all. But this is only the corporate body of citizens; therefore, the authority of making laws pertains to it. The first proposition of this proof is very nearly self-evident, for law would be useless if it were not observed. For this reason, Aristotle says in the *Politics*, Book 4, Chapter 8: 'For a well-fashioned law not to be obeyed means that the law is not of a good disposition.' Aristotle also says in Book 6, Chapter 8: 'Nothing is achieved by forming a given judgement regarding justice, yet not perceiving its application.' I prove the second proposition as follows: that law is better observed by every citizen which each one seems to have imposed upon himself; such is the law decreed on the basis of the hearing and command of the general multitude of citizens. The first proposition of this syllogism is virtually self-evident: since 'the city is a community of free persons', as is written in *Politics*, Book 3, Chapter 6, each person ought to be free and ought not to endure the despotism of another, that is, servile

lordship. This would not happen if some one or a few citizens decreed the laws over the corporate body of citizens on their own authority; for in thus decreeing the laws, they would be despots over the others, and therefore regardless of the goodness of such laws, the remaining citizens (namely, the larger part) would endure them with difficulty or not at all, and they would protest against that contempt they endured, and not a single person would observe a proposal not approved by him. Yet something decreed as a result of the hearing and consensus of the entire multitude, even though less useful, would be more readily observed and endured by anyone, because each one would seem to have established this by himself and therefore is not able to protest against it, but instead will tolerate it calmly. Furthermore, I prove the second proposition of the first syllogism by another means: the power of guarding the laws pertains entirely to those who are empowered to coerce transgressors; but this is the corporate body or its more dominant part; therefore, the authority of making law pertains to it alone.

7. Moreover, one may defend the principal claim thus: that practical concern, in the right institution of which consists the greatest part of the communal sufficiency of citizens in the present life, and by the bad institution of which damage to the community is threatened, ought to be instituted only by the corporate body of citizens; but this is the law; therefore, the institution of it pertains to the corporate body of citizens. The major premise of such a proof is nearly self-evident, and is supported by the immediate truths which are stated in Chapters 4 and 5 of this discourse. For human beings gather into the civil community on account of the pursuit of benefit and the sufficient life and the avoidance of the opposite. Therefore, those matters which can touch upon the benefit and inconvenience of everyone ought to be known and heard by everyone, so that they can obtain benefit and repel the opposite. Yet laws are such matters, as was taken up by the minor premise of the syllogism. For the greater part of the total and communal sufficiency of human beings consists in the correct formation of laws; under bad laws, however, the unbearable servitude and oppression and misery of citizens occurs, as a result of which the dissolution of the polity eventually comes to pass.

8. Once more, the previous proofs may be presented in a somewhat abbreviated and summarized form: either the authority of decreeing law pertains solely to the corporate body of citizens, as we have said, or it pertains to one or a few human beings; but it does not pertain to one person, because of what was said in Chapter 11 of this discourse and in the first proof which we have adduced in the present chapter; for on account of ignorance or malice or both, one person could decree a bad law, namely, looking more towards his own rather than the common advantage, for which reason it would be tyrannical. On account of the same reason, this does not pertain to a few people; for they could sin in framing the law, as before, for the sake of certain people (namely, the few) and not the common advantage, just as is seen in the case of oligarchies. Therefore, this pertains to the corporate body

of citizens or its more dominant part, in regard to which the reasoning is otherwise and opposed. For since citizens ought to be measured by law in accordance with due proportion, and no one knowingly harms oneself or wills an injustice upon oneself, therefore all or most people desire the law to be advantageous to the harmony of the community of citizens.

9. On the basis of these same proofs, changed only with regard to the minor premise, one may demonstrate that approval, interpretation and suspension, and other matters related to the law outlined in section 3 of this chapter pertain solely to the seat of the legislative authority. And the same is to be supposed of everything which is established by means of election. For those to whom pertains the primary authority of electing, or those to whom that authority has been conceded, should themselves approve or disapprove in regard to the same matters; for otherwise the part would be greater than the whole, or at least equal to it, if the part could dissolve by its own authority that which was instituted by the whole....

Chapter 17: Regarding the numerical unity of the supreme ruler in the city or kingdom, and the necessity for it; for which reason the numerical unity of the city or kingdom is made evident, as well as the numerical unity of the individual primary parts or offices of the city or kingdom

1. This will be the occasion for speaking about the unity of the ruling body or ruler; in advancing towards this, we say that there ought to be only one ruling body in a single city or single kingdom; or if more numerically or in species, as would seem expedient in larger cities, and especially in kingdoms taken according to the first meaning of the term, there ought to be among them one numerically supreme over all, with regard to which and by which the rest are guided and regulated, and also according to which errors occurring in them are corrected.

2. Now I say that this ruling body, namely, the supreme one, will only be numerically one, and not many, by necessity if the city or kingdom is to be rightly disposed. And I say the same about the ruler in accordance with this body – not that the ruler is to be numerically one with regard to the supposition of his humanity, but with regard to office. For there are certain numerically singular supreme and well-tempered ruling bodies within which more persons than one exercise rulership, such as aristocracies and polities, about which we have spoken in Chapter 8. Yet these many persons are numerically one ruling body in regard to office, on account of the numerical unity of every action, judgement, decision or precept arising from them; for no such action can arise from any of them separately, but only as a result of the common decree and consensus of them or their dominant part in accordance with the laws established in connection with such matters. And on account of the numerical unity of such actions thus arising from them, the

ruling body is and is called numerically one, whether it is ruled by a single person or many. Yet such unity of action is not needed in any other one of the remaining offices or parts of the cities; for in each one of them any actions of a similar or different sort can and ought to arise separately from different people attached to them. Indeed, such unity of action within them would be burdensome and harmful to the community and to the individual.

3. And so the numerical unity of the ruling body or ruler must be solely a numerical unity in the city or kingdom or, if many, there must be a numerically single such one supreme over all, rather than many. We shall first show this in the following way: if there were to be many ruling bodies in the city or kingdom, and it was not guided by or ordered under some supreme one, the execution of judgements, commands and matters of advantage and justice would cease; and as a result of this, there would be fighting, division and ultimately the disintegration of the city or kingdom. Such a consequence is a disadvantage to be most greatly avoided, yet it is a conclusion which can be shown clearly on the basis of the given antecedent, namely, the plurality of ruling bodies. First, transgressors of the laws cannot reasonably be judged except when called before the court of the ruler for the sake of the examination of the charges or accusations against them. But assuming a plurality of ruling bodies, none guided by some supreme one, no one called before the court of a ruler could adequately be present. For it may be, as frequently occurs, that on account of some transgression of the law someone is called to appear in court simultaneously by several ruling bodies, none ordered one under the other, since one ruling body can and is bound to call or summon an offender for the same reason as another; and as one person called for a reason is bound to appear in the court of one ruling body lest he be held in contempt, so he is bound for the same reason to appear in the court of another ruling body or of others, if there were more than two. Therefore, either he will appear in all of their courts at the same moment, or in none of their courts, or in a certain court but not in the court(s) of the other or others; of course, he cannot appear in all of their courts simultaneously, since this is an impossibility of nature and art; for the same body cannot exist simultaneously in different places nor can one speak or appear simultaneously before several people who are probably posing different questions at the same time. Moreover, it may be that, although impossible, one is called to be present at the courts of many rulers, and one says nothing about or responds to different charges at the same time; yet perhaps that person will be condemned by one ruling body while absolved of the same crime by another; or if one is condemned by both, they do not do so in the same fashion. On account of this, one may be bound and not bound to be punished, or if one is bound, this may be to a greater or a lesser extent, and thus in a certain measure and not in a certain measure. For this reason, one will either perform contradictory acts at the same time or not be punished. For the precepts of one or another ruling body ought to be observed for the same reasons. No

one has any better reason for appearing in the court of one ruling body than in the court of another or others. If a person appears in the court of one, spurning the others, however, and perhaps is absolved by it of guilt and civil punishment, he may still be condemned by another on account of contempt. Therefore, when thus called or summoned, one will neither appear at all courts simultaneously nor will one suitably be able to appear at the court of a certain ruling body and not at the court of some others. Thus, it follows that a person ought never to appear in the court of a ruling body by which he is called or summoned; therefore, no one can be judged. Therefore, such a plurality of ruling bodies not subordinated amongst themselves renders the city or kingdom impossible, if civil justice and advantage are to be preserved.

4. Moreover, on the presumption of a plurality of such ruling bodies, the entire common utility would be disturbed. For rulers ought frequently to consult with the whole assembly of citizens, especially those of leisure, in order that the common advantage be sought and determined, or on account of the avoidance of inconvenience and emerging threats such as those posed by persons who wish to oppress the common liberty from within or without; and just as citizens or subjects called for a certain reason by the command of one such ruling body are bound to convene at a given location and time, so the same people are bound to convene on account of the mandate of another ruler at a given location and time; and the hour could be identical, while the location could be different; and moreover, that which one ruling body wishes to carry out might perhaps be different from what the other one desires; and yet it does not seem possible to be in different locations simultaneously, or to aim at different goals at the same time.

5. Once again, from this there would occur the division and opposition, fighting and separation, of citizens and ultimately the dissolution of the city, some people wishing to obey one ruling body, while others wish to obey another; likewise, conflict would occur between ruling bodies themselves, on account of the fact that each one of them will wish to be superior to the others; besides, the ruling bodies will wish to subject citizens resisting them; and furthermore, the above mentioned obstacles would arise from dissension between the ruling bodies or their mutual competition in the absence of a superior judge.

6. Once again, on the presumption of this plurality, the greatest discovery of reason and art will be useless and superfluous, for whatever civil utility may be produced by many ruling bodies can be produced perfectly well by a single one, or a single supreme one, without the damaging effects resulting from a plurality of them.

7. Furthermore, on the presumption of such a plurality of this sort, no kingdom or city will be one. For these are and are called one on account of the unity of the ruling body, to which and according to which all the remaining parts of the civil body are ordered, as will be made apparent from that which we will discuss immediately hereafter. And once again, there will

be no order among the parts of the city or kingdom when they are not ordered to a first part, because they are bound to be subjected to no one, as has been made clearly apparent as the basis of the previous arguments, and there will be the disturbance of them and of the whole civil body; for one will select for oneself whatever office one desires, whether one or many, with no regulation of or distinction with regard to such matters. So many disadvantages would result from this that it would not be easy or possible to enumerate them.

8. Furthermore, just as in the arrangement of the animal, there is one primary source directing and moving it as regards changes of location, as is evident in the book *On the Movements of Animals* [by Aristotle] – since should there be several sources of leadership and should contrary or different motions be directed simultaneously, it would be necessary for the animal either to be carried in contrary directions or to remain entirely immobilized and hence to be deprived of those things which are procured for its needs and benefit by means of movement – so the same is the case for the suitably ordered civil body, which we have said in Chapter 15 has characteristics analogous to an animal well-formed according to nature. And therefore, just as a plurality of such leading principles would be useless, indeed, injurious, in the case of the animal, so the identical thing may be firmly believed in the case of the city. The same thing is also apparent to those wishing to inquire with regard to the primary source of alteration within animals, just as with regard to changes of location and similarly the patterns of changes and moving bodies in general. But these matters are to be overlooked, since they pertain more to the phenomena of the natural world; what we have said concerning them is adequate for the sake of present considerations.

9. Furthermore, since 'art generally perfects certain sorts of things which nature cannot finish, while it otherwise imitates nature', as is written in Book 2 of Aristotle's *Physics*, and since among the entities of nature, the ruler is numerically singular, rather than plural, because 'entities do not wish to be badly disposed', just as is maintained in Book 12 of the *First Philosophy* [Aristotle's *Metaphysics*], therefore the ruling body instituted in accordance with human reason and art will be only numerically one. Along with the reasons stated, this is apparent from true, useful and necessary experiences perceived by everyone: inasmuch as a place or province or human assemblage lacks a united ruling body, it seems impossible for any of these to be well-disposed in the way we have described, as appears clearly to virtually all people in connection with the kingdom of the Romans, as was demonstrated to some extent in the remarks of the introduction.

10. Whether it is appropriate to have a numerically singular supreme ruling body over everyone who lives in a civil fashion universally and throughout the whole earth, or whether it is at certain times appropriate to have different such ruling bodies in those different areas of the world which

are almost necessarily situated in separated localities, and especially among those who are unable to communicate by words and are greatly distanced by customs and habits (towards which the heavenly cause perhaps inclines lest there be an overabundance of human propagation), poses a matter for rational examination, although at a time and place different from the present line of investigation. For it would probably seem to some people that nature has moderated the propagation of human beings and other animals by means of wars and epidemics in order that there may be adequate resources for their raising.

11. Returning to our intended plan, however, we are to discuss, on the basis of that which is somewhat apparent from what has already been said, what constitutes the numerical unity of the city of kingdom, since this is not a unity in an absolute fashion, but is a unity of order according to which a plurality of individuals, which is called one, or other things which are called numerically one, are so called not because they are numerically one in a formal sense by reference to some form, but instead they are called numerically one because they are defined in relation to a numerical unity, namely, a ruling body, in relation to which and on account of which they are ordered and governed. For neither the city nor the kingdom is singular by reference to some singular natural form, as in the case of those things which are composite or compound, since its parts or offices, and the substratum or parts of those parts, are widespread in their activities and are numerically separated from each other in a formal sense on account of their location and also their individuality. For this reason, they are neither one-as the result of something inherent which is formally one nor as the result of some one thing which holds or contains them, such as a wall. For Rome along with Sicily and other communities are numerically one kingdom or empire for no other reason except that each and every one of their subjects is ordered through volition towards a numerically singular supreme ruling body. The world is said to be numerically one, rather than many worlds, in virtually the same manner, not on account of some numerically singular form inherent formally in all entities; but instead all entities in the world are said to be numerically one on account of the numerical unity of the first entity, since every entity is naturally inclined towards and is based on the first entity. For this reason, the declaration that all entities in the world are said to be numerically one means not that some numerical unity exists formally in all entities, nor that some universal is ascribed to them in accordance with oneness, but a certain sort of plurality is called one because it exists in relation to one and on account of one. In this way, human beings within one urban area or province are called one city or kingdom, because they consent to numerically one ruling body.

12. Yet human beings are not one part of the civic body in number by virtue of the fact that they are numerically one kingdom or one city, since although they consent to numerically one ruling body (on account of which they are called one city or one kingdom), still they are directed towards this

numerical oneness by means of different active and passive arrangements, which are nothing other than the different commands handed down by the ruler through which different people are appointed to different offices. On the basis of these differences of commands, the parts and offices of the civic body are themselves also formally different. That each of the offices is called numerically one or one numerical part of the civic body does not stand opposed to the numerical plurality of the component parts within it, nor does it mean that something inheres in them through numerical oneness, but rather they are directed by means of one active command of the ruler in accordance with the determinations of the law.

Chapter 19: Regarding the efficient causes of the tranquility and intranquility of the city or kingdom, and that which beyond customary sorts of causes especially upsets kingdoms, and regarding the transition from the first discourse to the second

1. The remaining and final topic of this discourse is to infer the causes of tranquility and its opposite in the city or kingdom on the basis of the preceding conclusions. For this was to be the principal line of inquiry in accordance with out plan as proposed at the beginning. And first we shall demonstrate what these causes which arise in the customary manner have in common, based upon the unrivalled conclusions about them by Aristotle in Book 5 of his *Politics*. Consequent upon this discussion, we shall draw conclusions in outline regarding an unusual cause of the discord or intranquility of civil governments, which (as we have said in the remarks of the introduction) has for a long time disturbed, or rather is perpetually agitating and disturbing, the Italian kingdom.

2. On account of this, it is necessary to go over once again the definitions of tranquility and its opposite already stated in Chapter 2. For tranquility was the good disposition of the city or kingdom by which each part can perform its own appropriate function in accordance with reason and its institution. From this definition, its nature is apparent. For when it is called a 'good disposition', its general intrinsic essence is denoted. Inasmuch as it is said that 'by means of it each part of the city can perform its appropriate function', its end is signified, which also renders intelligible its own essence or identity. Yet although it may be a sort of form or disposition of the city or kingdom, it is no more one than we said the city or kingdom to be in Chapter 17, parts 11 and 12, and it does not have a formal cause; for the latter is only fitting for composites. We can understand its efficient or active cause from the remarks in Chapter 15 and from other points which necessarily follow from it in regard to the city or kingdom: these include, for example, the mutual intercourse of citizens, and the interchange of their functions amongst one another, and mutual aid and assistance, and generally the power, unimpeded from without, to exercise their private and common functions, and also

participation in the common benefits and burdens according to the appropriate measure of each one, and along with this the other benefits and desirable ends expressed in the words of Cassiodorus which we have quoted at the beginning of this book. The contraries of all or especially some of these follow from its opposite, intranquility or discord.

3. Therefore, because the proper activity of the ruler constitutes the effect and conserving cause of the aforementioned and of all forms of civil benefit, as is demonstrated in Chapter 15, parts 11 and 12, it will be the efficient cause of tranquility; the Apostle was undeniably cognizant of this when he said in 1 Timothy 2[:1–2]: 'Therefore, I beg that prayers first be made... for kings and all those who are of lofty position, in order that we may live a quiet and tranquil life.' Insofar as the activity of this part on its own has been impeded, a sort of efficient cause of intranquility or discord within the city emerges therefrom. This cause may be seen in its genus, although it is varied by many species or modes, concerning the customary actions emerging from which Aristotle has made sufficient note, as was stated, in Book 5 of the *Civil Science*, which we have called the *Politics*.

There is, however, a certain unaccustomed cause of the intranquility or discord of the city or kingdom which occasionally takes place on account of an effect produced by the divine cause beyond all of its customary actions in things and which, as we recall having touched upon in our introductory remarks, could be perceived neither by Aristotle nor by any other philosopher of his time or earlier.

4. This cause, having obstructed up to the present time, and even now continuing to obstruct, the proper actions of the ruler in the Italian kingdom, that realm has been deprived and is deprived of its peace and tranquility and of its already mentioned benefits and the other things following therefrom; and it has been plagued and is plagued by every inconvenience, and has been overwhelmed with virtually every kind of misery and iniquity.

In accordance with the plan initially proposed by us, which involves the necessity of determining the special nature of this singularly obstructive cause on account of its habitually hidden malignity, one must recall the points which we stated in Chapter 6: namely, that the son of God, one of the three divine persons, the true God, assumed a human nature on account of the transgressing sins of the first parents and consequently restored the entire human race from the fall, was made a true man long after the time of Aristotle, and the Christian faithful worship the same man existing simultaneously as God, who is called Jesus Christ. This Christ, I say, the blessed son of God, living as God and man simultaneously joined together, was domiciled among the human beings of the Jewish people, from whom he was descended in regard to his carnal origins; he tried to teach and did teach the truth of what is to be believed, done and avoided for the sake of the achievement of the eternal life by human beings and the deflection of misery. Finally suffering and dying on account of this through the malice and insanity of the Jews during the reign of Pontius Pilate, vicar of Caesar, he was resurrected from the dead three days after his death, and shortly thereafter ascended into the heavens; yet beforehand, while he was living a corruptible life, he had, on account of the salvation of the human race, received into his presence certain colleagues for the job of teaching the truth, who are called Apostles, and he commanded them to preach throughout the entire world the truth which he had taught and imparted to them. For this reason, in the twenty-eighth and final chapter of Matthew [28:19–20], he had said to them after his resurrection: 'Going forth, therefore, teach all people, baptizing them in the name of the Father, and the Son, and the Holy Ghost, teaching them to believe anything whatsoever I have ordered of you.' By means of these apostles, I say, whose names are sufficiently known among those faithful to Christ, and by means of certain other people, Christ willed the Evangelical Law to be composed, and through their writing it was composed as though by means of a sort of organ moved and directed towards this by immediate divine strength; in virtue of this law, we are able to grasp the precepts and counsels of eternal salvation in the absence of Christ and of the apostles and evangelists themselves. In this and according to this has also been prescribed and established the sacraments which cleanse original and actual sin, cause and preserve divine grace, and recover its loss, and institute the ministers of this law.

5. He also instituted the already mentioned apostles as the first learned teachers of these laws and the ministers of the sacraments according to them, conferring on them through the Holy Spirit this ministerial authority which believers in Christ call priestly. By this means, the power was conferred upon these same persons and their successors in this office, and upon no one else, subject to a fixed formula of words to be said by one or more of them, to transsubstantiate bread and wine into the true body and blood of Christ. Along with this, he conceded to them the authority of loosing and binding human beings on account of sin, which they are accustomed to calling the power of the keys, and the power of appointing others with the same authority. This authority was also conferred by the apostles upon certain persons, or rather by God through their praying and laying of hands on others. These others are also endowed with the power of doing likewise, and they have done, are doing and will do the same things up until the end of the world. In this way, moreover, the Apostle Paul ordained Timothy, Titus and many others and taught them to ordain still others, For this reason, he says in 1 Timothy 4[:14]: 'Do not neglect the grace that is in you, which was given to you by the prophets when the presbyters laid hands.' And Titus 1[:5] states: 'For the sake of this I left you in Crete, that those matters which were wanting you might correct, and that you might designate presbyters throughout the cities, just as I assigned you.' And this authority of the priesthood or of the keys, whether single or multiple, is a sort of characteristic or form stamped upon the soul by the immediate action of God.

6. In addition to this, however, there is another sort of authority handed over to priests by human concession in order to avoid scandal on account of the multiplication of their numbers, and this authority involves the pre-eminence of one among them over the others to give direction in the temple for the sake of the proper performance of divine worship, as well as the ordination or distribution of certain temporal goods which are established for the use of the aforementioned ministers. In regard to the efficient cause of this authority, and whence its authority is derived, there will be adequate discussion in Chapters 15 and 16 of the second discourse, since this is not appointed through God immediately, but through human will and mind, just like the other offices of the city.

7. And so, once the origins of ecclesiastical ministers and the efficient cause of their offices have been reviewed and in some ways clarified, it is furthermore necessary to note that among the aforementioned apostles of Christ there was one named Simon, also named Peter, who first accepted from Christ the promise of the authority of the keys, just as the *Gloss* according to Augustine on Matthew 16[:19] says about the prophecy of Christ: 'And I will give to you the keys to the kingdom of heaven'; and the *Gloss* states: 'He who professed faith before others', namely, that Jesus Christ is the true son of God, 'is given the keys before others', that is, prior to the others. After Christ's passion, resurrection and ascension, this apostle arrived at Antioch, and was made bishop by the people of the same city, as is stated in his history. Yet from there, as the above mentioned history has it, he departed to Rome for some sort of reason that is not specified (because of which there are many different opinions regarding the matter), and he was elevated to bishop by those faithful to Christ in the same city; ultimately, he was killed by decapitation on account of his profession and teaching of Christ, and with him at the same time and place was the Apostle Paul, according to the above mentioned history.

8. On the basis of this prerogative, therefore, which this disciple or apostle is seen to have in relation to the others (because he was given the keys ahead of the others by means of the words in Scripture previously presented, as well as certain other things said to him by Christ, which will also be brought out in what follows), certain bishops following after him in the apostolic or episcopal seat of Rome, particularly after the time of Constantine, Emperor of the Romans, claim and assert themselves to be in command of all the other bishops and presbyters of the world in regard to all types of jurisdictional authority; and some of the more recent of them claim not only this, but also jurisdiction over all the rulers, communities and individual persons of the world – although they do not express this so equivocally nor state it so explicitly with regard to everyone as with regard to the ruler called the Emperor of the Romans and all the provinces and cities and persons sub-jected to him; in accordance with the truth, however, the expression of singular lordship or coercive jurisdiction over this ruler would seem to have

received an initial shape and support from a certain edict and donation which some people say was made by Constantine to the Roman pontiff St Sylvester.

9. Still, because that donation or privilege did not hold this clearly, or since it has perhaps expired as a result of later occurrences, or even because, although being valid, the force of that privilege or concession did not extend to the other ruling bodies of the world nor to that of the Romans in all of its provinces, thus afterwards the more recent bishops of Rome have assumed also for themselves this coercive jurisdiction over the whole world with a certain all-encompassing title, namely, 'plenitude of power', which they assert to have been conceded by Christ to St Peter and his successors in the Roman episcopal seat, as the vicars of Christ. For Christ, as they truly say, was 'King of kings and Lord of lords' [Revelations 19:16] over all persons and the whole world of things, although by no means does there follow from this what they wish to infer, as will be evident with certainty in the following. This is therefore thought among Roman bishops to indicate that, just as Christ has a plenitude of power and jurisdiction over all kings, rulers, communities, associations (*collegia*), and individual persons, so also those who call themselves vicars of Christ and of St Peter have this plenitude of coercive jurisdiction, limited by no human law....

11. Entering into secular affairs in this way, the bishops of the Romans have, first of all, excommunicated certain people who refuse to submit to their judgements on the pretence of procuring peace among Christian believers; then they have brought judgement to bear upon their property and persons, with a greater amount of pressure applied to those who are least able to resist their force, such as individual persons and communities among the Italians, whose kingdom is so divided and shattered in virtually all of its parts that it can be more easily oppressed; they have been more lenient, however, with those kings and rulers whose opposition and coercive power they fear. Yet even in regard to the latter they creep up gradually and they attempt the usurpation of jurisdictions by continuous creeping, not daring to invade everywhere at once, on account of which their stealthily penetrating conspiracy has escaped even the notice of the Roman rulers and the peoples subject to them. For the bishops of the Romans have gradually occupied one jurisdiction after another, above all with the imperial seat vacant; in this way, they now ultimately declare themselves to possess total coercive temporal jurisdiction over that ruler. Most recently and most clearly, the current already mentioned bishop appointed himself to hold supreme jurisdiction in regard to the ruler of the Romans in the provinces of the Italians as well as the Germans, and also in relation to the already mentioned inferior rulers, communities, associations, and individual persons of whatsoever rank and condition they may be, and also over all their feudal rights (*feudalia*) and the rest of their temporal goods; and he openly ascribes to himself the power of giving and transferring their rulerships, as can clearly be seen by everyone from certain writings by this bishop which he calls 'edicts' or 'sentences'.

12. And so such an incorrect judgement about, and perhaps perverted desire for, rulership on the part of certain Roman bishops, which they assert is due to them on the basis of a plenitude of power passed on to them (as they say) by Christ, constitutes that singular cause which we have described as the efficient cause of the intranquility or discord of the city or kingdom. For while prone to creep into all kingdoms, just as was said in the introduction, its troublesome action has long plagued the Italian kingdom, and has diverted and continually diverts it from its tranquility or peace by hindering with all its efforts the appointment or institution of the ruling body, namely, the Roman emperor, and its activity in the said Empire. In the absence of this activity, namely, the rendering of justice in regard to civil acts, injuries or conflicts readily result. Without the measurement of just rules or laws, on account of the absence of a measurer, fights are caused, for which reason the separation of citizens and eventually the dissolution of the Italian polities or civil life will occur, just as we have said. Therefore, by means of this opinion regarding, and possibly what we have called a desire for, rulership, the Roman bishop struggles to make the ruler of the Romans subject to his temporal or coercive jurisdiction; yet the emperor neither wishes to be subject to him in such judgement nor ought rightfully to be so, as will be clearly demonstrated from what follows. For this reason, so much quarrelling and discord is springing up that it cannot be extinguished without great risk to soul and body and great expenditure of resources.

For no Roman bishop or other bishop, priest or any other spiritual minister as such is suited to the office of coercive rulership over any individual person regardless of condition or any community or association whatsoever, just as is demonstrated in Chapters 15 and 17. And this was observed with regard to the priesthood under any law or religion by Aristotle in Book 4 of the *Politics*, when he says: 'On account of this, not everyone who is elected or selected by lot is to be regarded as a ruler, take for example priests. For these are to be regarded as something apart from political rulers.... Certain of these executive duties', that is, offices, 'are political....' And a little later he adds: 'Certain of these are economic.'

13. Because this pernicious disease, which is entirely hostile to all human quiet and happiness, could certainly infect the other Christian kingdoms of the world on account of the defect of its corrupt root, I judge it of the utmost necessity to repel it, just as was stated in the introduction. First, the mask of the already stated opinion is to be revealed as the root of evil deeds up to the present and in the future; then, its unjust or ignorant patrons or sponsors and pernicious defenders are to be restrained, by external action if necessary. All those with the knowledge and power to deflect this opinion are obligated to do so; those neglecting or failing in this on any pretext whatsoever are unjust, as Tully testifies in *On Duties*, Book I, Chapter 5, when he says: 'There are two types of injustice: first, of those who inflict injury; or else, of those who, when injury is inflicted upon others, do not repel it when they can.' Behold,

then, that according to this noteworthy statement by Tully, not only are those who inflict injury on others unjust, but so are those who know how to and can prevent the infliction of injuries upon others, yet do not prevent them, since every person is bound to others in this regard by a certain quasi-natural law, namely, the duty of friendship and human society. Lest I be called unjust (at least to myself) for knowingly transgressing this law, I propose to repulse this disease from the brotherhood of Christian believers, first by instruction and thereafter by those external actions of which I am capable. For, as I seem indubitably to recognize, there is given to me from above the power to know and reveal the sophism of the distorted judgement, and along with it perhaps the perverted desire, upon which certain previous Roman bishops have supported themselves up to the present and upon which the present Roman bishop and his accomplices endeavour to continue sustaining themselves, thereby nurturing the already mentioned scandals.

12

THE MIRROR OF KING EDWARD III
William of Pagula

INTRODUCTION

Among the vast number of political treatises dating to the late Middle Ages, none is more unusual than *The Mirror of King Edward III*. For many centuries the authorship of the treatise was disputed, but it is now safely attributed to William of Pagula (*c.* 1290–1332). A native of Yorkshire, William spent most of his career as vicar of the parish of Winkfield, near Windsor. But he was also an accomplished scholar who earned a doctorate in canon law in about 1320 and who wrote both *The Eye of the Priesthood*, a popular guidebook on theology and canon law designed for parish priests, and *The Summary of Summaries*, a more academic treatment of theological and legal questions.

William's *Mirror of King Edward III* is actually composed of two separate and distinct, but thematically related, treatises which are ordinarily regarded as alternate versions of the same work. The first version has been dated on internal evidence to early 1331, while the second edition, which differs from its predecessor in both language and tone, seems to have been written the following year. The two texts are united by their unremitting insistence on the hardships which royal taxes have imposed upon the peasantry of England. In particular, Pagula objects strenuously to the system of purveyance, that is, the customary right of the king to provide for his household and troops when touring his realm by confiscating local goods or purchasing them at a fixed, non-negotiable price. During the early fourteenth century, the English Crown had repeatedly abused this prerogative in order to avoid paying costs of its military entourage out of the standard sources of royal income. In arguing against purveyance, Pagula cites empirical examples of prices paid for agricultural goods and details the dire consequences for the poor.

The Mirror of King Edward III is of considerable interest as a work of political theory. William reshapes many of the standard conventions of the medieval advice-book or 'mirror' genre – such as teachings about royal justice, the bond of love between the people and their ruler, and the obligation of monarchs to remain within the bounds set by law – in order to defend the lowest and most humble subjects of the kingdom from the thievery of their superiors. Theological, moral and legal arguments are brought together as evidence that even the poorest man deserves and can demand the respect and protection of his government. Pagula's text represents a remarkable example of how the learning of Christian scholars and clerics, which often counselled quietism to the meek, could be subverted and converted to the articulation of popular grievances. In doing so, *The Mirror of Edward III* goes so far as to imply the legitimacy of rebellious expressions of discontent amongst the people of the realm who are subjected to ongoing oppression by the royal household.

THE MIRROR OF KING EDWARD III
(First Version)

1. Lord, my King, insofar as the republic is committed to you for governing, you ought to think of the many ways and means by which you will be able to order its affairs better and with more discretion for the sake of the honour of God and the utility of the kingdom, and also in order to acquire the love of the people. In order to do this, I give you a way so that you may indeed do justice to each individual. And justice is to return to each what is his own. For justice never sells another's goods, but gives to each one what is his own; it neglects its own utility so that it might serve the communal equity. And according to this, justice pertains first to God, second to the fatherland, third to parents, and fourth to all, according to Saint Ambrose. Likewise, the justice of the king is the peace of the people, the defence of the fatherland, the immunity of the commoner, the defence of the nation, the care of the sick, the joy of all, the solace of paupers, the heredity of sons and the hope for the king's own future happiness, and the war with the vices, as Cyprian says. Likewise, whoever does justice is also loved by God, for which reason the Psalmist says: 'The Lord loves those who are just' [Psalms 146:8]. And justice knows neither father nor mother; it knows truth, it does not respect the person, it imitates God, as Cassian says about this, and he is occupied with justice. Likewise, Lord King, if you desire to pursue justice, first fear and love God so that you might be loved by God; for you will love God if you imitate Him in this as insofar as you will justice to be done to everyone and to injure no one, and then all who follow you will call you just; they will venerate and love you. And so that you might be just, not only should you not injure, but also you should prohibit injuring, as Seneca says. And Gregory says in the *Register*. The highest good in kings is to worship justice, and to deliver right to each one, and not to allow to be done to subjects what is of power, but to keep to what is just. But where is the justice or equity these days to buy something for a lesser price than the seller wishes to give it, when buying and

selling pertain to the law of nations and are brought about through consent? For where there is no consent, there is not selling but extortion, no justice but seizure, no equity but falsehood and iniquity. And therefore, those from whom goods are taken cry to God. Yet what they cry to God, I need not express. Indeed, God knows and God freely hears those paupers; for this reason, the Psalmist says: 'You will pay heed to the prayers of paupers, Lord, your ear will hear the fears of their hearts' [Psalms 10:17]; and elsewhere: 'On account of the misery of the destitute and the laments of the poor, I will come, says the Lord' [Psalms 12:5]; 'The poor call to him and he answers.... And he is not forgetful of the cries of the poor' [Psalms 34:6, 9:12]; and Ecclesiastes 21[:5]: 'Prayers reach the ear of God directly from the mouth of the poor and the cries of the innocent rise to God'; and Exodus [3:7]: 'The cries of the children of Israel ascend to God regarding the Egyptians under whom they are burdened and God hears their laments.' For this reason, Job [24:12] says: 'The spirits of the wounded cry out to God and God does not permit the unavenged to depart.'

2. Therefore, so that justice may be done to each one, nothing may be taken for a lesser price than that which the seller wishes to give it. And if it is said that this is a royal prerogative, I also say to you, King, that it is destructive to your kingdom and against the will of God, since it is a great error, even though the law would allow it, for which reason Wisdom 14[:16] says: 'The iniquitous habit grew stronger, and finally the error was protected in law and was protected by the commend of tyrants.' But you, King, diligently avoid this. Understand that you would have nothing except from God, and still he does not remove from you what you have, but multiplies it greatly every day, just as you ought to be instructed to give to your subjects, and not to take anything away from them. But look out lest you provoke God to anger, since he has placed all good things into your hand, as is said in Job 1. Yet if it is said that all things are of the ruler, understand this to mean for the sake of defence, not of seizure. It is said near the end of Ecclesiasticus [33:31, 30]: 'If you have a slave he is to be like your soul, because you purchased his soul along with his blood', that is, it is a danger to your soul if 'you have treated him badly'. Moreover, 2 Kings [2 Samuel] 7[:7] says that David was made king in order to increase the flocks of the people of God, not to despoil them. Ezekiel 46[:18] says: 'The ruler does not acquire anything from the goods of the people by means of violence'; and Proverbs 22[:22–3] says: 'Do not do violence against the poor because the Lord will pass judgement on their case and he punishes those who are punishing the poor', and this sin is completely hateful to God since not only has he prohibited violence, but also that evil will to plunder. Exodus 20[:17] pronounces: 'Do not desire the cattle or donkeys of your neighbour or any other goods which are his.' And, King, you ought to know that whatever plunder of this sort is done constitutes murder, for he eats and drinks the pauper himself when he devours those things without which the pauper cannot live. Ecclesiasticus 34[:22] says: 'He who

snatches away hard earned bread from the mouth of the labourer is like someone who murders his neighbour'; and Micah 3[:2,3] states: 'Those who violently take the goods of my people eat the flesh of my people and they strip off their skin'; and it follows in the same text: when they are faced with tribulation and danger, 'they will cry out to the Lord and he will not heed them and He will hide His face from them, inasmuch as they have acted badly in their deed.' The Lord said this to rulers, kings, and each and every man. Therefore, so that your good fame may be maintained unharmed by others, you should wish to be loved both by God and by the people and also to be honoured, and it seems good and useful that those serving you take nothing against the will of the sellers, and then wherever you go in your kingdom, men will come from all sides and will bring all sorts of victuals to you and your servants and all necessities to your gate.

3. For men behaved in this way during the time of the last King Henry [III]. And if your own men behaved likewise, where previously there was sorrow and sadness, now and in the future there would be joy and happiness on account of your coming. Those men from your household who agree that this should occur are your friends, since they wish your honour and it may be presumed that they are from the household of God. However, those who disagree are not your friends, but are enemies, and from the devil's household, for such men have four or five horses on the land where they ought to have but one or two, and they seize the goods of others and they release virtually nothing, for which reason, according to Augustine, because they seize the goods of others, they are seized by the devil and by holding their injustice, they are held by the devil. Again, according to Augustine, for the sake of things belonging to others which they thus seize, they sell themselves to the devil. For often there has been a pauper who had sold his own hand or foot on account of his poverty, but even more poor is he who sells his whole self, both body and soul. For thus do many from your household, seizing goods of others against their will and knowing that their servants have committed these sorts of extortions and robberies throughout the land, refuse to apply any remedy. By reason of doing this, he is guilty who was able to correct the situation yet has neglected to amend it. And to neglect something when he can make trouble for evil people is nothing other than to favour them, and he who neglects to prevent a clear crime makes no secret of his lack of concern for society. And the king would seem to agree with wrongdoers [when] it happens that those who ought to be corrected are not restrained. And on account of the sort of purchasing and pillaging which go on at the hands of your ministers, indeed servants of the devil, your status is no little defamed. Therefore, so that your reputation be good and be preserved unharmed by the rest, it is necessary that you should act to correct all the things mentioned before without delay, since good reputation produces more than infinite wealth, for which reason Proverbs 22[:1] says: 'A good name is better than great wealth.' And you ought to work towards this goal,

so that you might have a good reputation, since according to Augustine, two things are necessary to you, that is, just conscience and honest reputation. Conscience for you, reputation on account of your neighbour. For he who neglects his reputation is cruel. Again, according to Cassiodorus, whatever effects the measure of good reputation neglects the increase of wealth, and one's faculty for ruling would then be more powerful when one strives to acquire a treasure of good reputation, to the neglect of the utility of valuable possessions. And you, King, if you wish to acquire for yourself the love of the people through your work, you should show this. For this reason, Gregory [the Great] asserted, our love towards our neighbour accomplishes more good work than words, so that the neighbour may be seen to be loved by you through this good work; and when we are not able to do as much as we would wish to do, the secrets of our heart suffice to Almighty God, and through love of God love of our neighbour is born, and through love of neighbour, love of God is sent. For who neglects to love his neighbour truly does not know how to love God, his Creator....

9. O Lord, my King, behold the kind of deception that occurs on account of your court. Recently, a proclamation was made publicly by a certain member of your court in the market-place to the effect that no one should seize any goods from others unless he paid for them and he should be held under heavy penalty. Nevertheless men of your court – not men, precursors of the Antichrist, that is, against Christ – and various subordinates of your court – that is, subordinates of the devil and completely bound to him because they are his slaves (for which reason it says in John 8[:34]: 'Whoever sins is a slave of sin', and as a consequence of the devil) – seize many goods by violence from the owners of those goods, namely, they seize bread, beer, fowls, cocks, beans, oats and many other things, for which practically nothing is paid; and because of extortions of this kind, many poor people will not have what they need to sow their fields. And behold the malice of these subordinates. It has been ordered or ordained tacitly and expressly among those same subordinates who have been deputed to one village that one evil doer and the worst of them should carry out robberies of oats, bread, beer, fowls, cocks; and from these they shall make their feasts in common and rejoice, and let the people be sad. But, certainly, joyful feasts of this kind are changed to sorrowful mourning and wailing according to that said by Amos 8[:10]: 'I will turn your festivals into funerals and all your songs into lamentations'; and by Luke 6[:25]: 'You who are full now: you will go hungry. You who now laugh: you will mourn and weep.' But if a complaint be made in your court concerning this sort of servant, that servant who has taken the aforesaid goods will absent himself and then he will not be found, and the other servants will excuse him completely, since all of them have been conspiring concerning robberies of this kind. But would that it be ordered in your court that, if one man is thus guilty, all and sundry should be held responsible, since that guilty man commits robberies of this kind by the

authority and with the defence of the others. Those consenting and committing should be punished with equal penalties, and in the same way their masters should be punished, because by doing this they merit blame because those who can correct neglect to amend; and not only those who do, but those who consent, are judged to be participants, and he who neglects to prevent a clear crime makes no secret of his lack of concern for society.

10. But it is commonly said that masters do not wish to have servants other than such men, because they know that they live well from robbery, because it is well known by means of the household that the lord is of this kind; for as the lord, so the household. These things are known publicly throughout the land. And unless these aforesaid things are amended quickly, your great damnation must be feared, or at least the damnation of those who allow these things to happen and do not impose any penalty; concerning this sort of damnation, it is said in Ecclesiasticus 10[:8]: 'Kingdoms are transferred from family to family on account of injury, injustice, abuse and other troubles.' And this is clear from Saul 1, Kings 15 and thereafter from Jeroboam 3, Kings 12, and from many other passages, and also from the example of many great lords formerly governing this kingdom in England. Think, think and think deeply about the foregoing and think that many evils have happened to Eli on that account, because he knew that his sons had committed great evil and he did not correct them, just as it is read in 1 Kings [1 Samuel] 3 and 4. Thus, it may be feared for you that many evils may happen to you and your kingdom, unless you take steps to amend the aforesaid. And if those men of your household persevere in their malice, and you do not correct them, since you have the power, you and they will perish, as it is said in 1 Kings 12 [1 Samuel 12:25], in the last chapter where it is said that 'if you continue to sin, you and your king will be destroyed.' And I warn you, King, and all of your household who consent to robberies of this kind, tacitly and expressly, that when the tribulation and anguish come upon you, you will cry to the Lord and He will not hear you. According to Isaiah [1:15]: 'When you lift up your hands to me, I will avert my eyes from you; and when you multiply your prayers, I will not heed you; for your hands are covered in blood'; and Proverb 1[:24, 27–30] states: 'I have called and you refuse'; and later: 'When tribulation and distress come over you, you will cry to God; and He does not heed you, because you have detested instruction from God, and you have not submitted to fear of the Lord, and you have not acquiesced to good counsel.'

11. 0 Lord, my King, you must know that your dignity consists in the multitude of the people and your ignominy in the poverty of the commoner, as is said in Proverb 14. But those of your household who seize any goods against the will of the owners, and those consenting to them, in truth are not of the household, although they seem and are said to be of your household. This I prove as follows. For it is said that the faith and the strength of the king rests upon the multitude of the people. But also the strength of faith rests

upon truth and fear of the Lord, as is said in Proverb 14. Therefore, those seizing the goods of others against their will do not have fear of the Lord, as has been noted above, because as is said in Ecclesiasticus 1[:27]: 'Fear of the Lord expels sin.' Therefore, it follows that because they are neither of your household nor of your people, and on account of robberies and injustices of this kind, it is as if the whole people sorrows in the face of your coming, wherever you may come in your kingdom, and they are not of one mind with you, although they seem to be of one body with you; and indeed, if they had some leader they would rise up against you, just as they did against your father, and in truth you will not have any multitude of people with you. But if you keep as many as thirty or forty good men with you in your household, and not such men as those who commit robberies of this kind, then you will have the whole land with you, and you will acquire the love of the multitude of the people, and in no other way. And you, King, look diligently, and understand what happened to the King Nebuchadnezzar and his son, Belshazzar, in Daniel 3 and 5.

13

WHETHER A RULER CAN ACCEPT THE PROPERTY OF CHURCHES FOR HIS OWN NEEDS, NAMELY, IN CASE OF WAR, EVEN AGAINST THE WISHES OF THE POPE

William of Ockham

INTRODUCTION

Although William of Ockham (*c.* 1285–1349) is known primarily as one of the most accomplished philosophers and theologians of the fourteenth century, and in particular as the most influential early proponent of the metaphysical doctrine of 'nominalism', he also composed a substantial body of political writings. Born in the village of Ockham (or Occam), Surrey, he seems to have been educated at the colleges of Oxford University. The first mention of Ockham in an extant document is his ordination as subdeacon of St Mary's, Southwark in 1306. When he joined the Order of St Francis is uncertain, but it was his involvement with the Franciscan movement which was to stimulate much of his later political activity. From about 1310 until 1324, William pursued a course of study and writing at Oxford which earned him a considerable reputation and the honourific title of 'Venerable Inceptor'. But he had also made enemies there, one of whom, the deposed Chancellor of the University, John Lutterell, arranged for a papal enquiry into Ockham's teachings. William was called before the papal court at Avignon, where he spent the period from 1324 to 1328 under house arrest answering charges of heterodox teachings. However, he also encountered at Avignon many of the leaders of his own Franciscan order, who were present for another inquisitorial process regarding the Franciscan doctrine of 'spiritualism', which required its members to live in imitation of Christ's absolute poverty. In 1328, William escaped with these Franciscan leaders from Avignon to the imperial court of Ludwig of Bavaria, who had already afforded protection to Marsiglio of Padua and numerous other proscribed intellectuals. Tradition recounts that Ockham commended himself to Ludwig with the words, 'Protect me with your sword, O Emperor, and I shall protect you with my pen'.

Whether an accurate report or a mere legend, Ockham devoted the remainder of his career to the twin pursuits of defending the Franciscan ideal of apostolic poverty and advancing the imperial claims of Ludwig. It was the first theme which primarily held Ockham's attention during the 1330s, when he composed a series of stinging attacks on the papacy's policy towards spiritual Franciscanism. But at the end of the decade, he turned his pen more directly to matters of secular government and its relation to the Church. The first attempt to address these issues was the treatise *Whether a Ruler Can Accept the Property of Churches for His Own Needs, namely, in Case of War, even against the Wishes of the Pope*, a work occasioned by the negotiation of an alliance between English King Edward III and Ludwig in 1337 and its solemnization the following year. The tract defends Edward's right to tax the churches of England in order to raise money for his military ventures (in this case, for his war with the French), and denies that the papacy can interfere with the royal authority to act for the good of subjects (priests included). This requires William to dispute the papal claim to a 'plentitude of power', that is, an all-encompassing lordship over the offices and properties of the laity, which had long been a mainstay of the papacy's defence of its temporal prerogatives. He attacks the 'plenitude of power' doctrine in general terms in Chapters 1–6 of *Whether the Ruler...*, and turns to the special circumstances of England in the seven remaining sections. The text breaks off in the middle of Chapter 13, and does not seem to have been completed by William, the explanation for which is perhaps circumstantial: the alliance between Edward and Ludwig did not last long.

Ockham went on to produce an impressive body of political writing during the following decade, including the *Dialogue* (c. 1339–41), the *Short Treatise on Tyrannical Government* (1341), the *Eight Questions on the Power of the Pope* (c. 1341) and *On Imperial and Pontifical Power* (1346/1347), as well as a number of occasional pieces and works of questionable attribution. But the basic outlines of William's political theory are contained already in *Whether the Ruler...*. His later writings largely embellished, refined and extended the views about the temporal community and its relation to clerical and papal power which he had proposed in 1338.

WHETHER A RULER CAN ACCEPT THE PROPERTY OF CHURCHES FOR HIS OWN NEEDS, NAMELY, IN CASE OF WAR, EVEN AGAINST THE WISHES OF THE POPE

Prologue

To the extent that the truth is expressed in abbreviated fashion, inquiry into it sometimes seems to be cut short and in particular is not dealt with carefully, and occasionally it is supported by obscure and invalid arguments, or at other times it is vulnerable to sophistic attacks. And therefore, manifest falsity is sometimes upheld to such a degree that those who resist the truth are not restrained in any way (and especially those affected by or accustomed to false and erroneous doctrines), but rather the truth is ridiculed by less profound minds and, at the same time, the simple are provided with an opportunity to err, and, even while they free themselves from obscurity, they are shown to tie themselves in larger knots. Nevertheless, because the moderns rejoice in brevity, in preference to sickeningly prolix works, I will try to illustrate, by creating a brief discussion, that our most serene and glorious ruler and lord, Lord Edward, by the grace of God King of England, legally, lawfully and indeed deservedly, must be helped, not only by laymen, but also by secular prelates, religious and other clerics within his lordship from the property of the Church, in his battle against enemies attacking him and usurping his rights unjustly; that if his intent is pure, no human statute, judgment or legal process, even if it should come from the pope himself, stands in his way; that any judgment brought against him because he pursued justice for himself, even if it comes from the pope himself, is null and void and neither to be feared nor obeyed; and that the Roman emperor is permitted to call to his aid those who support and obey him and that pious men who adhere to imperial justice and who pursue the causes of the faith are in no way bound by judgments brought against them.

If I say anything in contradiction to the truth, I will add a correction for whomever it concerns and, whether this error is noticed by myself or by someone else, I will not delay in retracting it at the proper time and place.

Chapter 8

Seeing this, it is to be proven that the prelates and clergy subject to the King of England are obliged to come to his assistance even with the property of the Church in his just war. For with respect to the possessions, especially the surplus, conferred on the Church by the kings of England and their subjects, the will and intent of the donors must be respected, since anyone can make some agreement as he pleases with respect to a donation of his property, according to the second remark above. But the will and intent of the kings of England and of their subjects in conferring their temporal property on the churches was that they be used in righteous causes, especially in causes that would spill over into the common good of everyone falling under the lordship of those kings, as can be seen in the charters and privileges which the churches receive and possess concerning these matters. If these documents should only state righteous causes, for which these goods were given to the churches, in a general way, the term must be understood in a more benign and humane way, according to the fourth remark made above. But the defence of one's country and its royal laws must in no way be considered unimportant among righteous causes. Therefore charters and privileges of this sort must be interpreted in such a way that they are extended to the defence of the country and the laws of its people. For this reason, prelates and clerics are obliged to come to the assistance of the king in the defence of the country and the laws of the people, something which is acknowledged to be for the good of everyone in the kingdom. For the prelates and clergy are entrusted with the dispensation of Church possessions, and not with lordship over them.

Furthermore, not only the property which is handed over to secular persons, but also that which is handed to ecclesiastical persons – especially the surplus – is transferred with its condition unless the person who has the power to do so dissolves this condition. But the condition imposed on the property conferred on the churches was that it be used to aid the king in the defence of the country and the laws of the people. In no way are the goods conferred on the churches by the kings of England free from this condition. Therefore the clerics are obliged to use them to come to the aid of the king in the defence of the country and the laws of its people.

It is not valid to say that church property has a general immunity from the kings of England and that consequently the clerics are in no way obliged to aid the king with the property of the Church. Because, as in a general promise everything forbidden and not expressly stated by the one promising is understood to be excepted according to both canonical and civil laws, so too in a general concession of immunity everything forbidden and not expressly conceded by the one making the concession is held to be excepted from the concession. But not to aid the king in such grave circumstances is illegal, and kings would not give such special immunity to ecclesiastics. Therefore this should be considered an exception to the general concession of immunity. Proof: just as, as was proven before, a kinder and more reasonable interpretation must be made with respect to general donations or concessions to righteous causes, so too in the matter of the concession of immunity must a similar interpretation be made. It is reasonable and kind that the clergy help the king in his hour of need. Therefore, the general concession must be understood in this way.

Again, the canonical sanctions say that all privileges cease in times of need. For if both divine and human laws stop in times of need and if need is cited as an exception to them, so much more surely should human privileges stop in times of need. Therefore, if the king now or hereafter found himself in a situation of need, the privileges of immunity conceded to the clergy by kings would cease.

Now it is proven that the clergy should help the king with the property of the Church in this case. For ecclesiastics are no more exempt with respect to the property of the Church than they are with respect to their own persons or at least the persons of their servants. But in times of need the servants of the clergy ought not to be freed from the defence of the kingdom. According to Saint Gregory [the Great], when the need is imminent, no man of the Church should excuse himself from guarding the city so that the city be better guarded with everyone on the lookout. Therefore, even the clergy are obliged to aid the king with the property of the Church.

Again, the clergy should pay the wages of the soldiers guarding their possessions out of the property of the Church. This is borne out by many sacred canons. So much more, then, ought they to help in defending their lord in temporal things for through him they and the property of the Church is defended. Proof: because, just as 'what affects everyone ought to be approved by everyone', so too what affects everyone ought to be guarded against by everyone. But an attack on the kingdom and the royal laws affects everyone in the country, clergy and laymen alike. Therefore everyone ought to lend a hand in defending the kingdom and the laws of the king. Moreover, since the goods of the Church are conferred on it for righteous causes, it is better to defend the country than to nurture poor people. For according to Tully in his *Rhetoric*, through piety a benevolent and diligent worship is given to the country and consequently piety directs itself to the country [*On Invention* 2.53]. And in *Ethics* [of Aristotle] 1.1, it says that the common good is 'better and more divine than the individual good'. From this it is inferred that the good of the whole country is better and more divine than the good of the poor of that country. From this it is concluded that it is more pious to come to the aid of the whole country than to the aid of the poor of the country. For it is agreed that the clergy are obliged to help the poor with the property of the Church. So much more, then, when the resources of laymen do not suffice, should they help the king in the defence of the country and the laws of the people. Again, the clergy ought to help the king more for the sake of the care he takes of the country and those in it than for the sake of his own person. But if the king is in need of the help of the clergy for the sake of his own person, they ought to help him not as any other needy person, but as someone more special than others in need, because of the charge invested in his person, a charge which is extended to the clergy itself. They ought to help him because of the generosity of his predecessors who conferred goods on the Church. The Church ought to aid its patron when the need arises more specially than others in need. Therefore, so much the more are they obliged to offer the necessary aid from the property of the Church if the king should need help from the clergy in the defence of the country and the laws of the people.

Chapter 9

It has been demonstrated that the clergy are obliged to offer the aid of subsidy from the goods of the Church to the king in his just war. Now it must be proved that they are obliged to do this, without the obstruction of any papal statute, nor any prohibition or command, nor any sentence or proceeding, even if it were to come down from the highest pontiff.

As evidence for this, it should be known that it is not from divine authority, but only from human authority, that the pope has regulating power over the temporal things, especially the surplus, which have been gathered by kings and the other faithful for the Church, if the donors had conceded any power to him over the gifts; and consequently he possesses only as much power as, and no more than, what the English kings, or those inferior to them, gave to the pope over the ecclesiastical goods which they have given to the churches.

This can be shown in a number of ways. For, as it was shown earlier, in Chapter 7, the clergy do not possess temporal goods, especially the surplus, by divine authority, but only by human authority, which is the authority of emperor and king; therefore the pope does not have ruling power over temporal things given to the English churches, unless by the authority of the king; therefore, he has only as much as the kings have given to him, and no more.

Further, as it is clear from those things which were demonstrated earlier, the pope does not have any ruling power over temporal goods solely by the ordination of Christ, other than the power and authority of seeking from the laity what is necessary for his sustenance and for the execution of his office; and if he has any other power, he has it from men. But, the temporal goods given to the English churches by the English kings were not designated for the sustenance of the pope nor for the execution of his office; therefore, if he holds any ruling power over temporal goods of this kind, he does not hold it solely by the ordination of Christ, but from men, and from no one else other than the kings of England; therefore the pope holds as much power over temporal goods of this kind as the English kings might have given, and no more.

Again, as it is clear from the preceding, anyone can impose an agreement of law with respect to one's own property as one wishes, in a donation or endowment, and consequently one can ordain how much power the one receiving, or anyone else, should have over it. But the things given to the English churches were first those of the English kings, and not of the pope; hence, when the kings gave them to the English churches, they were able to ordain how they should be expended and how much power the clergy and popes should have over them, nor should anyone have any power over these things, except what the English kings have bestowed upon him. Wherefore, if the English kings neither tacitly nor expressly gave any power over these things to the pope, then the pope has no ruling power over them. But I say 'tacitly or expressly', because, should the English kings, or others whom the English kings, by virtue of their authority and in such an event, could not resist, have consented, if it at first had been ordained that the pope should have for himself the established power over the matters which have been and should be conceded to churches other than that of Rome, and that the English kings bestowed temporal goods upon the English churches, and that they did not expressly ordain that the pope should have power in any way over temporal goods, then in some way they tacitly ordained that the pope should have power over these things, namely, that power which it is deemed worthy to have over the things which have been conceded to other churches. But they could ordain that the pope should not have more power over these things which they gave to the English churches than over the other temporal goods of their own kingdom, if the English churches, under such an agreement, were able to, and wanted to, receive the goods themselves. But if the churches, under such an agreement, either were unable to, or did not wish to, receive the temporal goods themselves, and nevertheless the kings, under a lawful agreement, bestowed them upon the churches, it should be conceded that the pope has some power over temporal things of this kind, although only insofar as the kings gave it to him: so that the pope may have power over temporal goods of this kind, which have been conceded by the English kings to the churches within the lordship of the same kings, only in virtue of the authority of the kings, and he has only as much as has been granted to him through the privileges of kings.

This having been demonstrated, it must be proved that, insofar as there is no papal statute, prohibition or command, or sentence or proceeding whatsoever, obstructing them, the clergy are bound to give aid to the king in his just war from the goods of the Church, especially its surplus. For, as has been shown, the pope does not have any power over the temporal goods given to the English churches, unless by human authority, and as the English kings have conceded it to him. But the English kings have not given to the highest pontiff any power, by any statute, prohibition or command, sentence or proceeding, to forbid the clergy subject to the king to give aid to him in his just war. Because, if the English kings gave such power to the pope through a special or even a general privilege, then either this is contained, distinctly, explicitly and specifically in some special or general privilege, which belongs to the king and not to the pope, or it is held only implicitly and in general terms.

The first cannot be said: in the first place, because no specific intention can be found in any privilege, concerning such power; in the second place, because if a specific intention should arise in any privilege concerning such power, such privilege is not to be held to be a privilege, because it would contain an obvious vice. It is vicious, unjust, and contrary to natural as well as divine law, to transfer the whole treasury for the defence of the country and of the public rights from those who have enough from other sources to those who, not having other sources, are known to be wanting. Since, therefore, the laity along with clergy, and not without them, have enough for the defence of the kingdom and of the law of the kingdom, it follows that such a privilege of whatever human power should be reckoned a vice, in the event that it is conceded to the pope, and consequently the privilege should be in no way valued; because a privilege is a private law; but a law is not a law unless it is just, a right is not a right unless it is just. Therefore, in no special or general privilege, which is in fact to be judged a privilege, is it either specifically or explicitly expressed that the English kings gave the pope such power over the temporal goods which they bestowed on the Church.

Neither can the second be said, namely, that the English kings should give such power to the pope through a general or special privilege, implicitly and in general terms. Because general terms placed in a privilege of this kind should not be increased, but rather they should be restricted, so that it is not to be understood that such powers were conceded to the pope. Because, as is clear from the fourth point above, in Chapter 7, in such matters the interpretation is to be made more moderate and more generous. But it is also more reasonable and more generous that he should offer the aid of subsidy to the king, when he has such need, from the goods which his predecessors liberally bestowed upon the churches, rather than that he should deny him such aid; therefore, the general terms of his predecessors are to be restricted in such a way that the power of impeding such aid may be in no way conceded to the pope.

Furthermore, as was treated earlier in Chapter 8, these exceptions are grasped in a general endowment, although those which are illicit and which the endower should in no way have conceded are in no way specifically expressed. But it is not licit to impede the clergy from giving support to the king during such time of need, although it is impious and cruel, and displays open ingratitude. Even the kings who were predecessors of the king who now gloriously holds the government of the kingdom should in no way have conferred this, especially because although it is not self-contradictory, it should be presumed that they should have conceded nothing vicious or dangerous or prejudicial to the common good of the kingdom; therefore, the English kings did not give such power to the pope in general terms.

Again, contemptible privileges, and those which diminish the power and authority of others, are not to be increased but restricted; this especially contains the truth when something is conferred through these privileges and, since no restrictions prevent it from being increased, it could detract from the common good. But the privileges conceded to the pope by English kings concerning the holding of power over temporal goods, especially the surplus, which the English kings conferred upon the English churches, are contemptible, because they diminish the rights of others. For through them, the right of the king, and even the rights of the clergy in the region of that king, are diminished because, through privileges of this kind, the clergy would be made subject to the pope with respect to many things, in which otherwise they would not be subject, but they would have freer administration over these things, if the kings were to concede less of such powers to the pope; for then they could do many things without the permission of the pope, even against the pope's command, which now they cannot. Therefore such privileges which have been conceded to the pope are not to be increased, but restricted.

But the way in which they should be restricted can be made clear from what has been written before: namely, in such a way that, for the sake of the common good of the king and of those subject to the king, the pope himself should not be able to impede, by any statute, prohibition or command, procedure or sentence.

Chapter 10

Indeed, in order that the truth of what was said before appears more clearly, I might adduce what should be replied to some objections which can be brought forth against these things. For it seems that the clergy and prelates should not offer aid from the goods of the Church to the king, without the permission of the pope.... From this it is to be inferred all the more that if the pope prevents them from helping the king, they should obey the pope, and not offer aid. Furthermore, the pope has held neither power, nor any privileges, at any time from the English kings; therefore, everything which was said in the preceding chapter concerning the power and privileges conceded by the English kings to the highest pontiff has been introduced into the present treatise uselessly and to no purpose.

Again, the pope alone can and should interpret the privileges of the highest pontiff; therefore, if any privileges should be conceded by the English kings to the highest pontiff concerning the things given to the churches and to anyone else, he himself, and no other, should seek to interpret them; and consequently, interpretation of them should be maintained. If, therefore, he should decide that the clergy should not give aid to the laity from the goods of the Church without his permission, it follows that the English clergy should not give aid to the kings from the goods of the Church contrary to the command or prohibition of the pope.

Thus, 'the benefits of the ruler' are to be 'interpreted' most broadly [*Decretals of Gregory IX*]; therefore, should there be any privileges, through which the English kings, in general terms, gave power to the chief pontiff over the things which they gave to the churches, these privileges should be interpreted broadly, so that through them the power of prohibiting the clergy from aiding the king with these same things, in any case whatsoever in which no express and special mention is made of these privileges, should in no way be taken away from the highest pontiff, but is understood to be granted to him. For this reason, if it is in no way expressed in such privileges that the clergy should come to the king's aid in his wars, then the pope can prevent them from coming to his aid in this event.

Furthermore, the goods of the Church are the goods of poor; therefore, they should not be expended in battles. Again, only four portions should be made from the goods of the Church, among which there should be no intention of expending any temporal goods in battle; therefore ecclesiastical goods should not be expended in battles.

Further, 'the sentence of the pastor, whether just or unjust, is to be feared' [Gregory the Great]; therefore, whether a sentence is brought forth by a canon or by the pope upon everyone giving subsidy to the king from the

215

goods of the Church, that sentence should be upheld; and consequently they should not give aid to him against the express command of the pope, just as they should not act against his sentence.

Chapter 11

These things may be easily refuted. To the first objection, it can be said that the clergy should not give aid to the king from the goods of the Church without papal permission, and unless the Roman pontiff is first consulted concerning those matters in which the pope has the power to obstruct the clergy from conferring subsidies for the purpose of alleviating the needs of others. On the other hand, in those matters in which the pope does not have the power to prevent the clergy from alleviating the needs of others, the clergy may give aid to the king and to others from the wealth of the Church without the permission – indeed, against the command – of the Roman pontiff. It follows, moreover, that if the king should for any reason be in dire need so that his life could not be saved unless the clergy were to give him aid from the wealth of the Church (even if it were to be given liberally), the clergy ought to assist him before consulting the Roman pontiff, lest they petition the Roman pontiff and the king pass from this life before they receive an answer. Moreover, if the king were taken captive and the wealth of the laity could not suffice for setting him free, the clergy may be obliged to give the wealth of the Church for his redemption before the highest pontiff can be consulted, if it were the case that he who holds the king captive should desire to have him killed directly if the king's ransom were not immediately offered. Furthermore, if the English kings had ordered that the wealth of the Church be conferred, because by its surplus captives could be delivered, bridges constructed, and whatever other common necessities and demands could be lightened, then the clergy, without such permission of the Roman pontiff, would be bound to spend those goods endowed upon them by royal generosity, and they would not be obliged to consult the Roman pontiff; for pacts and laws which are imposed by donors in their donation of things must be observed without exception.

Therefore, since the pope does not have the power of preventing the clergy from assisting the king when there is such a necessity, they are in no way obliged to consult the Roman pontiff in this case; and, if they were to consult him and he were to prohibit them from providing the aid for the king, they ought not to obey him, either because such a prohibition is wrong or because in this matter the power does not extend itself to the pope. In those matters, however, in which the pope has the power of preventing the clergy from alleviating common needs or the needs of others, the clergy should not confer subsidies for alleviating common necessities and demands unless the pope is consulted first. In such cases, moreover, in which the pope has such legislative power, it can be known by human judgement what the jurisdiction of the kings is, or what cannot be instituted without the express or tacit consent of the king, as will become clear in the response to the second objection.

To this objection it can be said that if the English kings or even individual inhabitants of the kingdom, by themselves separately without other of the faithful, had never given any power or jurisdiction to the pope over the temporal wealth which they gave to the churches, then the pope would have no legislative power over those things unless the English kings or the inhabitants of the kingdom, together with the other faithful, had given such power to the pope, either through a general council or through some other form of assembly or by any other means, tacitly or expressly, or unless the pope had acquired such power from precedent and reasonable practice without any revocation on the part of the English kings and inhabitants. And for this reason it has been already said of the pope's right to control the wealth given to the churches by the English king that it is a right of the kings, and that it was not instituted without either the express or tacit consent of the kings; for the kings granted such a right expressly, either individually, or in common with other kings established in other regions, since, together in a general council or assembly with the English kings, they desired that the pope should have such power over those things which they had given or would possibly give to the churches; it must be the case that, on the one hand, the English kings agreed either expressly or tacitly to the ordination passed in a general council or in another assembly or by other means, to the effect that the pope should have such power over ecclesiastical goods; or that, on the other hand, the pope acquired the power over such things legitimately from precedent and reasonable practice, without revocation on the part of English kings.

Therefore, the objection becomes fallacious when it states that the pope never had any power or privileges from the English kings. For any power which the pope has for legislation over the ecclesiastical wealth that the English kings gave to the churches, he acquired from the English kings in any of the manners listed above. Moreover, if in general councils there are issued any statutes, through which power is granted to the pope over those goods which the English kings gave to the churches, it can somehow be said that these statutes are privileges which are given to the pope by the English kings through express or tacit consent, and therefore all the statutes of general councils, and any other ones in which it is stated in general terms that the pope may have power over wealth given to the churches by the English kings, are to be interpreted and restricted in the same way as would be the privileges which the individual English kings under their own seals or otherwise gave to the pope concerning the holding of power over temporal wealth which had been granted to the churches. And therefore, those statements are not empty which have been inserted in the preceding chapter concerning the power or privileges granted by the English kings to the highest pontiff, since through these things it can be known how whatever statutes or decrees, by which it is asserted that the pope has power over the wealth given to the churches by emperors, kings, rulers and any other faithful, are to be interpreted and restricted; since they are to be interpreted in such a way that they exclude no piety and include no ingratitude or iniquity.

To the third objection it may briefly be replied that only the pope may interpret the privileges which he himself concedes to others legitimately and properly when the interpretation is necessary for the express reason that the intention of the giver of the privileges is unknown. But the privileges which are granted by others to the pope himself must not and cannot be interpreted by the pope, but rather by the givers, when the interpretation is necessary because the intention of those giving the privileges is forgotten. If, however, the interpretation of such privileges is necessary for someone or some people because of their ignorance of the power which the pope has from divine or human authority, such an interpretation pertains to those who have a truer, keener, more subtle and more profound understanding of human and divine laws, rather than those in whom the memory of divine and human laws blossoms little. It pertains especially to them to judge – not by discriminating in an authoritative and judicial fashion, but by affirming with doctrine and simple assertion – how much power the pope may attain over things given by the faithful to the Church, on the basis of reasonable and customary practice (not unreasonable or unprecedented practice), as a result of which the pope would be regularly able to exert power over such gifts to the churches, at least to the extent that the faithful who gave such things to the churches did not revoke but consciously allowed it. Those others who understand divine and human laws less profoundly, although they may understand the truth expressed through them, should be bound to follow any divine and human laws or human customs that might blossom in memory.

To the fourth objection it may be said that the privileges and benefits of rulers, insofar as special rights of rulers are concerned, are to be interpreted broadly so that they might not involve any vice, and so that those privileges which the rulers had in no way granted specially might be excluded; insofar as the common rights of others are concerned, they are to be strictly interpreted. And just as this applies to privileges, so it also applies to the power which one obtains either through the express or tacit permission of the rulers or through reasonable and customary practice: this must be most strictly understood insofar as the rights of others are concerned, especially where great harm could befall them. And thus, if the pope should have power over the things given to the churches by the English kings, either through the express or tacit concession of those kings or through reasonable and customary practice, then it is to be understood that he has power thereby, yet he still has no power in a particular case in which he has not legitimately used such power and in which this has not been made explicit in the concession or commission made to him which could generate great harm to common needs or to the rights of the clergy who are subject to the king. And thus, since the clergy could not be prohibited from aiding the king in such necessity without great harm – indeed, without great danger – to the common needs and even to the needs of the clergy who are subject to the king, it follows that the pope cannot make this prohibition, and should he make such a prohibition, it would be void and the clergy ought to resist him openly and in no way obey him as far as this is concerned, for they would sin mortally if they were to presume to obey him.

To the fifth objection, it may be replied that the goods of the English Church do not belong only to the poor but rather to the entire community, including the poor as well as the rich, and they also belong to all those others from the same kingdom who are in such dire or almost dire necessity that there can be no aid to them except through the goods of the Church. And so, in accordance with the assertions of the holy fathers, the ecclesiastical vessels and vestments, not only those of the poor but also those of the rich, may and should be sold for the release of captives, when they cannot be saved by any other means. And thus, the Church goods should be given not only to the poor but also for common needs, namely, for the defence of the land and the public rights; in this event, the goods may and should be expended. And just as the pope may not decree that the goods of the Church should not be issued to the poor (either since this would be against the intentions of those who gave these same goods to the Church, or since this would be against charity and brotherly love), so too he may not decree that these goods should not be expended for the defence of the homeland and of the public rights, either because this would be against the intention and will of the givers, or because this would be against the fervour and love of the communal good and salvation – not only that of the laity, but also that of the clergy and of things that pertain to them.

To the sixth it can be said that in earlier times it was customary in certain churches that only these four parts should be made from ecclesiastical goods, yet on special occasions, should be expended in another way; for according to the true assertion of the fathers, they were to be expended for the release of captives. And thus, although goods of the Church may not be customarily offered to the king, they are nevertheless to be placed at the king's disposal in the case of necessity for the defence of the homeland and of all laity as well as clergy who are native in the land, and for the defence of their belongings and of the rights of the kingdom and of the king; and at his disposal they can be expended in just battles, legitimately – even meritoriously – if this action is directed by justice alone.

To the seventh, which is the last, it is replied that the sentence of the pastor who is true (not merely according to human opinion) is to be feared, namely, that sentence which by its own right and deed is not void so as to be unqualified to pass judgment; the sentence of the false pastor, however, no matter how good a pastor he is according to human opinion – even the majority of Christians – is not to be feared. Even the sentence of the true pastor is not to be feared, should that sentence be void by its own right and deed, so he is not qualified to pass judgment, even though the sentence has not been suspended by an appeal. Such pertains to the sentence of even the true pastor when it contains a grievous error against justice and when it is brought into a case in which even the true pastor has no power. Such, moreover, pertains to the sentence of the true pope, when it is brought against the English prelates on account of their having assisted the king in the aforesaid case; since it contains a grievous error and is brought into a case in which even the true pope has no power, as may be understood from the preceding statement, and as will become more evident from things which will be discussed below.

14

ON THE DUTY OF THE KING
John Wyclif

INTRODUCTION

The life and career of John Wyclif (*c.* 1330–83) was in many ways para-
digmatic of the later medieval secular (or non-monastic) scholar. Born in
Yorkshire, Wyclif was educated and taught at several Oxford colleges, supporting his scholarship by means of absentee clerical offices, upon which
medieval scholars commonly relied for income. Wyclif's intellectual interests
were encyclopedic: they included all the major branches of philosophy and
theology, as well as political theory. In fact, when Wyclif's opinions were in
due course examined by church authorities, it was his theological teachings
regarding the Eucharist that caused the greatest stir. That Wyclif himself was
never directly condemned seems to owe much to his political connections
with the English royal family, especially John of Gaunt, the powerful son of
King Edward III. Wyclif performed various services for John and the Crown,
for which he was compensated with both financial support and protection
from hostile ecclesiastical opponents. In the end, however, Wyclif's increasingly unorthodox theological positions cost him many of his friends and
advocates at court, and he prudently withdrew from Oxford in 1381 just prior
to a purge of his followers from the University.

Wyclif's contributions to political theory were primarily an extension of
his theology. His best known works on secular government are *On Civil
Lordship* (1374/1375) and *On the Duty of the King* (1378/1379), which form
self-contained treatises within his massive *Summary of Theology*. Wyclif
develops in these works the political implications of his theology. He holds
that the legitimacy of lordship (meaning both political office and tangible
property) is dependent upon the condition of one's soul. In *On Civil Lordship*, Wyclif argues that the divine gift of temporal goods extends only to
those who avoid sin. Hence, just persons alone can rightfully exercise the
offices and prerogatives ordained by God. Such 'civil' lordship, as well as the
further 'evangelical' lordship enjoyed by individuals who are in a state of

grace, must be distinguished from mere 'natural' lordship, that is, the factual possession of temporal goods in the absence of a right to them. Individuals whose lordship is neither 'civil' nor 'evangelical' may justly be punished and deprived of it. *On Civil Lordship* also gives voice to a number of other characteristic Wyclifite political doctrines, including the articulation of a 'minimalist' conception of human law (according to which the divine law articulated in scripture should be sufficient in the main for just government) and the defence of monarchy as the prefered type of regime. Wyclif returns to these themes in *On the Duty of the King*. Taking largely for granted the superiority of kingship, he inquires into the nature and extent of authority within a monarchical system, especially in relation to the ecclesiastical hierarchy. His arguments in *On the Duty of the King* reflect, in particular, his desire to place priests under royal direction without, however, reducing the Church to an arm of the secular power.

ON THE DUTY OF THE KING

Chapter 3

...The rule of the kingdom consists in the institution of few and just laws, in their wise and precise execution, and generally speaking in the defence of the status and rights of each and every one of its loyal subjects. For the kingdom must be ruled not only by a king but by such laws if it exists in accordance with civil principles, to the extent that Aristotle seems to say that law is more necessary to the community than the king, since law is the perpetual unyielding provision of a prompt remedy for every sort of general injury against human beings. For this reason, Augustine in his Letter 32 to Boniface says, 'For because he (a king) is a human being, he serves God by living faithfully; yet because he is a king, he serves God by prescribing just laws and prohibiting the contrary, thus rigorously ordaining harmony.' And he refers to the examples of five kings (as has been demonstrated in Book 3, Chapter 26 [Wyclif's *On Civil Lordship*]). 'In this way', Augustine says, kings 'are servants of the Lord inasmuch as they are kings, since that which they do for the sake of serving Him they could not do except as kings.' The king must, therefore, establish just laws and as a consequence the rule of the law of the Lord, so that as a result of this he as well as his subjects are servants of God in His justice. And prudence makes clear that there are to be few laws. The first reason is that they [laws] are in excess of the original state of innocence; but the servant of God must be strictly limited to matters of necessity, because a surplus distracts in many ways from the law of God. The second reason is that a multitude of such laws would generate confusion and perplexity in regard to the understanding and execution of them, and the business of the wise men of the kingdom would be set aside for the sake of interpreting them. And hence the laws of the kingdom of England excel imperial laws, since there are few of them, because beyond a few basic precepts the remainder are left to the equitable judgement of the wise. And third, it may be inferred that a multitude of such laws would be dangerous and harmful to the kingdom: dangerous because men of arms would be distracted from their proper purposes on account of private profit, and especially so because, according to worldly wisdom, they would increase injuries within the kingdom on account of accusations and the desire for domination; and that would threaten the ruin of the kingdom, since according to the wise the kingdom of God is transferred from one dynasty to another on account of such injuries. Therefore, a multitude of such laws beyond what is necessary would be harmful and injurious. But second, the execution of the laws of the kingdom is to be wise and precise, for if the law were not to be executed but instead ignored, then the royal dignity would be humiliated, misdeeds and injuries would spread throughout the kingdom, and as a consequence the Christian religion would be everywhere impeded. For proportionately as one loves the king one loves his laws, just as was the case with the statement of Christ in John 14[:15]: 'If you love me you will obey my words.' And the same is the case with regard to whomever is his vicar, who not only commands his kingdom on the basis of his own person but also out of the strength of the whole community, so that he is thus to proceed in accordance with law. God thus condemns the king and kingdom which render useless such rational and established commands, since in that case law is said not merely to be superfluous but to be instituted foolishly and profanely. For this reason, [pseudo-]Aristotle in Chapter 3 of the *Secreta Secretorum*, teaching how the reputation of the king may be preserved through the display of wisdom and prudence, writes thus:

> Every king who subjects his kingdom to divine law is worthy to rule and to hold sway honourably; yet he who reduces his laws to servitude, subjecting them to his arbitrary command, is a transgressor against truth and a despiser of his own law; moreover, he who despises his law is to be despised by everyone, because he is condemned in the basis of his law.

From the first part of this, it is evident that the king so acquires the friendship of God as His true vicar that he is made to be most rightfully dominant over human beings; and from the second part of this, it is evident that the law is known to be despised when he who is bound to the law restrains or binds law without abandoning it, as though it were dead. Insofar as every king who suspends his law subjects it to his servants, so that its course is not free, he reduces the law itself to servitude because he subjects it to a person or community and he diminishes the benefits of law to those over whom law is executed. From the third part of these words of the Philosopher, it is evident that the king, by thus despising his own laws, despises God and also himself. Therefore, it is necessary that he is to be despised as sacrilegious by the people of God through condemnation by law. 'Sacrilegious', I say, because he who diverts the execution of sacred matters by means of the sacred law commits an injury against God and the kingdom. Therefore, the king, who ought to ordain his laws and their execution to be just and rational, creates an obstruction in respect to God and his own people, who accordingly desire the accomplishment of justice. Moreover, although the king can on occasion dispense with the execution of law, inasmuch as he is superior to his law, still he should never seek this except on account of a dispensation of reason, for otherwise crimes could be multiplied in the kingdom to the extent that it would be turned into a den of traitors to God and the king. Therefore, Aristotle says above that the wise philosophers and excellent speakers have said that, in the first place, it befits the majesty of kings to obey instituted laws not in the mere semblance of fiction but in the clearness of fact, so that everyone knows him to fear God on high and to be subject to divine power. For then humans grow accustomed to revering the king when they see him fearing God. Moreover, if he reveals himself to be religious in mere appearance and is an evil doer in his works, since it would be difficult for nefarious deeds to be concealed from and unknown to the people, he will be reproved by God and disdained by everyone. This judgment of the philosophers is supported on the grounds of the principles of faith and from the experiences which the kings of the Old Testament underwent. Therefore, since the law is to be executed by a virtuous soul over those subject to the law, do not be surprised if the king who abolishes such execution of his own laws destroys virtue and causes the vices of impiety to grow. And both elements are evident with regard to the royal laws and the execution of them. But in connection with the third point, it may be noted that, although the king in the rule of his kingdom cannot match God, still since he is to be vicar of God he ought to administer his kingdom along similar lines inasmuch as he can. God omnipotently creates the world in a manner corresponding to the Father, he wisely preserves the created beings belonging to the world in a manner corresponding to the Son, and he benevolently governs the progress of the preserved beings within His creation in a manner corresponding to the Holy Spirit. Likewise, the king ought to act along similar lines in regard to the corporeal affairs entrusted to his rulership, for he ought to establish his loyal subjects in their ranks, he ought to defend them in the goods of nature, and third he ought to govern them carefully in regard to their temporal possessions through his law. Concerning the first point, it is clear that it is necessary for the parts of the kingdom to be coordinated in quantity and number, since if all were to be lords, who would be workers or servants? If all were to be presbyters, who would be the lords governing or functioning secularly? Therefore, it is necessary for there to be a three-fold hierarchy in the kingdom through which all are arranged into one person of one heart, namely, the priests or those who pray, the secular lords or defenders, and the common people or labourers. The first group forms the roof of the house of the church for the reason that the level of their intercourse ought to be nearer to heaven, the burden of their temporalities ought to be lighter and their defence of spiritual affairs ought to be loftier. For they ought to protect the inferior parts from the heat of carnal desire, from the storms of worldly molestation, and from the winds of hollow boastfulness. The second level, just like a rectangle, ought constantly to defend the kingdom physically from the four plagues in a manner corresponding to the four walls of a house. Two separate walls running up to the ceiling and down to the ground are specifically reserved for priests. The third level ought to attend to working the land and therefore, by sustaining the kingdom in temporal goods, it may be compared to the foundation of the house. When this three-fold hierarchy is proportionately arranged in quantity and quality, according to God's standards, the kingdom will proceed to prosper. Therefore, the king ought to direct his wisdom and prudence most diligently to this goal. For although it may fall to God to create these three ranks, still it pertains to his Vicar to assist with their administration. But the first and more necessary level pertains to the dissemination of the Word to us. Thus, if the king rules himself along with his subordinate officials humbly, trusting completely in divine rulership; if, second, he honours the clergy by granting their income in accordance with the teachings of the law of the Lord; and if, third, he abhors and punishes harshly those who dishonour their station; then his kingdom will be erected under a very stable roof directed by the spirit of God....

Chapter 5

...The entire kingdom including the king is a single person, as has been here assumed, whose head or heart is the king, flowing out of whom is the preservation of sensation and movement from defect. But all of the functions, from the secondary members all the way up to the more primary members, are administered by the principal member itself. Therefore, all of the functions that are performed under the influence of royal laws and royal authority are performed as by the king himself. For in this way, we rightly say the heart pumps life into the other members, the head guides forward movement, and so forth. This would seem to confirm thoroughly, therefore, that a captain of the people does whatever is done by his people as though it were his act. Yet if something is done which is not subject to the reason or authority which one has or ought to have from the captain himself, then the act is not to be ascribed to the captain himself, just as sinning is attributed neither to God nor to Christ. This follows insofar as the head itself neither has the authority nor has the duty to act in such a manner. Yet it may be noted that, just as what is done within one body is preordained and foreknown not on account of moral but of natural differences [among members], so the parts of the body are united together in regard to material actions and not in regard to merit or demerit. If a temporal or spiritual leader permits subjects to perform any disordered acts whatsoever on account of disregard for their rulership, then the deeds of subjects ought to be imputed to their leader for the sake of assigning blame, and therefore the condition of both sorts of leaders is perilous, as is generally agreed. And I do not see why holy persons who cooperate with someone else for the sake of moral goodness do not create that goodness, just as everyone who is foreknown to cooperate with sinners for the sake of evil creates that evil. For in this manner, many people and each one of them may haul a ship, and although it may be that in the case of spiritual conduct theirs is no impediment of distance, still the king or other leader or curate has concern for spiritual matters on the basis of the singularity of the rulership undertaken by him. Hence, he receives a reward proportionately according to what is imparted by his rulership for the sake of happiness or what is lacking as a result of the defect of his rulership, and in this way the condition of both kinds of leaders is not only more elevated but also more perilous than the condition of his subjects, because just as one's merits increase from the accomplishment of one's duties, so one's demerits increase with their omission. And therefore, learned teachers say that the king, in respect of his resemblance to God, has a triple existence in the kingdom, namely, an individual existence, an environmental existence, and a virtual or potential existence. He has an individual existence in the space in which he is extended, just as every other substance which is individuated is known to us by means of place and time. He has a more extensive environmental existence in those situations in which he is present, and this presence is immediately felt in relation to the place within which he is perceptible [as in the aura of royal presence]. He has a virtual existence on account of being more greatly extended throughout his entire kingdom which is civilly ruled by his lordly virtue. And in this way, Proverb 20[:8] can be understood: 'The king who sits on the seat of judgement drives away all evils from his gaze.' For these evils concern the king on account of the unyielding justice for which his coercive power is to be used, and therefore the wise saying from the above text is to be revered: 'You dread the growling lion, so also dread the king; whoever provokes him sins in his soul' [Proverbs 20:2]. And in this way I understand the words of Augustine and the other saints when they say that the Holy Church is spread throughout the whole earth. For since every member of that Church is a spiritual king dominating the whole world, do not be surprised if power over the whole world is spread across a more extensive distance than that of the civil lord, however powerful a monarch he may be. But furthermore it may be objected to this that the king would seem to be subjected to his own law, and regulated by his own law, which is superior to the king, even though he is the chief part of the kingdom and inferior only to the priesthood. Yet it would seem, on the contrary, that no one would rationally establish law for the cancellation of his own liberty. Therefore, it is necessary that the creator of law is to be above the law, as Aristotle says regarding the king in Book 3 of the *Politics*. It is necessary to note here how human law, since it is a reason or truth above all human beings, obligates all human beings, even Christ in human form inasmuch as he was not God, although on account of divinity he is above all laws, as I have explained elsewhere. But law created by civil bodies connotes, beyond such truth, a human ordination and promulgation for the sake of regulating civil lordship, and in this sense, the king is the principal creator of his law. Second, it is necessary to note how 'subjection to law' can be understood in two ways, namely, as a duty purely on the basis of the binding character of the law itself or as a duty on the basis of an obligation to a superior law. The first form of subjection is called 'coercive', and the second is called 'voluntary'. In the first way, all Christians are subject to the law of Christ, and in the second way, the human Christ himself is subject to his own law. From this it is clear, thirdly, that the command of divine law subjects a king to his own law, rather than a command of his own law. For in accordance with the law of nature, and as a consequence in accordance with divine law, it is necessary for the king to defend his own law and to serve as an example to others of how it is to be followed by obeying it and carrying it out himself. Nor is this a disgrace to the king, since his law is to be understood essentially as eternal truth, although law viewed formally and equivocally is established by finite beings. Therefore, it is necessary to distinguish between different meanings of subjection and obedience to law and reason in the process of clarifying these matters. Thus, the king, as the head of the kingdom, ought to execute his own law voluntarily in accordance with the command of a superior law, and the loyal subjects of the king, if they refuse, ought to be coerced by the command of his law, even in the case of priests, although according to other reasoning they are superior to [temporal] law. And it is clear that the condition of the king is, according to one argument, more impaired for the sake of earning merit, while according to another argument it is more elevated for the sake of earning merit, just as is explained in comparable fashion by Augustine in *On Questions of the Old and New Testaments*, Chapter 124.

If the pauper and the rich person are both ashamed, the shame of the pauper is more insignificant; for humility can recall the pauper lest he will what he desires to satisfy himself, just as fear of the law can recall him; yet the rich person, since he can entertain more opportunities for illicit pleasures, is more laudable if his soul averts these. Therefore, one reward is earned by the shame of the rich person, another by the shame of the pauper. Thus, there is more glory if the king is ashamed, inasmuch as by having everything in his power, it does not happen that he seeks with impunity to do what he can for himself. In this, he truly fears God; in this, God's precepts protect him who, having the law in his power, takes into consideration the future judgement of God. Whatever passes over into the realm of delights merits many rewards, but the greatest of these are earned by those who are lords of laws and men in the present world. For the rest are afraid of men and laws; this is the purpose for which they are watched over. Yet in the case of he who fears neither domination nor laws and who does not show respect to human beings, it is the greatest glory if he abstains.

From these words it is clear, first, that the king has his own laws in his power in the sense explained; second, it is evident that there is no specific rank that God has approved that does not have its own particular merit to be praised more by reason of a certain superiority in comparison with other ranks. For this reason, it seems to be very true that the clerical rank, which Christ instituted, is more worthy of and suited to reward than the rest of the ranks following after it, on account of its assistance to humanity. And third, it is clear that a person of such rank is not to be more praised absolutely as a result of his condition, but in relation to the substantial merits which are suited to his superior rank. For, while a rank endures without change, a person of such rank is infinitely more praiseworthy or blameworthy on account of virtue or vice than on account of great eminence or inferiority of status which is brought about by such a disposition. For, as Augustine states in Chapter 34 [of Augustine's *On Questions of the Old and New Testaments*], a person of minimal virtue at the lowest station of the Church earns more praise and honour than a person of supreme rank so long as he has persevered in sin. And thus would eternal wisdom be enhanced, inasmuch as the condition of the Church would not be disparaged nor would a person be praised in a proportionately more elevated fashion than his rank permits; but to the extent that virtue and perseverance are unknown to us, so is the source of human praise, insofar as it derives from the Lord, concealed and all praise of finite beings is imputed by the Creator from whose source praise prudently and principally arises.

And so in the temporal realm the royal station is more elevated and in the spiritual realm the apostolic station is more elevated. But who has been thrust lower than Pharaoh or Judas? Therefore, it is necessary that the just king establish just laws and execute them virtuously after the example of the law of God, prudently honouring each person according to the dignity of his station and merit – such as the good dukes, counts and barons, and knights of the same sort, and faithful workers of the same sort, and clerics of the same sort, who duly proceed within their station – and in turn honouring with suitable punishment those who are a disgrace to their rank. For the body of the kingdom endures in political health when its heart, which is the royal power, pushes the superior clergy as well as the inferior masses towards what is just. And because the human animal pays a great deal of attention to temporal goods, thus those inferiors who look after temporalities are to be prudently moderated in regard to temporalities, just as the sizeable provisions of those superiors who plainly and gently look after the animate spirit ought to be removed from the embrace of holy men and measured out equally among those in possession of temporalities and offices. For this reason, nothing more powerfully destroys the premier part of the kingdom, which exists for the sake of political life, than the immoderate removal of the goods of fortune from inferiors. For undermined foundations must surely ruin a house. For this reason, [pseudo-]Aristotle says in Chapter 4 of the *Secreta Secretorum*: 'Just as the royal lordship is preserved by the unwavering obedience of subjects, so the power of those holding sway is debilitated and depressed by their disobedience.' And I will reveal to you the causes on account of which subjects are led to obey. The first cause is that the king exercises justice in regard to the meagre and wretched possessions and financial affairs of subjects. It is necessary, I say, that the king distribute his wealth to them, conferring it with wise generosity according to the merits of individuals. The second cause is moderation in deeds and possessions lest these be multiplied to excess; for he must prudently master his subjects for the sake of the honour of God and the utility of the kingdom and himself. And these two, namely, limitation to more appropriate functions and defence of the rights of subjects, make the people duly obedient to their lord. Nor is this contrary to, but instead consonant with, the claim that the king in times of need for himself or the kingdom may draw (although with discretion) upon the temporal goods of both his laymen and his priests, as well as himself. For in this way, the heart draws warmth and moisture for its own needs from every possible external member. And in regard to priests, who are the neck of the Church or kingdom, the king ought to give them temporal goods more unconditionally, without burden or responsibility, insofar as it is necessary for their duties according to the standards set by the law of God. For the excessive inclination of priests towards temporal goods induces a sort of giddiness, just as ruination and overindulgence produce a troubled humour in the head, causing laziness and other afflictions in the head, as a result of which the body is abandoned by the ruling head. And hence Aristotle in *On Animals*, Chapter 14 [1.15] says that the human being alone among the multitude of animals has a head erected towards the heavens, on account of the divine substance in which it participates. For the erection of the head on high over the stomach renders its humours purer and achieves what is contrary to evil. And on account of such refinement, the prophet would seem to say in regard to the mingling of the senses, 'The whole head is weak and the whole heart is sick' (Isaiah 1[:5]). The king is, therefore, to reflect on the words of Deuteronomy 19[:14]: 'Do not take it upon yourself and move the property line of your neighbour which your ancestors had fixed.'...

15

THE BOOK OF THE BODY POLITIC
Christine de Pizan

INTRODUCTION

Considered to be the first woman of letters of France, Christine de Pizan (*c.* 1365–*c.*1430) was born in Venice, daughter of Thomas de Pizan, medical doctor and astrologer, whose training at the prestigious University of Bologna brought him an appointment to the court of Charles V of France. He settled his young family in Paris, and there they stayed throughout his career. Christine's love of learning and familiarity with court life brought their reward when she was suddenly left a young widow at the age of twenty-five, with three young children, a widowed mother, and an orphaned niece to support. Christine turned to a life of letters both for consolation and for income, writing a series of remarkable works that included poetry, biography, politics, chivalry, warfare, religion and philosophy.

The works for which she is best known today were written both to defend and instruct women: *The Book of the City of Ladies* and *The Book of the Three Virtues* (also called *The Treasury of the City of Ladies*). For this volume, we have chosen a work written for a young man, the fourteen-year-old heir to the throne, Louis of Guyenne. This political treatise, *The Book of the Body Politic*, is an example of a 'mirror for princes'. Its purpose was to instruct as well as entertain the prince, with the goal of transforming him into a model king.

Body Politic takes its name and organizing theme from John of Salisbury's *Policraticus* (see pages 30–60) where the political community is described as a body, with king as head, soldiers and administrative officers as the hands, and the peasants are the feet. The metaphor had been used since the twelfth century to express interdependence and hierarchy, depending on the author's political views. In Christine's work the metaphor is used primarily as an organizing theme, but there are suggestions in the text that she also meant it as a warning: if the prince is not caring for his people, they will revolt.

Body Politic is arranged in three parts, corresponding to the major classes or 'estates' of French society. Part I considers the education of the prince in detail – what he should eat, how he should dress, as well as the books, experiences, and ideas to which he should be exposed. Part II treats knights and nobles, and considers the nature and behaviour to be expected of this class. Part III, the selection chosen for this volume, examines the common people: merchants, clergy, students, and artisans as well as peasants. While it is the shortest part of the book, it shows us a rare glimpse of the life of common people – of whom Christine was one. The politics, however, reveal her princely audience. The work conveys a politics of seigneurial responsibility, and contains an implicit warning – if you do not act responsibly, your people will revolt.

THE BOOK OF THE BODY POLITIC

PART III

(Here begins the third part of this book, which is addressed to the universal people.)

Chapter 1: How the estates must [unite] and come together

In the first part of this book concerning the instruction of princes, as we have said, we have depicted the aforementioned prince or princes as the head of the body politic, as planned before. Thereafter followed the second part, on the education of nobles and knights, which are the arms and the hands. In this part, with God's help, let us continue with what we can pluck from the authorities on this subject of the life of the body of the afore- mentioned polity, which means the whole of the people in common, des- cribed as the belly, legs, and feet, so that the whole be formed and joined in one whole living body, perfect and healthy. For just as the human body is not whole, but defective and deformed when it lacks any of its members, so the body politic cannot be perfect, whole, nor healthy if all the estates of which we speak are not well joined and united together. Thus, they can help and aid each other, each exercising the office which it must, which diverse offices ought to serve only for the conservation of the whole community, just as the members of a human body aid to guide and nourish the whole body. And in so far as one of them fails, the whole feels it and is deprived by it.

Thus it is appropriate to discuss the way the final parts of the body should be maintained in health and in well-being, for it seems to me that they are the support and have the burden of all the rest of the body, for which they have the job of having the strength and the power to carry the weight of the other parts. This is why, just as we said earlier, the good prince must love his subjects and his people, and we spoke of the office of nobles which is established to guard and defend the people.

It is suitable to speak of the love, reverence, and obedience that his people should have for the prince. So let us say to all universally, all the estates owe the prince the same love, reverence, and obedience. But after I have said something about the increase of virtue in their life and manner of living, perhaps I will discuss the three ways the different classes ought to express the generalized principle. And because sometimes there are complaints among the three different estates – princes, knights, and people – because it seems to each of them that the others do not do their duty in their offices, which can cause discord among them, a most prejudicial case, here is a moral tale told as a fable:

Once upon a time there was great disagreement between the belly of a human body and its limbs. The belly complained loudly about the limbs and said that they thought badly of it and that they did not take care of it and feed as well as they should. On the other hand, the limbs complained loudly about the belly and said they were all exhausted from work, and yet despite all their labour, coming and going and working, the belly wanted to have everything and was never satisfied. The limbs then decided that they would no longer suffer such pain and labour, since nothing they did satisfied the belly. So they would stop their work and let the belly get along as best it might. The limbs stopped their work and the belly was no longer nourished. So it began to get thinner, and the limbs began to fail and weaken, and so, to spite one another, the whole body died.

Likewise, when a prince requires more than a people can bear, then the people complain against their prince and rebel by disobedience. In such discord, they all perish together. And thus I conclude that agreement preserves the whole body politic. And so attests Sallust, 'In concord, little things increase, and by discord, great things are destroyed'.

Chapter 2: On the differences between the several peoples

Although the writing of books and especially those on manners and instruction must be general and relate to the inhabitants of all countries (since books are carried to many places and regions), because we reside in France, we will restrict our words and teaching to the French people, although these words and instruction would seem generally to serve as a good example in all other regions where good and correct understandings are desired.

Throughout the whole world, lands which are governed by humans are subject to different institutions according to the ancient customs of places. Some are governed by elected emperors, others by the succession of kings, and so on. Also there are cities and countries which have rule and are governed by princes which they choose among themselves. Often these make their choice more by will than by reason. And sometimes, having chosen them by caprice, they seem to depose them the same way. Such government is not beneficial where it is the custom, as in Italy in many places.

Other cities are governed by certain families in the city that they call nobles, and they will allow no one not of their lineage to enter their counsels nor their discussions; this they do in Venice which has been governed thus since its foundation, which was very ancient. Others are governed by their elders which are called 'aldermen'. And in some places, the common people govern and every year a number of persons are installed from each trade. I believe that such governance is not the most profitable for the republic and also it does not last very long once begun, nor is there growth or peace and for good reason. But I will not say more for reasons of brevity. Such was the government of Boulogne of Grasse. I would have too much to do to speak of each people separately, but when it comes to choosing the most suitable institution to govern the polity and the community of people, Aristotle says in Book III of the *Politics* that the polity of one is best, that is, governance and rule by one. [Rule by] a few is still good, says he, but [rule] by the many is too large to be good, because of the diversity of opinions and desires.

On our subject, I consider the people of France very happy. From its foundation by the descendants of the Trojans, it has been governed, not by foreign princes, but by its own from heir to heir, as the ancient chronicles and histories tell. This rule by noble French princes has become natural to the people. And for this reason and the grace of God, of all the countries and kingdoms of the world, the people of France have the most natural and the best love and obedience for their prince, which is a singular and very special virtue and praiseworthy of them and they deserve great merit.

Chapter 3: The obedience to the prince that a people ought to have

It pleases the good to have their merits be praised, although to be praised scarcely matters to those who are wise. As I have said before, no matter what anyone said to diminish their worth, it causes them to be pleased and delight more in goodness. For just as prudent men who are curious about their health would like the advice of doctors, even though they have no symptoms of illness, but so they may live in health, it pleases them to have a regimen to preserve their health. Likewise, we will comfort the loyal people of France in order to preserve them in the good and faithful love that they are accustomed to and always have for their very noble, venerable, and above all, praise-worthy and redoubtable princes. And so that they understand and know that by doing so they act as virtuous and good people, this will be demonstrated here by quotations on the subject from Holy Scripture and other examples.

The Holy Scriptures in many places advise subjects to render themselves humble subjects and to be readily obedient to their lords and rulers. So St Paul says in the thirteenth chapter of the Epistle to the Romans: 'All living creatures ought to be subject to powerful rulers, for those powers that princes have are commanded by God. And he who resists their power, he is recalcitrant or rebellious against the command of God.'

And this same St Paul, in Chapter Three of the Epistle to Titus, admonishes those of the common people to hold themselves subject to princes and high powers. And this adage is given by St Peter in his first epistle, Chapter Two, where he says, 'Be subject to your lords in fearful dread.' But, so that no one can excuse oneself by saying that this only applies to princes that are good, St Peter declares plainly, 'Suppose that the princes were bad,' he says, 'then subject yourself for the love of God, and especially to the king as most excellent and to the leaders sent by God for the punishment of evil doers and for the glory of the good and of their good deeds.'

And for those who may complain about the tribute and taxes that it is suitable to pay to princes, they are to understand that it is a thing permitted and accepted by God. And so Holy Scripture gives an example to demonstrate how subjects ought not to refuse to pay that which is commanded. In Chapter Twenty-two of his gospel, Saint Matthew tells how the Pharisees asked our Lord if they must pay taxes to Caesar the emperor, to which our Lord answered, saying 'Give to Caesar that which is Caesar's and to God that which is His', which means that taxes are due the prince. In the seventeenth chapter of his gospel, Saint Matthew also tells how our Lord sent St Peter to the river and told him to look in the mouth of the first fish which he caught and he would find a coin. And He told him to take this coin to those who collected the taxes of the emperor in payment for the two of them. Thus, our Lord himself gave an example of being subject in deed and in word to revere and obey lords and princes. On this point of loyalty towards the prince, I believe that God has saved the people of France from many perils, because of their goodness and merit.

All subjects ought accordingly to be loyal towards their prince, and evil comes from doing the opposite. Therefore let us return to Valerius and other authors on this subject. In Chapter Eight, Book Six, Valerius tells of the loyalty which a person named Papinion [Urbinus Panapion] had towards his lord. He knew that his lord was spied on by those who hated him to death and he could not escape if he were found. And so, in order to save him, he took his lord's robe and his ring, and wrapped him in his own and secretly took him out of the palace and stayed there in his place. When his enemies came, he let them kill him in order to save his lord and master. Valerius said that although the narration of this deed was brief, as a subject for praise, it is not.

On the topic of the evils that come to a people that rebels against the prince, so that one can guard against it, in Book Eighteen, the book of Trogus Pompeius tells how the people of a great city rebelled so much against their lord that they wanted to kill him, his wife and children and all his lineage. None the less there is always one person who is less evil than the rest. One of the citizens named Strato, when he found his lord hidden in fear, did not want to kill him but had pity on him and wanted to keep him from death. He hid him to save him and the people believed he had fled. And when the people had done this, they wanted to choose one of themselves to be king. But because they were divided on who it should be, they ordered that they assemble in a field the next day before sunrise, and the first to see the sun rise would be their king. Strato, who had saved the king from death, took counsel with him that night about how he could see the sun first in order to be king. His lord, who wanted to return the courtesy for the life that he had saved, advised him that when everyone looked to the east, Strato should look to the west towards the city. So they were all together, looking towards the rising sun, when Strato, who was looking in the opposite direction, saw the rays of the sun hit the top of a high tower. And so he showed it to the others who could not see it yet. Then everyone was much amazed and asked him who had given him the advice and he told them how he had saved his lord, and everything.

A long time after, in the time when Alexander the Great reigned, the treason of this people to its lord was spoken of. And Alexander wanted to avenge the king and went to assail the city and take it by force and punish them severely. Because the king that he had saved was dead, he confirmed Strato in his kingdom and ordered that his children would reign after him because of the kindness he had done his lord.

Chapter 4: Here we begin to discuss the third estate of the people, and first, clerics studying the branches of knowledge

In the community of people are found three estates, which means, especially in the city of Paris and other cities, the clergy, the burghers and merchants, and the common people, such as artisans and labourers. Now it is suitable to consider the things to say that are beneficial as examples of good living for each of the distinct estates since they are different. And because the clerical class is high, noble, and worthy of honour amongst the others, I will address it first, that is, students, whether at the University of Paris or elsewhere.

Oh well advised, oh happy people! I speak to you, the disciples of the study of wisdom, who, by the grace of God and good fortune or nature apply themselves to seek out the heights of the clear rejoicing star, that is, knowledge, taking diligently from this treasure, drinking from this clear and healthy fountain. Fill yourself from this pleasant repast, which can so benefit and elevate you! For what is more worthy for a person than knowledge and the highest learning? Certainly, you who desire it and employ yourself with it, you have chosen the glorious life! For by it, you can understand the choice of virtue and the avoidance of vice as it counsels the one and forbids the other.

There is nothing more perfect than the truth and clarity of things which knowledge demonstrates how to know and understand.

There is no treasure of the goods of fortune that he who has tasted of the highest knowledge would exchange for a drop of the dregs of wisdom. And truly, no matter what others say, I dare say there is no treasure the like of understanding. Who would not undertake any labour, you champions of wisdom, to acquire it? For if you have it and use it well, you are noble, you are rich, you are all perfect! And this is plain in the teachings of the philosophers, who teach and instruct the way to come by wisdom to the treasure of pure and perfect sufficiency.

The very worthy philosopher Cleantes, having already experienced the true desire to taste of wisdom, had such love that though he was too poor to buy books or even something to live on, drew water all night for the needs of students in order to have enough to live on; by day, he listened to the study and the lessons of Chryssipus, who was a very fine philosopher, so that his learning would be complete. Thus by industry and long patience he became a very noble man, who was worthy of the highest praise as much for the constancy of his labour as the knowledge he acquired. Thus, in a letter, Seneca said that Cleantes, by the labour he had undertaken, helped himself to come to the perfection of knowledge.

On the subject of the love of knowledge and diligence and care needed to learn, in order to have the great good that comes to those who acquire it, we will tell a little of other philosophers to whet the appetite of those who study.

The philosopher Plato loved knowledge so much that by the hard work of acquiring it, he filled himself with wisdom and learning. This Plato was Aristotle's teacher and lived during the time of Socrates the philosopher. He benefited so much from learning that because of the nobility of his mind, he was reputed to be the wisest of all mortal men. And he showed that he was fond of knowledge, for he went everywhere looking for books, even to Italy. About this, Valerius says that his great diligence and desire for learning took him to collect books everywhere, and so, by him, knowledge was expanded and dispersed around the world.

This eminent man died at the age of eighty-one. His death showed the love he had for all kinds of books, for found near him were the books of a woman poet, named Sappho, who wrote about love in joyous and graceful verses, so Orosius says. And so, perhaps he looked at them to take pleasure in her pleasant poems.

Valerius' book tells of the philosopher Democritus, who, according to what Aristotle says in the first book of *On Generation and Corruption*, was concerned about everything, that is, that he wanted to talk and debate about everything that he said. Therefore, Aristotle recommended his natural philosophy and his opinions in many places. He is praised and recommended so much by Valerius because, first, he despised riches, which many times are an impediment to the acquisition of philosophy, and also he tells how Democritus was able to abandon his riches, which were so great that his father could give food to Xerxes' entire army. None the less, so that he could retire to study, he threw aside the concerns and occupations that come to men with

236

wealth; he distributed all that he had and retained scarcely what he needed to live on.

Secondly, Valerius recommends him because he did not desire worldly honours, which are an impediment to the conquest of knowledge. And because he lived a long way from Athens and employed all his time in educating himself, he lived unknown by those in the city. As he testifies in one of his volumes, he chose the solitary life to be outside the tumult that impedes thought. So it appears that he had a great desire for wisdom, for he avoided with all his power anything which could hinder his acquisition of it.

On the subject of the love of knowledge and study, Valerius says of the philosopher Carneades that he was the upright, hardworking knight of wisdom, because for 80 years he lived as a philosopher. So amazing was his concentration on works of learning that he often forgot to take his meal at table. He was so abstracted that his loyal servant, Meleisa, would put the food in his hand. This philosopher cared for nothing in the world but virtue.

I could speak of other noble philosophers and seekers of wisdom, but will not, for the sake of brevity. I tell the above stories to bring them to the memory of good students so that they see that books of such topics can teach them knowledge in order that they may increase in goodness and virtue. For there is no doubt that the sciences perfect the habits, so that if there is someone so perverse that it is suffices for them that others think that they know the sciences, and they teach it to others, then they resemble such people who die of hunger with food near them. And no doubt, such people are more to blame when they are mistaken than are others.

Chapter 5: More on the same subject

Because it is an important subject and appropriate to know, and because not everyone has the book by Valerius to study at his pleasure the subjects of which he speaks, it pleases me to speak about study.

As I said before, the student ought to have great diligence in order to acquire wisdom. Valerius teaches how one ought to have moderate diligence and not be too excessive in this exercise. He says that Scaevola, who was an excellent jurist and expert in common law in Rome, and who composed many laws, after his arduous work and study, took recreation in a variety of games. And this ought to show that Valerius is correct when he says that the nature of things does not allow a person to work continually, but that to rest is not at all to be lazy. Leisure does not mean to do nothing physical, but means any joyful work or sport will refresh his understanding, because the sensitive qualities of the soul become weak from long attention to study, and they are better refreshed by rest and peace than by complete cessation of all activity. If they give themselves no recreation, those whose work is study become melancholy because the mind is overworked, and if they go to sleep they will suffer from bad dreams. And so the remedy for such labour is to rejoice the spirit in games and play. Just as rich food pleases us more when alternated with plain food, so the work of study is best nourished when one sometimes plays, and so Cato says, 'Vary your work with diversions'. In Book Four of *Ethics*, Aristotle says: 'one should exercise the virtue of temperance and moderation in work and play'; to which Seneca, in his book *On Tranquility of Mind*, adds: 'fertile fields are soon exhausted by continual and uninterrupted cultivation'. So continual mental work destroys the strength and leads to frenzy, and so nature gives humans an inclination to play and relax from time to time. It is for this reason there are laws establishing certain holidays so that people come together in public to bring joy and a cessation of work. On this, it is said of Socrates, from whom no part of wisdom was hidden, that he was not ashamed when Alcibiades mocked him for playing with little children, because it was because of this recreation that his understanding was clearer and more lively at study. This is why in his old age he learned to play the harp.

Chapter 6: On the second estate of people, that is, the burghers and merchants

I said before that the second estate of the people is composed of the burghers and merchants of the cities. Burghers are those who are from old city families and have a surname and an ancient coat of arms. They are the principal dwellers and inhabitants of cities, and they inherit the houses and manors on which they live. Books refer to them as 'citizens'. Such people ought to be honourable, wise, and of good appearance, dressed in honest clothing without disguise or affectation. They have true integrity and are people of worth and discretion, and it is the estate of good and beneficial citizens. In some places, they call the more ancient families noble, when they have been people of worthy estate and reputation for a long time. And so, in all these places, one ought to praise good burghers and citizens of cities. It is a very good and honourable thing when there is a notable bourgeoisie in a city. It is a great honour to the country and a great treasure to the prince.

These people ought to be concerned with the situation and needs of the cities of which they are a part. They are to ensure that everything concerning commerce and the situation of the population be well governed. For humble people do not commonly have great prudence in words or deeds that concern politics and so they should not meddle in the ordinances established by princes. Burghers and the wealthy must take care that the common people are not hurt, so that they have no reason to conspire against the prince or his council. The reason is that these conspiracies and plots by the common people always come back to hurt those who have something to lose. It always was and always will be that the end result is evil and detrimental. And so, if there is a case sometime when the common people seem to be aggrieved by some burden, the merchants ought to assemble and from among them choose the wisest and most discreet in action and in speech, and go before the prince or the council, and bring their claims for them in humility and state their case meekly for them, and not allow them to suffer, for that leads to the destruction of cities and of countries.

So, to the extent of their power, they should quiet the complaints of the people because of the evil that could come to all. They take care of themselves this way as well as others. And if sometimes the laws of princes and their council seem to them to appear, according to their judgement, to be wrong, they must not interpret this as in bad faith, and there may be danger in foolishly complaining, but they ought to assume that they have good intentions in what they do, although the cause might not be apparent. It is wisdom to learn when to hold one's tongue, said Valerius, citing Socrates, the most noble and praiseworthy philosopher. Once he was in a place where many complained of the laws of princes, and one of them asked him why he alone said nothing when the others spoke. 'Because', said he, 'I have sometimes repented of speaking but never of holding my tongue.'

It is a noble thing to keep from speaking, from which evil can come and no benefit. Likewise, wise Cato said, 'The first virtue is to hold one's tongue.' For one is close to God who by the teaching of reason knows to keep quiet. And in the fifth book of the last work, Seneca said that 'he who would be one of the disciples of Pythagoras must be silent for five years, because only thus could he learn when to speak.'

Chapter 7. How the wise burghers ought to counsel the simple people in what they should do

As was said before, the wise should teach the simple and the ignorant to keep quiet about those things which are not their domain and from which great danger can come and no profit. And as testimony to this, it is written in Chapter Twenty-two of the book of Exodus that the law forbids such complaints and says also 'you will not complain about great rulers nor curse the princes of the people'. And Solomon confirms this in the fifth chapter of Ecclesiastes, saying 'Do not betray the king in your thought', which means that no subject ought to conspire against his lord. It is also dangerous to complain about or disobey the laws of princes. In his twelfth chapter, Justin tells about Alexander, who became ruler of Persia due to the great victories that he had won. He wanted to be greeted according to the custom of the place, which was a kind of adoration, as we would call kneeling or speaking on one's knees, which was not the customary thing in Macedonia or other regions. But because there were complaints, Cantilenes the philosopher (who had been sent to him by Aristotle, because he could no longer tolerate the burden of travelling with him himself) harshly reproved Alexander, for which Alexander had him executed. And this means, says Valerius, that when Aristotle left Alexander, he left this Cantilenes in his place, for he was his

239

disciple and was very wise. But Aristotle counselled his disciple not to speak of the vices of the prince behind his back for two reasons. First, it does not become a subject to shame his lord. Secondly, that as soon as these words have gone out of his mouth, they are reported to the king by flatterers. He advised him to speak little to Alexander, but when he did, he ought speak cheerfully, so that his words could not put him in danger. Nor should he flatter him, but if cheerfully phrased, what he said would be acceptable. But this disciple did not follow his master's teaching, and he repented later.

Another example from Valerius of not disobeying the laws of the prince, and concerning the philosopher that Alexander had killed because he contradicted his law, was the philosopher Demades in Athens. When Alexander wanted to be adored as described above, he sent word to Athens and said that he wanted to be worshipped in this way. The Athenians, who were more accustomed than other people to respect ceremonies and laws, went to their council on this. It was the common opinion that they could not do him such an honour which was appropriate only for the gods. Then the wise man Demades, who knew well what could happen if they disobeyed the prince, said to them: 'Be careful not to be so careful of the heavens that you lose the earth.'

These things could be given as an example in any country but merciful God has not put cruel and bloody princes against their people in France. For of all the nations of the world, I dare say without flattery, it is true that are no more benign and humane princes than in France, and thus they ought all the more to be obeyed. And even if sometimes by chance it seems to the people that they are aggrieved and burdened, and that other places are less so, and even supposing that were true because of their chartered liberties, yet they may have other services and usages that are more detrimental, like great wrongs done to them, or murders amongst themselves, because there is no justice which guards them or treats them in another way. And in spite of those who contradict me, I hold that of all the countries in Christendom, in this one the people commonly live better both because of the benevolence of princes without cruelty, and because of the courtesy and amiability of the people of this nation. And I do not say this out of favouritism, because I was not born here. But, God be my witness at the end, I say what I think! And since I have enquired about the government of other countries and I know there is no paradise on earth, I know that everywhere has its own troubles.

One could speak of these cruel princes of times past, and even in the present times there would be enough to find. But because this could not be turned to good example, I will pass over them lightly. But on the subject of people burdened by the ruler, an amazingly false and dishonest trick was played on his people by the tyrant Denis. This Denis was defeated in battle, so afterwards he went and plotted in great malice and evil, in order to recover his losses and expenses. He publicly announced to all his people and citizens that he believed that the loss was due to sin; he had not fulfilled his vow to the goddess Venus. The vow was that if she would give him help and grace in battle so that he would be victorious, then on the feast day of the goddess and in her honour, all the ladies and young women of the country would give pleasure to any man who requested it. But because he had not fulfilled his vow after the victory in battle, Venus had avenged herself on him for having defrauded her. In this most recent battle, she had caused his defeat. And so to satisfy the goddess, on her solemn feast day, he ordered all the ladies and young girls to dress themselves in their richest apparel and with all their jewels. And those who had no jewels of their own were to borrow some. Then they were to go to the temple and from there they would be brought to the public square. But every man should be made to swear not to touch them. Because of this vow, the foolish people of this land believed the king and consented that their wives and daughters be brought there because it seemed to them that this would appease and satisfy the goddess without threat to either the honour or the chastity of their wives and daughters. So all the women, dressed as well and as richly as they could, went to the temple. But Denis their king, had a different plan in mind. Having lied about this, he knew by their clothing and jewels the riches of his people and his burghers. So it seemed to him that he could burden them with greater taxes, and with that he sent some people to the temple to rob them of their rich robes and jewels and the richest matrons were forced by beatings and torture to reveal the savings of their husbands.

This Denis, who was king of Sicily, could well be called a bad prince. But so that no one has the desire to imitate him, it should be known that, as often happens, an evil life attracts an evil end, and his end was very bad. After he had done this evil deed, he was villainously slain by his own people. His son, who was also named Denis, succeeded him but also had a bad end: he was deposed as ruler and afterwards taught children at a school in Corinth to earn his living. Thus the child bears the burden of the misdeeds and evil of his father. As it is written in Holy Scripture, 'The fathers eat sour grapes and their children suffer from toothache'. It is also written, 'Our fathers sin and we bear their iniquities'.

Still on the subject of bad princes, from which God guard us, there was once a king in Egypt named Ptholomeus Phiton, who among other vices was debauched and lecherous. And he was named Phiton, says Valerius, because Phiton is synonymous with increase and augmentation of vice, for because of his lechery, he committed many crimes and infinite evils, for which reason he died a villainous death and is defamed in memory.

Chapter 8: On merchants

As we discussed before, merchants are those people whose estate is very necessary and without whom neither the estate of kings and princes nor even the polities of cities and countries could exist. For by the industry of their labour, all kinds of people are provided for, without their having to make these things themselves, because, if they have money, merchants bring from afar all things necessary and proper for human beings to live. For it is a good thing that in the world people can have different duties. For otherwise, one would be so busy with trying to make a living that no one could attend to other aspects of knowledge – thus God and reason have provided well.

And for the good that they do for everyone, this manner of estate of people – loyal merchants who in buying and selling, in exchanging things one for another by taking money or by other honest means – are to be loved and commended as necessary, and in many countries are held in high esteem. And there is no great citizen in any city who is not involved with trade, however, they are not considered thereby less noble. So Venice, Genoa, and other places have the most rich and powerful merchants who seek out goods of all kinds, which they distribute all over the world. And thus is the world served all kinds of things, and without doubt they act honestly. I hold that they have a meritorious office, accepted by God and permitted and approved by the laws.

These people ought to be well advised in their deeds, honest in their labour, truthful in their words, counselled in what they do by those who know how to buy and resell things at such a price as not to lose money, and ought to be well informed about whether there are enough goods and where they are going short and when to buy and when to sell – otherwise their business will be gone.

They ought to be honest in their work, that is, that they ought not, under threat of conviction and awful punishment of the body, treat their goods by any trick to make them seem better than they are in order to deceive people; that they might be more expensive or more quickly sold, because many crafts are punished when there is fraud. And those who practise deception ought not to be called merchants but rather deceivers and bad people. Above all, merchants should be truthful in words and in promises, accustomed to speak and keep the truth so that a simple promise by a merchant will be believed as certain as by a contract. And those who keep their promises and are always found honest would rather suffer damage than fail to keep an agreement, which is a very good and honest custom, and it would please God, if others in France and elsewhere would do the same. Although there may be some who do wrong, I hold that by the mercy of God, there are those who are good, honest, and true. May God keep them rich, honourable and worthy of trust! For it is very good for a country and of great worth to a prince and to the common polity when a city has trade and an abundance of merchants. This is why cities on the sea or major rivers are commonly rich and large, because of the goods that are brought by merchants from far away and delivered there. So these people ought to be of fair and honest life without pomp or arrogance and to serve God in courage and reverence, and to give alms generously from what God has given them, as one finds among those who give a tenth of their goods to the poor and who found many chapels, places of prayer, and hospitals for the poor. And so there are those of such goodness that if God pleases, they truly deserve merit in heaven and goodness and honour in the world.

Chapter 9: The third estate of people

Next comes the third estate of the people who are artisans and agricultural workers, which we call the last part of the body politic and who are like legs and feet, according to Plutarch, and who should be exceptionally well kept and cared for so that they suffer no hurt, for that which hurts them can be a dangerous thing for the body. It is therefore more necessary to take good care and provide for them, since for the health of the body, they do not cease to go 'on foot'. The varied jobs that the artisans do are necessary to the human body and it cannot do without them, just as a human body cannot go without its feet. It would shamefully and uselessly drag itself in great pain on its hands and body without them, just as, he says, if the republic excludes labourers and artisans, it could not sustain itself. Thus though some think little of the office of the craftsmen whom the clerics call 'artisans', yet it is good, noble, and necessary, as said before. And among all the other good things which exist, so this one should be even more praised because, of all the worldly estates, this one comes closest to science.

They put into practice what science teaches, as Aristotle says in his *Metaphysics*, because their works are the result of sciences, such as geometry, which is the science of measurement and proportion without which no craft could exist. To this a writer testifies, saying that the Athenians wanted to make a marvellous altar to the goddess of wisdom named Minerva and because they wanted a notable and beautiful work above all, they sought counsel of excellent masters. They went to the philosopher Plato as the most accomplished and king of all the sciences, but he sent them to Euclid as the highest master in the art of measurement, because he created geometry which is read every day in general studies.

And from this can one see that artisans follow science. For masons, carpenters, and all other workers in whatever crafts work according to the teachings of the sciences. 'To be praised is to master a craft', says Valerius, 'so that art will follow nature.' When a worker properly copies a thing which nature has made, as when a painter who is a great artist makes the figure of a man so lifelike and so well that everyone recognizes him, or when he makes a recognizable bird or other beast, so too the sculptor of images makes a likeness, and others. And so some say that art is the 'apess' or the 'ape' of nature, because a monkey imitates many of the ways of a man, just as art imitates many of the works of nature.

But none the less, they say, art can not imitate everything, so one ought to praise the skilled in art and believe those who have experience, for there is no doubt that no one speaks as properly of a thing as the one who knows it. And

I believe that the most skilled artisans of all crafts are in Paris because more commonly there than elsewhere the most beautiful and noble things are made.

But to speak a little of the fact of their habits: I would to God they pleased God in themselves, because it would be pleasing to God if their lives were more sober and less licentious as is appropriate to their estate. For lechery in taverns and the luxuries they use in Paris can lead to many evil and unsuitable things. Aristotle speaks of the voluptuous life that such people and those like them lead, saying that many seem like beasts, because they choose lechery before any other pleasures.

And on the false opinion that gluttons have, in the second chapter of Wisdom, Holy Scripture says that they believe

the time of our life is short and full of troubles and in the end we have no rest, and so we use our youth to follow our desires, and we fill ourselves with wine and meat, and in everything leave the traces of our joy.

And without doubt, similar foolish and vain words can often be heard not only from simple people but from others believed wise for their estate. So the people especially ought to follow preaching and sermons on the Word of God, since for the most part they are not learned in the teachings of Holy Scripture.

Good exhortations and sermons are beneficial for Christians to hear, as Justin describes in the twentieth book of *Trogus Pompes*, about the city of Croton. They were pagans and unbelievers, and Pythagoras the philosopher, also a pagan, brought them back by his exhortations on their evil lives. For as the people there were corrupt and inclined to gluttony, vice, and lechery, they were brought to continence and a pure life by the intervention of Pythagoras. This philosopher most castigated the vice of lechery and showed that because of it many cities had gone to ruin. He taught ladies and men the doctrine of honesty and chastity, and to be sober in their food and drink. And so Pythagoras, by his wise admonitions, made the ladies put aside their fancy clothes and the men their gluttonous lives. And during the twenty years that he lived there he continued his instruction. Justin says that in the city of Methaponthus in Puilla, from which Pythagoras came, people had so great a reverence for the house in which he was born that they made it a temple and adored Pythagoras as God because of the good he had done.

Great is the need in many places for such a man, so that many people could put to work that which he taught.

Chapter 10: On simple labourers

On the subject of simple labourers of the earth, what should I say of them when so many people despise and oppress them? Of all the estates, they are the most necessary, such as those who are cultivators of the earth who feed and nourish the human creature, without whom the world would end in little time. And really those who do them so many evils do not take heed of what they do, for anyone who considers himself a rational creature will hold himself obligated to them. It is a sin to be ungrateful for as many services as they give us! And really it is very much the feet which support the body politic, for they support the body of every person with their labour. They do nothing that is unpraiseworthy. God has made their office acceptable, first, because the two heads of the world, from whom all human life is descended, were labourers of the earth. The first head was Adam, the first father, of whom it is written in the second chapter of Genesis, 'God took the first man and put him in a paradise of pleasures, to work, cultivate and take care of it.' And from this Scripture one can draw two arguments to prove the honesty of labour: the first is that God commanded it and made it first of all crafts; the second, that this craft was created during the state of innocence.

The second head of the world was Noah from whom, after the flood, all humans are descended. It is written in the ninth chapter that Noah was a working man, and after the flood he put himself to work on the land and planted vineyards. And so our fathers, the ancient patriarchs, were all cultivators of the earth and shepherds of beasts (whose stories I will not tell you for the sake of brevity), and in the olden days it was not an ignoble office nor unpraiseworthy.

In his *History of the Romans*, Florus tells us how Diocletian, Emperor of Rome, after many battles and victories, went for the rest of his life to the village called Sallon and his occupation was working on the land. Long after, the rulers of Rome were lacking good government, so Lentulius and Galerius sent to this worthy man to ask that he return to Rome and take over the empire. 'Ah,' he said, 'if you had seen the beautiful cabbages that I planted with my own hands, you would not require me to return to the empire.' And this was to say that he had more peace of mind in his state of poverty. And better to have things to one's liking than to carry a burden so large and perilous as an empire.

And on this subject, in the third chapter of the fourth book Valerius tells of Actilus, the very worthy Roman who was taken from his work to be emperor. As he worked at his plough in the field, knights came to seek him, and he was made chief and leader of the whole Roman army. And he whose hands had been hardened by labour at the plough, later left the leadership of the army and re-established the republic by his noble courage and with his hands. Said Valerius, 'The hand which had governed a team of oxen behind the plough took up governing battle chariots.' And after many noble and great victories, he was not ashamed to leave the dignity of emperor and return to the work he had left behind. Because of these stories, we can understand that the estate of simple labourer or others of low estate should not be denigrated, as others would do. When those of the highest estate choose for their retirement a humble life of simple estate as the best for the soul and the body, then they are surely rich who voluntarily are poor. For they have no fear of being betrayed, poisoned, robbed, or envied, for their wealth is in sufficiency. For no one is rich without it, nor is there any other wealth.

To confirm this, I will discuss what Valerius said about sufficiency and about a very rich man who was very poor in having it. And to tell of him and his sufficiency, he tells this story: There was, said he, a King in Lydia, who was named Gyges. His wealth was reputed to be so great that he went to ask the god Apollo whether there was anyone more happy than he. Apollo answered him that Agamis Soplidius was happier than he was. This Agamis was the poorest man in Arcadia and he was very old. He never left his little field and was content with the small yield on which he lived and that which he had. Thus one can see how Apollo took happiness to be sufficiency and not wealth, because in wealth one cannot have sufficiency, at least, not security, but instead a lot of concerns, and a plenitude of fears and worries. And so, King Gyges, who believed that the god ought to confirm that no one was happier than he, was mistaken in his vain opinion, and learned what pure and firm wealth and happiness were. Anaxagoras agreed that happiness is to have sufficiency. In the prologue to the *Almagest*, Ptolemy says, 'He is happy who never will have the whole world in his hands'. And that this saying is true is proven by all the sages, the poets, and especially, those perfect ones [i.e. those in religious orders] who have chosen a pure and poor life for their greatest surety. For although one can be saved in any estate, none the less it is very difficult to pass by flames and not be burned. There is no doubt that the estate of the poor which everyone despises has many good and worthy persons in purity of life.

Chapter 11: Christine concludes her book

I have come, God be praised, to the end I intended, that is, I bring to an end the present book, which began, as Plutarch described, with the head of the body of the polity which is understood to be the princes. Of them, I very humbly request first of the head of all, the King of France, and afterwards the princes and all those of their noble blood, that the diligent labour of writing by the humble creature Christine – this present work, as well as her others such as they might be – be agreeable to them. And since she is a woman of little knowledge, if by ignorance any faults be found, let her be pardoned and her good intention better known, for she intends only good to be the effect of her work. And I beg in payment from those living and their successors, the very noble kings and other French princes, who by remembrance of my sayings, in times to come when my soul is out of my body, that they would pray to God for me, requesting indulgence and remission of my defects.

And likewise, I ask of French knights, nobles, and generally of all, no matter from what part they may be, that if they have any pleasure in the hours they saw or heard read from my little nothings, that they think of me and say an Our Father. And in the same way, I wish the universal people – the three estates and the whole together – that God by His holy mercy desire to maintain and increase them from better to better in all perfection of souls and bodies. Amen.

Here it ends.

FURTHER READING: THE FOURTEENTH CENTURY

Primary sources

Christine de Pizan, *The Book of the City of Ladies*, trans. E.J. Richards, New York, Persea Books, 1982.

Christine de Pizan, *The Treasury of the City of Ladies*, trans. C.C. Willard, New York, Persea Books, 1989.

Christine de Pizan, *The Book of the Body Politic*, trans. K.L. Forhan, Cambridge, Cambridge University Press, forthcoming.

Dante Alighieri, *On World Government (De Monarchia)*, trans. Herbert J. Schneider, New York, Bobbs-Merrill, 1957.

Dante Alighieri, *The Banquet*, trans. Christopher Ryan, Stanford, Stanford University Press, 1989.

John of Paris, *On Royal and Papal Power*, trans. J.A. Watt, Toronto, Pontifical Institute of Medieval Studies, 1971.

Marsiglio of Padua, *Defender of the Peace*, trans. A. Gewirth, New York, Columbia University Press, 1956.

Marsiglio of Padua, *Writings on the Empire*, ed. and trans. C.J. Nederman, Cambridge, Cambridge University Press, 1993.

[Anonymous], *The Method of Holding Parliament*, ed. and trans. M.V. Clarke, *Medieval Representation and Consent*, Oxford, Oxford University Press, 1936.

[Anonymous], *The Mirror of Justices*, ed. W.J. Whittaker, London, The Selden Society, 1895.

Secondary sources

Boyle, L.E., 'William of Pagula and the *Speculum Regis Edwardi III*', *Mediaeval Studies*, 32, 1970, 329–36.

Canning, J.P., *The Political Thought of Baldis de Ubaldis*, Cambridge, Cambridge University Press, 1987.

Coleman, J. 'Medieval Discussions of Property: *Ratio* and *Dominium* According to John of Paris and Marsilius of Padua', *History of Political Thought*, 4, 1983, 209–28.

Coleman, J., '*Dominium* in Thirteenth- and Fourteenth-Century Political Thought and Its Seventeenth-Century Heirs: John of Paris and John Locke', *Political Studies*, 33, 1985, 73–100.

Condren, C., 'On Interpreting Marsilius of Padua's Use of St. Augustine', *Augustiniana*, 25, 1975, 217–22.

Condren, C., 'Marsilius of Padua's Argument from Authority: A Survey of Its Significance in the *Defensor Pacis*', *Political Theory*, 5, 1977, 205–18.

Condren, C., 'Democracy and the *Defensor Pacis*: On the English Language Tradition of Marsilian Interpretation', *Il Pensiero Politico*, 8, 1980, 301–16.

Daly, L.J., *The Political Thought of John Wyclif*, Chicago, Loyola University Press, 1962.

Fasolt, C., *Hierarchy and Council*, Cambridge, Cambridge University Press, 1991.

Forhan, K.L., 'Polycracy, Obligation and Revolt: The Body Politic in John of Salisbury and Christine de Pizan', in M. Brabant, ed., *Gender, Genre and the Politics of Christine de Pizan*, Boulder, Colo., Westview Press, 1992.

Gewirth, A., *Marsilius of Padua and Medieval Political Philosophy*, New York, Columbia University Press, 1951.

Hanrahan, T.J., 'John Wyclif's Political Activity', *Mediaeval Studies*, 20, 1958, 154–66.

Heiman, G., 'John of Paris and the Theory of the Two Swords', *Classica et Mediaevalia*, 32, 1971/1980, 323–47.

Holmes, G., *Dante*, Oxford, Oxford University Press, 1980.

Kenny, A., *John Wyclif*, Oxford, Oxford University Press, 1984.

Leff, G., *William of Ockham*, Manchester, University of Manchester Press, 1973.

Lewis, E., 'The "Positivism" of Marsiglio of Padua', *Speculum*, 38, 1963, 240–69.

Limentani, U., 'Dante's Political Thought', in U. Limentani, ed., *The Mind of Dante*, Cambridge, Cambridge University Press, 1965.

McDonnell, K., 'Does William of Ockham Have a Theory of Natural Law?', *Franciscan Studies*, 34, 1974, 383–92.

McFarlane, K.B., *John Wyclif and the Beginnings of English Nonconformity*, London, English University Press, 1952.

McGrade, A.S., *The Political Thought of William of Ockham*, Cambridge, Cambridge University Press, 1974.

Nederman, C.J., 'Royal Taxation and the English Church: The Origins of William of Ockham's *An Princeps*', *Journal of Ecclesiastical History*, 3, 1986, 377–88.

Nederman, C.J., 'Welfare or Warfare? Medieval Contributions', *International Journal of Moral and Social Studies*, 1, 1986, 219–34.

Nederman, C.J., 'Private Will, Public Justice: Household, Community and Consent in Marsiglio of Padua's *Defensor pacis*', *Western Political Quarterly*, 43, 1990, 699–717.

Nederman, C.J., 'Nature, Justice and Duty in the *Defensor Pacis*: Marsiglio of Padua's Ciceronian Impulse', *Political Theory*, 18, 1990, 615–37.

Nederman, C.J., 'Knowledge, Consent and the Critique of Political Representation in Marsiglio of Padua's *Defensor pacis*', *Political Studies*, 39, 1991, 19–35.

Oafley, F. 'The Three modes of Natural Law in Ockham: A Revision of the Text', *Franciscan Studies*, 37, 1977, 207–18.

Oakley, F., *Natural Law, Conciliarism and Consent in the Late Middle Ages*, London, Variorum, 1984.

Offler, H.S., 'The Origin of Ockham's *Octo quaestiones*', English *Historical Review*, 82, 1967, 323–32.

Peters, E.M., '*Pars parte*: Dante and an Urban Contribution to Political Thought', in H. Miskimin, D. Herlihy and A. Udovitch, eds, *The Medieval City*, New Haven, Yale University Press, 1977.

Saenger, P., 'John of Paris, Principal Author of the *Quaestio depotestate papae* (*Rex pacificus*)', *Speculum*, 56, 1981, 41–55.

Skinner, Q. 'Ambrogio Lorenzetti: The Artist as Political Philosopher', *Proceedings of the British Academy*, 72, 1986, 1–56.

Wilks, M.J. *The Problem of Sovereignty in the Later Middle Ages*, Cambridge, Cambridge University Press, 1963.

Willard, Charity Cannon, *Christine de Pizan, Her Life and Works*, New York, Persea Books, 1984.

Yenal, Edith, *Christine de Pisan; A Bibliography*, Metuchen, N.J., Scarecrow Press 1982.

NAME INDEX

Aaron 164
Abbey of Monte Casino 97
Abelard, Peter 21, 26
Abraham 163, 164, 181
Abel 181
Achates 44
Achior 59
Actilus 245
Adam 181, 245
Adrian IV, Pope 45, 46
Aeneas 44
Aesop 24
Agag, King of Amalak 32
Agamis Suplidius 246
Albertus Magnus 97
Alcibiades 230
Alexander the Great 235, 239, 240
Alfred the Great, King 6
Alps 173
Ambrose of Milan, St 130, 131, 132, 201
Amon 59
Anaxagoras 246
Antecletus, Pope 21
Antioch 196
Apollo 246
Apulia 46
Aquinas, St Thomas 97, 98, 99, 149, 157, 158
Aquino 97
Arcadia 246
Aristotle 1, 2, 3, 6, 9, 12, 71, 72, 73, 97, 98, 105, 112, 117, 118, 121, 125, 126, 127, 128, 130, 132, 136, 137, 138, 140, 144, 147, 149, 150, 151, 152, 161, 162, 169, 175, 176, 178, 179, 180, 182, 183, 184, 185, 186, 191, 193, 194, 198, 211, 222, 223, 226, 228, 233, 236, 238, 239, 240, 243
Asia 163
Assyria 163, 164
Athens 34, 35, 237, 240, 243
Attila 30, 31
Augustine of Hippo, St 1, 2, 3, 4, 5, 7, 8, 32, 54, 64, 108, 119, 120, 121, 123, 124, 127, 131, 132, 135, 160, 163, 171, 196, 203, 204, 222, 226, 227, 228
Augustinian Order 149
Augustus Caesar 38, 111
Avignon 173, 207

Balaam 42
Basil, St 55, 56, 130, 131
Becket, St Thomas 26, 27
Belgium 64
Belshazzar 206
Belus 163
Benedict, St 8, 9
Benedictine Order 8
Benevento 46
Bernard of Clairvaux, St 21, 47, 64, 65, 165
Boethius 2, 5, 6, 7, 158, 168
Bologna, University of 9
Bonne Esperance 64
Bonaventure, St 97
Boniface VIII, Pope 157, 158, 222
Boulogne of Grasse 233

Cain 181
Calcidius 2
Cambrai 64
Cambridge 9

Canterbury Cathedral 27
Cantilenes 239
Carneades 237
Carthage 44, 45, 143
Cassian 201
Cassiodorus 175, 178, 179, 194, 204
Catiline, Segius 50
Cato 92, 238, 239
Cham 33
Champagne 65
Charles, Count of Agno and Provence 76
Charles V, King of France 230
Charles VI, King of France 246
Charlemagne 9
Charondas 151
Chartres 23
Chaucer 6
China 16
Chrétien de Troyes 65
Christ, Jesus 21, 22, 23, 34, 46, 55, 56, 78, 81, 108, 109, 133, 135, 136, 157, 159, 160, 163, 164, 165, 166, 175, 177, 194, 195, 196, 197, 198, 204, 212, 225, 227, 228
Christine de Pizan 230, 231, 246
Chrysippus 31, 236
Chrysostum, St John 160
Cicero, Marcus Tullius 1, 3, 9, 27, 50, 56, 71, 72, 74, 77, 91, 121, 127, 163, 168, 176, 182, 198, 199
Citeaux 21
Cistercians 64
Clairvaux 64
Cleantes 236
Codrus 34
Cologne 97
Columna 149
Constantine I, Emperor 1, 33, 159, 196, 197
Constantinople 2
Cornificians 27, 29
Corinth 241
Crete 35, 195
Croesus 46
Crotonne 244
Cyprian 201

Damon 110
Dante 71, 168
David 32, 57, 59, 91, 102, 109, 161, 202
Demosthenes 31
Demades 240

Democritus 236
Denis 240
Dens, Guido 47
Descartes, Rene 5
Dido 44
Diolcletian, Emperor 245
Dionysius 36, 110
Dominican Order 97, 149, 157, 158
Dorians 34

Edward III, King of England 200, 201, 202, 204, 208, 209, 221
Egyachus, King of Sicyonii 163
Egypt 16, 37, 54, 107, 164, 202, 241
Eleanor of Aquitaine 24
Elizabeth I, Queen of England 6
England 11, 12, 24, 27, 61, 62, 72, 150, 200, 208, 209, 210, 212, 213, 214, 215, 216, 217, 218, 219, 220, 221, 222
Eucharist 157, 221
Euclid 243
Eugenius III, Pope 21, 47, 64, 165
Euripides 146
Europe 2, 3, 9, 10, 11, 12, 14, 16, 61, 97
Europs 163
Eutyches 158

Fabricius 47
Florence 47, 71, 168
Florus 245
France 21, 24, 26, 65, 71, 73, 97, 98, 157, 158, 166, 208, 230, 232, 233, 234, 240, 242, 246
Franciscan Order 157, 207, 208
Fulbert, Bishop of Chartres 12, 13

Galerius 245
Gaul 8, 160, 166
Gellius 51
Genoa 242
Germany 11, 15, 173, 197
Gethsemane 21
Giles of Rome 10, 149, 150
Greece 1, 2, 3, 7, 12, 149
Gregory I, Pope 8, 9, 201, 204, 210, 215
Gregory VII, Pope 15, 16
Gregory IX, Pope 129
Gregory of Nyssa 8
Gyges 246

Henry, Count of Champagne 64, 65
Henry I, King of England 16
Henry II, King of England 24, 26, 27, 61

Henry III, King of England 203
Henry IV, Emperor 15
Henry V, Emperor 16
Henry VII, Emperor 168
Herod 159, 160
Hezekiah 57
Holofernes 57, 58, 59
Homer 44
Honourius Augustodunesis 15
Horace 44
Hugh of Fleury 15
Hugh of St Victor 165
Huns 30

Illyricians 45, 46
India 163
Isaac 163
Isidore of Seville 116, 119, 125
Israel 42, 57, 202
Italy 73, 75, 97, 98, 149, 160, 173, 175,
    193, 194, 197, 198, 232

Japan 16
Jeremiah 103
Jerome, St 1, 57
Jerusalem 21, 22, 58
Jews 194, 195
Job 40, 105, 112, 175, 202
John of Gaunt 221
John of Paris 157
John of Salisbury 10, 24, 26, 65, 230
Josiah 57
Jovinian 160
Judah 57
Judas 228
Judith 58, 59, 60
Jugurtha 176
Julia 50
Julius Caesar 111, 160, 166, 234
Justin 239, 244

Lactantius 3
Laon 64
Latin 1, 2, 24
Latini, Brunetto 71, 72
Levi, Tribe of 114, 163, 164
Lentulius 245
Livy 24
Lombard, Peter 97, 121, 129
Lothair, Emperor 21
Louis VII, King of France 64
Louis of Guyenne 230
Lucan 54, 55

Ludwig of Bavaria, Emperor 173, 177,
    207, 208
Lutterell, John 207
Lycurgus 35, 151

Macedonia 45, 46, 239
Manegold of Lautenbach 15
Manicheism 4
Manipean 51
Mantua 44
Marie de France 24, 65
Marsiglio of Padua 173, 174, 207
Mary, St 81
Melchizedech 34, 164
Meleisa 237
Mercury 29, 39
Methaponthus 244
Methodius 164
Mexico 16
Minerva 44, 243
Mons 64
Moses 57, 184

Naples, University of 97
Nebuchadnezzar, King of Babylon 58,
    107, 206
Nero, Emperor 38, 172
Nestorius 158
Nicea, Council of 33
Nicholas of Clairvaux 65
Nicholas, Pope 33
Ninus 56, 72, 163
Noah 163, 245
Norbert of Xanten 64

Old Sarum 26
Olympus 53
Origen 8
Orosius 163, 236
Ossa 53
Ovid 53
Oxford 9, 207, 221

Papinian 31, 234
Paris 9, 29, 97, 98, 157, 173, 230, 235,
    244
Paris, University of 97, 149, 157, 158,
    173, 235
Paul, St 33, 35, 73, 92, 102, 105, 107,
    116, 117, 118, 128, 129, 132, 133,
    134, 136, 164, 194, 195, 196, 233
Pelagius II, Pope 8
Pelleas 54

Persia 239
Peru 16
Peter, St 22, 108, 129, 158, 196, 197, 234
Peter of Auvergne 98
Pharaoh 228
Philip of Harvengt 64
Philip III, King of France 149
Philip IV (the Fair), King of France 149, 157, 158
Photinus 54
Plato 1, 2, 4, 7, 12, 36, 40, 91, 149, 176, 236, 243
Plutarch 1, 37, 38, 39, 53, 56, 243, 246
Pompey 54
Pompeyus Trogus 234
Pontius Pilate 195
Porphyry 6
Premontre 64
Pseudo-Ausonius 129
Ptholomeus Phiton 241
Ptholomy 55, 246
Ptolomy of Lucca 98
Pythagoras 239, 244
Pythias 110

Quintillian 38

Ranulf of Glanville 61, 62
Robert of Leicester, Count 50
Rome 1, 2, 3, 8, 11, 13, 16, 38, 44, 46, 47, 48, 56, 61, 72, 76, 77, 81, 95, 106, 107, 134, 149, 163, 166, 168, 170, 173, 191, 192, 196, 197, 198, 199, 209, 211, 216, 237, 245
Roman Empire 1, 4, 8, 176, 198
Roman Republic 106, 107
Romulus 24

Southwark 207
Salem 163
Sallon 245
Sallust 106, 176, 232
Sappho 236
Saul 33, 57
Sammonicus 49
Samuel 32, 33
Scepticism 4
Scevola 237
Sem 163
Seneca 38, 90, 91, 134, 201, 236, 238, 239
Serenus, Quintus 49

Sicily 11, 36, 110, 192, 241
Sicyonii, kingdom of 163, 164
Silvester, Pope 48, 159, 197
Socrates 38, 49, 236, 238, 239
Solitae 165
Solomon 45, 57, 73, 85, 100, 102, 105, 106, 109, 111, 112, 113, 162, 239
Solon 151
Sparta 143
Stoicism 3, 4, 7, 32, 176
Strato 234, 235
Suetonius 111

Theobald, Archbishop of Canterbury 26
Theodosius, Emperor 33, 37
Tertullian 1
Thierry of Chartres 26
Thomas de Pizan 230
Tournai 64
Tracians 45
Trajan 37
Trojans 170, 233
Tyre 107

Ulysses 44
Urban II, Pope 128
Uriah 32, 59

Valerius Maximus 56, 65, 166, 234, 237, 239, 240, 241, 243, 245, 246
Varro 52
Vegetius 65
Venice 230, 233, 242
Venus 241
Vigilantius 160
Virgil 44, 45, 52, 54, 170

Waldensians 159
White Guelfs 168
William of Conches 26
William of Ockham 207, 208
William of Pagula 200, 201
Winkfield 200
Windsor 200
Wyclif, John 221, 222

Xerxes 236

Yorkshire 200, 221

Zedekiah 59

SUBJECT INDEX

aristocracy 74, 101, 103, 104, 106
artisan 43, 114, 124, 138, 147–8, 171,
  172, 231, 235, 243–4

body 4, 5, 25, 34, 36–7, 38, 40, 48–9,
  100, 101, 103, 104, 113, 134, 136,
  145, 165, 172, 179, 182, 198, 246
body politic 24, 25, 27, 38–9, 49, 51, 52,
  56, 73, 86, 100, 113, 115, 162, 191,
  206, 225, 228, 229, 230, 231, 232,
  243, 245
burgher 73, 75, 79, 80, 81, 235, 238

canon law 11, 13, 61, 158, 200, 210
Christianity 1, 12, 14, 15, 97, 135, 174,
  178, 196, 223
Church 9, 11, 14, 15, 21, 22, 27, 33, 46,
  47, 48, 52, 80, 92, 131, 157, 158, 159,
  160, 174, 208, 209, 210, 211, 212,
  213, 215, 216, 218, 219, 224, 226,
  228, 229
citizen 2, 9, 41, 44, 71, 73, 75, 78, 82,
  83, 84, 91, 93, 94, 96, 106, 108,
  141–8, 150, 151, 152, 162, 174, 184,
  185, 186, 187, 188, 190, 193, 198,
  238, 240, 242
city 2, 12, 14, 29, 31, 35, 39, 48, 54, 72,
  73, 75, 76, 77, 78, 79, 80, 81, 82, 84,
  85, 86, 90, 91, 94, 101, 102, 103, 106,
  115, 117, 118, 124, 128, 137, 138,
  139, 140, 141, 142, 144, 145, 146,
  147, 148, 161, 163, 169, 175, 176,
  177, 178, 179, 180, 182, 183, 184,
  188, 189, 190, 191, 192, 193, 194,
  196, 198, 210, 232, 233, 235, 238,
  239, 242, 244

common good 27, 29, 30, 32, 43, 49,
  85, 90, 100, 101, 102, 104, 106, 107,
  110, 114, 115, 116, 117, 118, 119,
  139, 145, 151, 152, 158, 161, 162,
  165, 166, 167, 168, 177, 178, 185,
  186, 187, 190, 194, 201, 209, 210,
  214, 219, 229
community 3, 12, 30, 31, 34, 43, 44, 50,
  52, 59, 72, 86, 89, 92, 93, 96, 98, 102,
  106, 117, 118, 119, 137, 138, 139,
  140, 144, 149, 150, 161, 162, 167,
  174, 176, 177, 180, 181, 182, 183,
  185, 186, 188, 189, 192, 196, 197,
  198, 219, 222, 223, 230, 231, 233
consent 10, 13–14, 16, 76, 93, 94, 172,
  174, 192, 202, 212, 217
court 24, 26, 27, 55, 61, 62, 65, 204, 230
custom 13, 61, 62, 72, 75, 79, 80, 81, 84,
  86, 88, 89, 92, 94, 95, 127, 185, 192,
  217, 218, 219, 232, 239, 242

democracy 101, 103, 104, 141, 143, 145,
  161, 233
divine law 12, 35–6, 55, 56, 114,
  119–20, 121, 123–4, 132, 135, 195,
  210, 218, 222, 223, 225, 227, 228, 229
duty 29, 32, 33, 36, 43, 45, 51, 53, 54,
  56, 98, 113, 114, 115, 116, 136, 148,
  181, 225, 226, 227, 229, 242

education 2, 7, 9, 27, 65–6, 79, 97, 114,
  140, 146, 149, 165, 235–8
emperor 3, 75, 107, 129, 134, 168, 170,
  171, 172, 191–2, 197, 198, 209, 218,
  232
equity 31, 32, 38, 41, 53, 62, 150, 151,

152, 171, 201, 202, 223

evil 5, 23, 25, 31, 47, 54, 74, 76, 78, 82, 85, 87, 90, 91, 93, 104, 105, 110, 125, 127, 132, 152, 198, 203, 205, 224, 226, 229, 234, 241, 243

family 43, 44, 54, 102, 117, 118, 134, 139, 140, 145, 161, 163, 165, 169, 180–1, 205, 233

fealty 11, 12, 51, 59, 78

feudalism 10–14, 197

fortune 37, 42, 55, 66, 73, 74, 91, 151, 229, 235

freedom *see* liberty

friendship 29, 44, 75, 105, 110, 111, 151, 152, 169, 199, 223

glory 36, 46, 47, 53, 54, 74, 77, 81, 82, 96, 107, 109, 110, 227

God 5, 6, 9, 12, 15, 22, 28, 29, 30, 31, 33, 34, 38, 42, 49, 50, 53, 54, 57, 59, 73, 75, 78, 82, 91–2, 99, 103, 104, 107, 109, 112, 113, 115, 119–20, 130, 131, 133, 134, 135, 159, 166, 170, 171, 183, 184, 194, 195, 196, 201, 202, 203, 204, 222, 223, 224, 229, 234, 242, 245, 247

good 5, 6, 7, 9, 23, 28, 31, 46, 47, 54, 78, 83, 85, 87, 92, 93, 104, 105, 108, 110, 115, 116, 121, 125, 132, 144, 145, 146, 147, 152, 170, 171, 178, 182, 201, 203, 221, 226, 233, 234, 237, 243, 246

government 9, 16, 53, 73, 77, 78, 85, 91, 100, 101, 102, 103, 104, 105, 110, 111, 112, 113, 114, 124, 140–1, 142, 143, 144, 145, 146, 161, 162, 169, 171, 174, 175, 176, 177, 179, 180, 184, 193, 201, 208, 240, 245

grace 27, 28, 42, 54, 66, 77, 81, 82, 135, 195, 233, 235

happiness 5, 7, 28, 108, 109, 114, 116, 117, 169, 174, 178, 198, 201, 226, 233, 246

heaven 1, 34, 109, 114, 164, 171, 176, 182, 196, 243

honour 25, 34, 35, 39, 51, 52, 53, 59, 66, 78, 79, 80, 81, 82, 83, 84, 85, 86, 90, 96, 105, 107, 109, 110, 151, 203, 235, 240, 241, 243

individual 4, 5, 28, 30, 37, 43, 44, 99,

100, 101, 106, 115, 116, 117, 118, 131, 132, 139, 145, 158, 161, 162, 166, 167, 169, 176, 189, 192, 196, 197, 198, 203, 211, 229

injustice 42, 56, 82, 101, 104, 110, 112, 135, 168, 188, 198, 199, 203, 205, 206, 209, 224

investiture 14–16

judge 13, 39, 41, 42, 47, 50, 56, 75, 77, 78–9, 82, 83, 84, 85, 87, 88, 90, 91, 95, 107, 113, 125, 126, 142, 143, 152, 189–90, 218

jurisdiction 10, 11, 12, 42, 87, 158, 159, 160, 171, 197, 198, 217

justice 3, 7, 13, 30, 31, 32, 35, 39, 41, 42, 44, 46, 48, 52, 53, 55, 62, 73, 74, 75, 76, 78, 82, 84, 90, 91, 93, 101, 103, 104, 105, 108, 110, 112, 113, 115, 122, 123, 124, 125, 126, 127, 128, 129, 135, 136, 142, 144, 147, 150, 151, 152, 166, 174, 181, 183, 184, 186, 189, 198, 200, 201, 202, 209, 211, 213, 222, 224, 226, 229, 240

kindgom 16, 29, 54, 62, 63, 113, 115, 128, 149, 150, 151, 152, 161, 169, 174, 175, 176, 177, 178, 179, 188, 189, 191, 192, 193, 194, 198, 201, 202, 203, 205, 206, 210, 211, 213, 214, 217, 219, 222, 223, 224, 225, 226, 228, 229

kingship 3, 9, 13, 12, 14, 15, 16, 27, 34, 39, 40, 45–6, 54, 56, 57, 61, 62, 73, 91, 98, 99, 101–2, 103, 106, 107, 108, 109, 110, 112, 113, 114, 115, 116, 124, 139, 150, 151, 152, 158, 159, 161, 162, 163, 164, 165, 166, 169, 179, 197, 200, 201, 203, 205, 210, 211, 212, 213, 215, 216, 217, 219, 222, 223, 224, 225, 226, 227, 228, 229, 232, 234, 241

knowledge 2–3, 6, 9, 29, 41, 71, 74, 79, 100, 119, 137, 138, 140, 146, 165, 171, 172, 184, 198, 235, 237, 242, 246

laity 9, 166, 167, 208, 209, 211, 213, 219, 229

language 27, 28, 29, 62, 74, 81, 84, 93, 100, 161, 163

law 3, 13, 30, 31, 32, 35, 36, 37, 41, 42, 43, 50, 51, 53, 54, 56, 57, 61, 62, 63, 72, 73, 75, 78, 80, 82, 84, 87, 88, 91,

92, 95, 99, 115, 116–19, 120, 121,
122–3, 124–5, 127, 128–30, 132, 133,
135, 140, 150, 171, 172, 174, 184,
185, 186, 187, 188, 193, 198, 201,
202, 209, 210, 211, 213, 216, 218,
222, 223, 224, 225, 226, 227, 228,
229, 239, 240, 242
liberty 6, 10, 12, 25, 46, 54, 55, 65, 76,
101, 106, 120, 139, 147, 148, 172,
176, 186, 190, 226, 140
lordship 10, 11, 12, 14, 25, 89, 101, 105,
112, 114, 130, 131, 157, 159, 166,
167, 187, 196, 205, 208, 209, 210,
221, 224, 225, 226, 227, 234, 239, 240
love 5, 7, 29, 34, 40, 54, 66, 73, 77, 90,
91, 96, 110, 111, 112, 132, 150, 151,
152, 158, 200, 201, 203, 204, 206,
223, 231, 233, 234, 236, 237

merchant 9, 235, 238, 241–3
monarchy 98, 104, 106, 149, 169, 179,
222, 233
monasticism 7, 8, 9, 21, 64, 131, 158
multitude 43, 99, 100, 101, 102, 103,
104, 111, 112, 113, 114, 115, 116,
118, 141, 144, 161, 162, 164, 186,
187, 205

natural law 118, 119, 120–1, 122,
126–8, 131, 132, 133, 135, 161, 162,
163, 199, 227
nature 3, 4, 5, 27, 28, 29, 30, 43, 76, 78,
90, 99, 100, 103, 108, 113, 115, 120,
121, 122, 123, 125, 127, 130, 134,
136, 137, 143, 161, 162, 170, 171,
176, 178, 179, 180, 182, 183, 186,
189, 191, 192, 222, 225, 233, 243
nobility 65, 66, 74, 101, 172, 231, 233,
235, 238, 246

oligarchy 101, 103, 104, 141, 145, 161,
187, 233

papacy 21, 33, 47–8, 75, 157, 158, 159,
160, 161, 167, 173, 174, 196–9, 208,
209, 211–20
peace 28, 49, 54, 62, 81, 82, 84, 90, 93,
94, 102, 103, 105, 115, 126, 131, 149,
162, 167, 169, 174, 175, 176, 178,
179, 180, 183, 193–9, 201, 232, 233,
237
peasantry 27, 39, 43, 200, 230, 231, 244–6
people 25, 30, 34, 35, 36, 37, 50, 53, 54,

57, 72, 76, 78, 80, 81, 83, 84, 93, 96,
101, 103, 104, 106, 117, 143, 150,
151, 152, 185, 200, 201, 203, 205,
206, 209, 210, 225, 229, 230, 231,
232, 239, 240
polity 101, 103, 104, 146
poverty 40, 53, 62, 74, 87, 91, 92, 133,
150, 151, 200, 201, 202, 203, 204,
205, 207, 211, 215, 219, 227, 243,
245, 246
power 12, 15, 16, 21–2, 30, 31, 33, 41,
54, 55, 56, 75, 81, 82, 91, 92, 101,
105, 107, 118, 128, 130, 134, 135,
136, 143, 151, 159, 164, 165, 166,
167, 177, 195, 196, 197, 198, 201,
204, 205, 208, 212, 213, 214, 215,
216, 217, 218, 220, 226, 227, 229, 233
priesthood 9, 14, 15, 27, 33, 34, 56, 57,
114, 163, 164, 165, 166, 195–6, 198,
208, 209, 210, 211, 212, 213, 214,
215, 216, 219, 222, 224, 225, 226,
227, 228, 229, 235
prince 27, 66, 73, 90, 92, 93, 151, 152,
230, 231, 232, 233, 234, 238, 239,
240, 241, 242, 246
property 10, 11, 75, 76, 81, 89, 92, 99,
104–5, 107, 110, 114, 130–3, 151,
158, 159, 160, 166, 167, 196, 197,
202, 203, 204, 205, 206, 209, 210,
211, 212, 213, 214, 215, 216, 217,
219, 221, 222, 224, 225, 228, 229

reason 4, 5, 27, 28, 29, 31, 33, 49, 62,
88, 97, 99, 100, 103, 106, 108, 111,
113, 114, 116, 117, 119, 120, 121,
122, 123, 124, 125, 127, 137, 138,
143, 145, 151, 161, 163, 170, 171,
174, 179, 181, 190, 191, 192, 193,
223, 226, 227, 232, 233, 242, 245
republic 30, 32, 38, 39, 42, 43, 44, 49,
50, 52, 53, 56, 75, 106, 108, 115, 201,
233
right 10, 12, 31, 33, 41, 42, 59, 63, 72,
134, 136, 152, 166, 167, 176, 181,
201, 209, 213, 214, 217, 218, 219,
220, 222, 229
Roman law 3, 13, 51, 61, 78, 168, 210,
237
ruler 16, 27, 30, 31, 32, 33, 34, 35, 36,
38, 39, 41, 43, 45, 50, 52, 53, 56, 57,
65, 71, 72, 73, 74, 75, 76, 78, 80, 81,
84, 85, 86, 87, 89, 91–2, 94–5, 102,
113, 115, 117, 119, 129–30, 135–6,

142–3, 146, 147, 150, 151, 159, 160, 162, 163, 170, 172, 188–93, 198, 204, 212, 218, 225, 226

salvation 108–9, 131, 135, 177, 195
slave 101, 134, 136, 139, 146, 147, 148, 172, 182, 185, 202
society 4, 7, 9, 27, 28, 100, 102, 113, 151, 162, 169, 170, 176, 181, 183, 199, 203, 205
soul 2, 38, 40, 52, 101, 103, 106, 109, 113, 136, 145, 162, 165, 182, 198, 202, 221, 224, 227, 237, 246, 247

tyranny 27, 30, 51, 53, 54, 55, 56, 57, 59, 91, 98, 101, 103, 104, 105, 106, 107, 110, 111, 112, 141, 145, 150, 161, 162, 167, 187, 202

vice 45, 51–2, 53, 54, 65, 72, 74, 78, 84, 90, 91, 92, 125, 178, 201, 213, 224, 228, 235, 240, 241, 243
virtue 2, 5, 7, 28, 34, 38, 40, 45, 46, 52, 55, 72, 74, 75, 76, 77, 78, 82, 87, 92, 101, 105, 106, 108, 111, 115, 117, 118, 125, 126, 129, 136, 141, 144, 145, 146, 147, 152, 161, 162, 164, 224, 226, 228, 233, 235, 237
voluntary *see* will

will 4, 5, 6, 7, 30, 32, 33, 41, 42, 81, 105, 108, 109, 115, 120, 125, 126, 129, 130, 134, 160, 161, 167, 171, 175, 181, 188, 202, 203, 219, 227, 232
women 7, 9, 24, 25, 50, 57, 59, 78, 80, 84, 92, 93, 146, 185, 230, 241